TRAILBLAZER

TRAILBLAZER
Perseverance in Life and Politics

CAROL MOSELEY BRAUN

WITH DONNA M. OWENS

HANOVER
SQUARE
PRESS

**HANOVER
SQUARE
PRESS™**

Recycling programs
for this product may
not exist in your area.

ISBN-13: 978-1-335-52383-9

Trailblazer

Hanover Square Press
22 Adelaide St. West, 41st Floor
Toronto, Ontario M5H 4E3, Canada
HanoverSqPress.com

Printed in U.S.A.

This book is dedicated to my grandmother and guardian angel, EDNA ROBERTA DAVIE, whose loving protection has allowed me the successes of my life.

"Trust in the Lord with all thine heart; and lean not unto thine own understanding. In all thy ways acknowledge him, and he shall direct thy paths."

—*Proverbs* 3:5–6

TABLE OF CONTENTS

Prologue 11

1. Barriers 17

2. The Birth Certificate 25

3. We, Too, Sing America 33

4. Welcome to the Neighborhood 41

5. Home Is Where the Heart (and Fighting) Is 49

6. Bucket of Blood 57

7. Marching with a King 69

8. College and the Cow 79

9. Love and Lawyering 93

10. Working Girl 107

11. A Baby and Bobolinks 123

12. Springfield 135

13. Brother John 147

14. Marriage and Divorce 159

15. Good Deeds 165

16. Historymaker Part One....................................... 177

17. Historymaker Part Two 191

18. Historymaker Part Three 205

19. Old Bulls and Sister Senators 217

20. Carol vs. the Confederacy.................................. 237

21. Courting Controversy 247

22. Reelection.. 255

23. Ambassador to Paradise 277

24. Take the "Men Only" Sign Off the White House............... 299

25. Letter to My Grandchildren 319

Epilogue   329

Acknowledgments   337

Bibliography   341

Endnotes   347

PROLOGUE

April 2022

On a sun-splashed spring day in our nation's capital, I was among the honored guests in attendance at a historic celebration on the South Lawn of the White House.

President Joe Biden was honoring Judge Ketanji Brown Jackson, whom he had nominated as the first African American woman to sit on the Supreme Court. This outdoor celebration, ahead of her official investiture, marked a momentous milestone in the long march toward justice and equality.

The mood was festive as members of Congress, the Judiciary, and Cabinet members mingled with fellow officials, as well as movers and shakers from academia to entertainment.

Against the backdrop of a soft blue sky, American flags fluttered in the breeze. Red, white, and blue bunting adorned the portico. The US Marine band, their uniforms crisp and brass instruments gleaming, played tunes brimming with pomp and circumstance.

As guests buzzed with excitement before the program began, I quietly navigated the manicured lawn and found a seat. A few people recognized me, with some cheerfully pointing or waving in my direction. I softly mouthed hellos and smiled, appreciative of the well wishes that still come my way.

Back in 1992, the outcome of a high-profile and controversial Supreme Court confirmation hearing led to me running for the United States Senate. The good people of Illinois saw fit to elect me, resulting in a historic breakthrough for our great nation. I became the first African American woman to serve in the upper chamber. Concurrently, I was the first woman Senator to represent the state of Illinois in Congress.

Now a new generation was picking up the torch of democracy and blazing new paths.

As Vice President Kamala Harris and Ketanji Brown Jackson flanked our commander-in-chief, my heart brimmed with joy at seeing these brilliant women, Black women, taking their rightful places in the annals of history.

What a blessing for me to bear witness, to be in the same space and time, breathing the rare air of progress, promise, and possibility. I have never been prouder and more humbled to be amid fellow trailblazers, knowing that each of us had the distinction of being able to proclaim: "I was the first."

That day at the White House is one of countless memories in my epoch-making journey.

My seven decades of life—and counting—have whizzed by in a Technicolor dream. As I reflect upon my experiences, it's hard for me to fathom that I have been a public servant and stateswoman for more than half a century.

My story is uniquely American.

Born in Chicago in the shadow of World War II, mine is the tale of millions who are progeny of the Great Migration, descending from Southerners on both sides of my family tree.

My people were New Orleans jazz and ragtime musicians and Alabama farmers whose labors in the field and lively music on Saturday night produced me. My clan has a long history of activism, entrepreneurship, and military service that dates back to the Civil War.

My life and those of my forebears intersects with the rich, diverse, and complex history of these United States.

In the 1950s, I was among the first "Brown babies"—Negro children who integrated schoolhouses around the country after a landmark Supreme Court case. In my neighborhood school, bullied and even placed in the "dummy row" by my teacher, I defied expectations and would do so for the rest of my life.

In my teens, I marched with Dr. King as part of the Civil Rights Movement. In high school, I benefited from federal programs and scholarships that helped me become the first in my family to graduate from college.

In my twenties, I had a front row seat to the women's and Black Power movements.

Along the way, I was one of the few women and Black students in my law school class, where I met my future husband. Our interracial marriage was a sign of the changing times, and our love child is my greatest treasure.

As a young, idealistic community advocate in the '70s, I won a longshot election for the Illinois General Assembly, beating a candidate backed by Chicago's notorious political "Machine."

I rose through the leadership ranks to become the legislature's first Black woman to serve as assistant majority leader.

A decade or so later, running on a "unity" ticket of multiracial candidates, I was elected the recorder of deeds for Cook County, Illinois, the first Black woman in this executive position.

Being elected to the Senate was one of the greatest triumphs of my life. Yet my arrival on Capitol Hill was rife with obstacles, controversies, and lessons learned. After one term, I lost my seat in Congress, but the universe still had more "firsts" awaiting me.

President Bill Clinton appointed me as the US ambassador to New Zealand and Samoa. As the first Black woman in the post, it was an opportunity to showcase our country's diversity on a global stage.

Afterward, I returned to a life unbound by politics and polls: teaching, consulting, and launching an organic food company. During that time, I vowed never to seek office again.

Yet in 2004, I leapt into the fray of politics yet again. This time I was running for president of the United States of America.

I was not the first woman, nor the first woman of color to seek the highest office in the land. However, I was the lone woman in a crowded field of Democrats during that political cycle. I followed in the footsteps of the legendary congresswoman, Shirley Chisholm, and became only the second African American woman in America's history to seek a major party nomination for president.

Truly, I have had experiences beyond my wildest dreams. From conferring with US presidents and First Ladies, to attending state dinners and meeting global leaders and royalty, to being named an honorary member of an Indigenous tribe in New Zealand, to visiting the South Pole as an ambassador representing our country.

Yet my outsized life, one in which I have frequently felt like an outsider, has always been an uphill climb.

I have had to overcome a learning disability. I'm a survivor of domestic abuse. I have lost a beloved sibling to the mean streets. When my parents split up, the family was torn asunder and we experienced days when there was no water or electricity in our home. I've been a divorced, single mother who parented long-distance. I've known loneliness and heartache and abandonment. I have suffered the sting of political defeat and crushing loss in my personal life.

What has saved me to see another day is a divine force, the Source that soothes every sorrow. I often say that my life has been filled with adversity, adventure, and serendipity, anchored by God's amazing grace.

Carol Moseley Braun is still here.

I joke about "flunking retirement." I still practice law periodically, and am active with a host of civic causes—from having stumped on the presidential campaign trail for fellow Democrats—to volunteering on a committee to build a new memorial for WWI veterans in Washington, DC.

In January 2023, I answered the call of public service when the Biden-Harris administration nominated me for a post that syncs with my longtime passion for international affairs.

A year later, I was confirmed by the Senate and sworn in as chair of the United States African Development Foundation.

This independent agency established by Congress has a worthy mission which encompasses community-led development, investment, and social entrepreneurism across the African continent.

The role, which is unpaid, is a continuation of my longtime interest in the African diaspora, as well as the leadership and service that has defined my career.

Through it all, self-determination, grit, and faith have enabled me to stay the course as a mother, daughter, sister, grandmother, friend. Mine is an American saga of a life with more trauma and despair beneath the surface than one might fathom. Yet my desire to be of service gave me the will to overcome sexism and racism, and persevere in politics and life.

Over the years, there have been so many stories written and broadcast about me that I've lost count. Admittedly, I've gotten angry about some of the portrayals and occasionally reacted in ways not befitting of a public servant. I've wept privately. I have railed about the vagaries of being in the public eye, and having others attempt to define your every move and motive.

Trailblazer is my only memoir. There have been other books written about me, or which include my story, but this one is my own. Finally, I can set the record straight about my life and times on the local, national, and global stage.

Memory can prove tricky. And sometimes facts are not always as they seem. I have tried to the best of my recollection to tell the truth and paint an accurate picture of what was happening at the time, and how it has impacted me personally, politically, and professionally. And how it has affected my loved ones, who did not choose this public life.

I hope that you will read *Trailblazer* with an open mind.

I hope you will laugh about the unusual encounter with a bird that launched me into politics.

I hope you will savor the power of sisterhood when I share how Gloria Steinem, Maya Angelou, and powerful women in Hollywood supported my groundbreaking Senate campaign. Or, how the handful of bipartisan women in my Senate class formed a bond as we battled antiquated rules about our clothing and one lavatory for the ladies.

You may feel my outrage about having to filibuster on the Senate floor about the Confederate flag. You may cheer the friendships and alliances I made in Washington, DC—from Joe Biden and Ted Kennedy to Hillary Clinton and Dianne Feinstein.

Trailblazer has musings about my one of a kind hometown, and the six degrees of separation between me and fellow Windy City figures: Reverend Jesse Jackson, Harold Washington, and Barack Obama, to name a few.

I believe you will glean inspiration from my remembrances of great humanitarians such as Rosa Parks, Nelson Mandela, and Dr. Martin Luther King Jr.

Last but not least, I believe you will enjoy meeting my extraordinary ancestors in these pages, and reading the optimistic letter to my grandchildren and future generations. I convey my thoughts about the gains we have achieved, the mountains we must continue to climb, and the unity we must nurture among all people to ensure that the United States—the greatest country in the world—lives up to its creed of liberty and justice for all.

BARRIERS

On a winter's day in January 1993, I practically glided up the steps of the U.S. Capitol, eager to report for my first day on the job. I was a United States senator, the first Black woman duly elected to the body in the history of our republic.

The moment felt divinely ordained, as if I had been carried on the golden wings of God's loving angels. As a proud American, as a descendant of enslaved ancestors who had toiled and sacrificed, as a woman who embraced the power of my gender, all of these identities had coalesced and catapulted me to this place and time.

The good people of Illinois had sent me to Washington, DC, as their junior senator—the first woman from the Land of Lincoln ever elected in this capacity. I was ready to get to work, to begin serving my constituents and country.

Apparently, however, no one had given security the memo that Carol Moseley Braun had a date with destiny.

A uniformed guard stationed near the entrance of the grand building looked me over as I approached. I smiled and was about to say, "Good morning." Before I could greet him, however, he uttered a few words that I shall never forget.

"Ma'am, you can't go any further," he said almost dismissively, gesturing toward a side entrance for visitors.

I stood there, stunned into silence. I was a newly minted senator, replete with all the responsibilities and privileges therein, yet the gatekeeper didn't want to let me in the door.

Days earlier, clad in a peach business suit, and clasping my Bible, I had been sworn in by Vice President Dan Quayle.

"I do solemnly swear that I will support and defend the Constitution of the United States against all enemies, foreign and domestic; that I will bear true faith and allegiance to the same; that I take this obligation freely, without any mental reservation or purpose of evasion; and that I will well and faithfully discharge the duties of the office on which I am about to enter. So help me God."

I was escorted down the center aisle of the senate's ornate, wood-paneled chamber by senior Illinois senator Paul Simon. He was a prominent lawmaker and gallant gentleman who wore bow ties and horn-rimmed spectacles. We would become close allies and friends.

The ceremony was among the whirlwind of official and unofficial events, receptions, and parties that marked the unprecedented occasion.

A large entourage of family, friends, supporters—some invited, some not, still others who simply wanted to witness history—had accompanied me to the nation's capital.

My wonderful son, Matthew, a baby when I launched my first political campaign more than a decade earlier, was ever by my side. My dear siblings—Marsha and Joseph—had flown in from the Windy City to cheer their big sister on.

Several pivotal members of the Moseley clan were missing. My precious mother, Edna, was quite frail from illness and sadly could not make the trip.

My father, Joseph Sr., did not live to see the day, although in his own way, he had always dreamt outsized dreams for me. Years earlier, we'd lost my beloved brother, John, following his battle with addiction. I could only pray that both Moseley men were in heaven, surveying the scene and proud of my accomplishment.

Besides my relatives, a number of my fellow Chicagoans were in attendance. The Rev. Jesse Jackson, whom I have known for decades, delivered a sermon-like prayer for me. Gwendolyn Brooks, the US Poet Laureate and Pulitzer Prize winner from my hometown, had graciously penned a special poem in my honor, terming me "a young giant."

Meanwhile, my campaign manager turned fiancé had come to witness the victory that his efforts and those of my hardworking campaign team and dedicated volunteers had helped make possible.

I was thrilled, of course, to have the honor and opportunity to serve in the Senate, but I was a little nervous and slightly overwhelmed.

Almost immediately, people had begun to treat me differently. Long before social media, influencers, and reality stars were a thing, I had become a political celebrity. The press was trailing me, calling out questions over the click, click, click of cameras flashing.

The media weren't the only ones buzzing about my first day.

I was the junior senator from Illinois, but it quickly became clear that many people, particularly women and Black Americans, viewed my constituency as national, even international.

Congratulatory phone calls, cards, letters, and felicitations poured in from Illinois, across the country, and from around the world.

Decades ago, I had no playbook, no primer to help me make sense of all this. Even though I'd served as a legislator at the state level, in retrospect I was fairly naive about national politics. Everything was coming at me fast, furious, and in real time. It all seemed surreal. Still, I was excited. I could not stop smiling.

After her recitation, Gwendolyn Brooks said something to me along the lines of "Hold on, Senator Carol."

I thought little of her words at the time. However, that wisdom would prove prescient, providing a warning to prepare me for whatever might be in store in the unpredictable world of politics on Capitol Hill. Hold on, indeed.

In 1787, George Washington, Benjamin Franklin, and fellow colonial leaders assembled in Philadelphia for the inaugural Constitutional Convention. It was during that seminal gathering, that the contours of our democracy took shape.

The framers—all of them white male landowners, and some, slaveholders—commenced their efforts in the spring and did not adjourn until the fall. They departed having established a national Congress. The legislative branch consisted of two distinct houses, the Senate and House of Representatives. Each chamber would craft laws designed to provide governance and direction for our young nation.

Centuries later, I was entering the Senate's exclusive one-hundred-member club. I arrived bringing the fullness of my humanity as a woman, African American, mother, daughter, sister, and child of the Most High. I perceived my electoral victory not merely in personal terms, but as a triumph that exemplified progress for all Americans, and our precious creed of one nation, under God, indivisible with liberty and justice for all.

I could not fathom what the framers, nor what the ancestors, might have thought of my literal and figurative arrival. Here I was, America. History had signed my name.

21

★ ★ ★

When I was born in the late 1940s, little girls of my generation did not grow up seeing considerable numbers of women in
elected office, as is commonplace in today's society. Yet, there
have always been smart, civic-minded women of every race,
color, and creed across America whose countless contributions
helped form the backbone of our homes, schools, churches, and
communities. Upon entering the Senate, I stood on their shoulders, and those of countless political pioneers who had persevered
and shattered barriers through the annals of time.

Women have walked the halls of Congress dating back to
1916 when Jeannette Rankin of Montana became the first. By
the early 1930s, two women had served in the Senate.

African American men have served as senators dating back to
the pivotal period of Reconstruction that followed the Civil War.

Hiram Revels, a pastor turned Union Army chaplain, held
local and state offices in Mississippi, before being seated in the
Senate in 1870. Newspapers of the era reported that when Revels took the oath of office, guests packed the Senate galleries and
loudly applauded his extraordinary achievement.

Revels would be followed by Blanche Bruce in the Senate,
and fifteen other African American men who served in Congress during the early nineteenth century.

Despite those advances, it would be another eight decades or
so before another African American senator, Edward Brooke of
Massachusetts, won an election in 1967.

One year later, the inimitable Shirley Chisholm of New York
blazed a trail as the first African American woman elected to
Congress. A valiant fighter for the people, a founding member
of the Congressional Black Caucus, she served seven terms before retiring in the early eighties.

A decade later, it was my turn to stride into history. That is,
if the gatekeepers didn't block my path.

After the words that stopped me in my tracks—"You can't go any further"—I was aghast.

The first African American woman ever elected to this august body deserved—as any human being would expect—common courtesy. Instead, mine was an inauspicious beginning rife with disrespect. My emotions swirled between indignation and humiliation. I took a deep breath and tried to remain calm. I happen to hail from a law enforcement family, and was taught to respect those who serve and protect the public. I studied the face of the gentleman. He did not appear to be malicious. Yet his words had been tossed out in such a casual manner, that perhaps it seemed wholly implausible to him that I might be a member of Congress, and specifically, the Senate.

There was a certain bitter irony. The Capitol, with its famous dome, neoclassical architecture, marble columns, and gilded sweeping ceilings, had been erected in the 1800s in part with the labor of enslaved and free Black men.

Our diverse nation exists because of the blood, sweat, and tears of countless ancestors, yours and mine.

But to this man, I was unknown, an interloper. I wasn't sure how to react. A few awkward minutes passed.

Fortunately, a second, pleasant guard stationed on the other side of the door recognized me. He turned to his colleague and said, "Oh, that's the new senator from Illinois," and waved me on in.

"Thank you," I said, making sure that I addressed them both. My tone was gracious.

Certainly, some senators might have become irate; reported the offending employee to his superiors; or even proffered—*ahem*—a few choice words.

Yet I was not about to let him throw me off my game. I was a US senator, and moreover, a lady. I chose to maintain my composure and exhibit the genteel manners that my lovely Southern mother had taught me.

I am not unaccustomed to ignorance, nor to what we now term "implicit bias." Security saw me coming through the main doors and unwittingly assumed that I did not belong in this space of power and privilege.

I credit his associate, who must have watched the news or read in the paper about my historic election, with quickly straightening out the situation. Yet that moment, of feeling unwelcome, out of place, and challenged near daily, was a harbinger of what I would encounter during my tenure in the Senate.

Some people were going to see a Black woman coming through and attempt to block me intentionally or inadvertently.

But I was not going to use the side doors for visitors. And the days of back doors were long gone.

I squared my shoulders. I walked through the door and took my designated seat in the chamber.

I was here, ready to do my job as an elected official in the legislative branch. I tried to brush off the earlier incident, but in retrospect perhaps it was an omen.

Looking back on my tenure in Congress, a powerful and seemingly glamorous position, few understood the magnitude of the pain, drama, and machinations that happened to me publicly and behind the scenes. I held one of the most important offices in the land, but grew increasingly miserable. I was grateful to the good people of Illinois for allowing me the privilege of representing them. I was patriotic and yearned to be of service to my constituents and country. In myriad ways, my six years in the Senate was an extraordinary experience. Conversely, it was also the worst period of my life, one I barely survived.

THE BIRTH CERTIFICATE

My journey has been one of adventure and adversity, sweetened by serendipity, and anchored by God's precious love.

I have often found myself propelled into places and spaces that were unexpected, including the US Senate and a global ambassadorship, in a series of divine twists and turns that have shaped my destiny.

Even my first breaths in this world seemed to foreshadow the extraordinary experiences that awaited me.

I was born in the late 1940s, part of the baby boom that followed World War II.

Reflecting on that era, it seems eons ago.

Harry Truman was the nation's thirty-third president. A loaf of bread cost about thirteen cents. The jitterbug was a popular dance.

Yet life was not so simple for Black Americans. Segregation, with its so-called "separate but equal" accommodations, which were anything but, cast a pall upon our society. What scholar

W.E.B. Du Bois famously termed the "problem of the color line" persisted in housing, schools, restaurants, and beyond.

As my parents-to-be excitedly prepared for the birth of their first child, the complexities of the color line became readily apparent.

On a sweltering August day, my mother's water broke. Daddy was out of town on a business trip, but she managed to make her way to Lewis Memorial Maternity Hospital. The renovated nineteenth-century building on South Michigan Avenue was once a luxury hotel. Now its "guests" were patients.

In my hometown and big cities elsewhere during that period, many hospitals had a "white" maternity ward, and a different area for "colored" women. The accommodations for Black women were usually shabbier, and subpar medical treatment was not unheard of.

Young and anxious, this being her first child and all, my mother had no idea what to expect.

Thank goodness, the reception she received from the staffers at the facility was genial. In fact, they took one look at my mother's fair complexion, hazel eyes, and curly tresses, and did not bother to ask her race.

She was promptly wheeled into the "white" maternity wing.

My mother braved hours of labor pains, awaiting the miracle of delivery, until I arrived, full of promise. Wailing and wrinkled, my skin tone was vague enough in infancy that the doctors and nurses never suspected that a "Negro" baby was cooing in their midst.

As my mother cradled me tenderly in her arms, love overshadowed any regret about her "passing" for white, a practice that was taboo, yet far from uncommon in that era.

We were discharged within a few days, our secret having been safely swaddled away. Unbeknownst to the hospital, we had skirted the rules around segregation and integrated its facilities.

Once we arrived home, caring for an infant round the clock

guaranteed that no one had time to dwell upon the matter. To her dying day, whenever my origin story came up in conversation, Mother swore that she did not intentionally "pass."

Her explanation was that she was simply a young expectant mother anxiously awaiting her firstborn, who seized the opportunity to receive top-notch medical care and be treated humanely, regardless of race. She desired the same for her precious newborn babe.

Decades later, my mother's concerns have proven predictive. The issue of Black maternal health has entered the public consciousness, underscoring long-standing disparities around mortality rates.

I never questioned her decision. As a devoted mother and grandmother, myself, I completely understand the instinct to protect one's child and provide them with every possible advantage.

My mother's intentions notwithstanding, the matter of the color line did yield unintended consequences for me. It would be the first of many fateful occurrences that have shaped my life.

On my official birth certificate, typed under my given name, Carol Elizabeth Moseley, was a stunning entry. My race was listed as "white." I would remain so for a very long time.

My parents—Edna Davie and Joseph Moseley—were children of the Great Depression.

Born in the 1920s, they both came of age in the shadow of a world war "over there," and amid economic upheaval, widespread unemployment, and food lines, here at home.

Mother was a student at Wendell Phillips, the oldest Black high school in Chicago. Founded in 1904 and named for a nineteenth-century abolitionist, the school initially educated the offspring of wealthy white denizens, and a few children of their Black servants.

By the 1930s, when she began matriculating, the student

body's complexion had changed. The school was predominantly Black, and its enrollees were a mix of native Chicagoans and youngsters whose families had fled the Deep South during the Great Migration.

My relatives, both maternal and paternal, were Southern sojourners who were part of this seminal movement. In the immediate aftermath of WWI, and for decades later, millions of people from the South flooded Chicago, as well as cities like New York City, Philadelphia, and Detroit, and states as far west as California. Black Southerners were lured by the promise of jobs, opportunity, and escape from the daily indignities, discrimination, and violence wrought by Jim Crow.

My mother's people from Union Springs, Alabama, were farmers who had talked about coming to the Midwest, so that the older children could attend high school. No such option existed for Negroes in their small rural community.

Tragedy hastened their plans. My mother's sister, Ollie Myrtle, was just ten years old when a truck ran her down and kept right on going. Little Ollie was left to die in the middle of the road.

Family members were beside themselves with grief, not to mention, rage. Apparently, they knew who the driver was, one of the town's white residents. But in a tiny community under the iron fist of segregation, they had little recourse legally or otherwise. The angels in heaven had Ollie under their wings, but her loved ones on earth had no way to hold the culprit accountable for the untimely death of an innocent child.

In her sorrow, my grandmother Edna Sr. packed up and fled to Chicago. She left her three surviving children behind with relatives until there was money enough to send for them. A few years later, Thomas Jr., nicknamed Tommy; Ruby ("Darrel"); and Edna Jr., her namesake and my mother, arrived in the Windy City.

We believe based on census records that my mother arrived

in Chicago sometime in the mid-1930s, when she was about thirteen years old.

My mother would come of age in the big city. She was a sepia version of the quintessential Southern belle: sweet, mannerly, and "purty."

A natural redhead, some of the family and friends called her "Red." She had a vivacious personality, a generous nature, and a quick wit.

In high school, my mother was an excellent student, and was inducted into the National Honor Society. Her 1940 high school yearbook lists a dizzying array of extracurricular activities: French Club, Student Council, reporting for the school newspaper and editing the yearbook. She was in the Drama Club and as a senior had a starring role as Miss Vanity Fair in the school play.

My father was a year older than my mother. Joseph was born in Chicago, and from Southern stock with roots in New Orleans, Louisiana.

He hailed from a family of professional musicians who were both performers and music teachers.

His upbringing among entertainers may be why my father commanded attention at an early age. Chocolate brown, he stood about five feet six, and had the sturdy build of a boxer, a sport he dabbled in as an amateur. Along with his physical attributes, my father had a steely demeanor to match.

Daddy's family was comfortable financially, and they doted upon the youngster, and indulged his whims. As a result, he comported himself in the manner of royalty, spawning a nickname: Little Lord Fauntleroy, a nod to the 1886 novel and 1930s Hollywood film.

The dignified lad grew into a cultured young adult. A Renaissance man, by contemporary standards. My father was an intellectual, who read books on philosophy and spoke several languages. A musical prodigy, he played seven instruments.

It's unclear if my father matriculated at Wendell Phillips or DuSable High School, which was the other high school for Black Chicagoans back then. Family lore says that Daddy was a classmate of jazz and blues legend Dinah Washington. Both studied under the tutelage of musician and educator Walter Dyett, whose renowned program in Chicago public schools trained the likes of Nat King Cole, Bo Diddley, Gene Ammons, and Redd Foxx, to name a few. Captain Dyett, as he was called because of his military service, taught at both schools. Wherever he studied, Little Lord Fauntleroy and "Red" eventually met, but did not immediately become a couple.

The specter of WWII loomed.

Some sixteen million Americans—men and women— served at home and overseas during the war and one million Black Americans were among those who did their duty.

Daddy enlisted in the army. He was a private first class in the field artillery branch of the National Guard. He served four years until America and its allies declared victory.

After the war ended, he sought higher education. Across the country, a wave of veterans were utilizing the G.I. Bill to purchase homes, attend college, and so on.

Benefits would prove to be unevenly distributed to Black vets, and we don't know if my father accessed them.

However, he stayed in town and enrolled at Roosevelt University. At that time a new campus, the university was named in honor of President Franklin Delano Roosevelt and First Lady Eleanor Roosevelt. I don't know if he graduated, but this erudite man aspired to be a lawyer.

At some point, he also pursued legal studies at John Marshall Law School, which was founded in 1899 and merged more than a century later with the University of Illinois. When it was discovered that the school's namesake—a former Supreme Court justice—had also been a slave trader, the institution removed his moniker and gained a new name: the University of Illinois Chicago School of Law.

Of course, in those days, Daddy would not have known any of this. He truly yearned for higher education.

My mother, who was smart and talented in her own right, also dreamed of attending college. After high school graduation, she headed back down south to enroll at Dillard University, a historically Black institution in New Orleans.

Dillard bears the name of James Hardy Dillard, an educational reformer who promoted racial harmony. The leafy campus was a bastion of higher learning where my mother and her peers could take such courses as history, psychology, and anthropology.

Mother had expressed interest in becoming a registered nurse. The talented thespian hadn't lost her passion for the theatre, but she surmised that a career in the health care arena was more realistic.

Alas, my mother's life as a coed ended abruptly after only a semester or two. Her family simply could not afford the tuition.

While heartbreaking, her withdrawal from college due to its affordability was not especially unique—then or now. In my parents' day, college was almost exclusively for the affluent. In 1940, for example, less than 5 percent of Americans held college degrees.

Still, my mother was crestfallen about leaving school. She tucked away her dreams, and headed back to the metropolis that was now her adopted home.

Likewise, Daddy's thirst to become a lawyer was a dream that died on the vine.

By the time my parents reconnected, they were twentysomethings who each had some life experience. College. Romances with other people. Dreams deferred.

Against that backdrop, my parents reunited, fell in love, snuck off, and eloped.

Mother and Daddy eased into life as newlyweds. Early in their marriage, they resided with Edna Sr., and while she was kind to her daughter and son-in-law, the young couple was saving up to purchase a home of their own.

It was a hopeful time for my parents. Young and in love, they had each other, and soon a newborn daughter—yours truly. Less than two years after my mother and I inadvertently broke the maternity ward color barrier, my brother, John, was born. Later, two more sweet, sprightly siblings—Marsha and Joseph John II—would join the fold.

The Moseleys had all the makings of a happy family. And for a time, we were.

WE, TOO, SING AMERICA

"I, too, sing America."

—*Langston Hughes*

I am descended from a pantheon of men and women who have sought to sing our own distinct songs in America, this land of opportunity. It's a song of faith in God, family, and freedom.

I sing of my remarkable Southern ancestors. These courageous, hardy, and industrious individuals contributed to the building of our manifold nation with their toil, ingenuity, and service.

There are generations of valiant veterans in my ancestry, American heroes whose branches spread across the family tree.

I sing the song of Andrew Day, a paternal ancestor born in Mathews County, Virginia. A blacksmith and carpenter, he was formerly enslaved. In 1864 at age twenty-two, he shook off the shackles of bondage to enlist and serve our country during the Civil War.

My second great-grandfather was a private in the 53rd Regiment of the United States Colored Troops in the Civil War.

The USCT was comprised of more than two hundred thousand Black men in the army and navy, along with smaller numbers of Native Americans and Latinos. Women provided support through roles ranging from nurses to scouts, and in the case of Harriet Tubman, as a brave military raid leader. Their collective valor would help defeat the Confederacy and reunite and save our country.

According to muster records, Private Day fought in the infantry and saw action in battles that spanned Mississippi and Arkansas. His discharge date was in 1866, three years after president Abraham Lincoln issued the Emancipation Proclamation. The document declared in part, "all persons held as slaves" in states which had seceded "are, and henceforth shall be free."

Oh, sweet freedom. After the war ended, my emancipated second great-grandfather continued to be of service to our country. An official Freedmen's Bureau letter in his military papers sought his skills as "the services of a carpenter are very necessary-particularly at this time." He later received a pension, which is recorded in the National Archives. Today, Andrew Day's name is inscribed alongside fellow USCT members at the African American Civil War Memorial in Washington, DC, and he is buried in Mississippi's Vicksburg National Military Park.

The boundless blessings of liberty enabled my people to build new lives in the aftermath of the Civil War. Miraculously, we became landowners.

The value of owning property, then and now, cannot be measured. Postwar, few African Americans received the promised forty acres and mule, but through the goodness of God, my maternal kinfolk were able to acquire hundreds of acres that remain in our hands today.

My mother's people hail from Union Springs, Alabama. It's a small town in Bullock County that dates back to the 1840s.

This community in southeast Alabama was once the domain of Native Americans who were forcibly removed by settlers. It is now part of a larger region famously known as the Black Belt. The moniker speaks both to the inky dark soil, as well as the plantations where cotton became "king" on the backs of enslaved human beings.

Our land initially belonged to my maternal great-great-grandmother, Isabelle McNair, born in 1856. She was the daughter of an enslaved African woman and a free mulatto father. The property was a gift from her husband, Charles Henry, circa 1894.

Upon Isabelle's death in the 1930s, the farm was deeded to her daughter, Ollie Henry, my great-grandmother. A spitfire who married three times, she was widowed when her first husband, with whom she bore two children, was killed in a mining accident.

One of her offspring was my maternal grandmother, Edna. The union of Bryant and Thomas Davie, Sr., produced four children including my mother, her namesake.

My grandmother Edna, sometimes called Alberta or Edna Sr., was a special woman, and practically a saint. A devout Catholic, she went to Mass every morning and exuded an inner calm. She was one of the city's early Black toll-takers and a savvy businesswoman who owned property. And her beauty was such that she turned heads.

Her husband, Thomas Davie, was my grandfather. He was a World War I veteran who was among nearly 5 million Americans who joined the Allied effort in Europe, and one of some 350,000 Black Americans who served.

Grandfather Thomas enlisted in his early twenties, later becoming part of the 366th Infantry of the 92nd Division, a segregated unit known as the Buffalo Soldiers. By the time they set sail on the ship *Covington* in the summer of 1918 from Hoboken, New Jersey, he was already a sergeant.

He would later fight in the Meuse-Argonne Offensive, one of the largest and deadliest battles of the war; after seven weeks, the Allies were able to declare definitive victory in November 1918.

Grandfather returned from France on the ship *Aquitania*,

reaching New York in February 1919. He was honorably discharged one month later and awarded the World War I Victory
Medal for his service.

The interesting cast of characters picks up on my father's side
of the family.

Daddy was the only child of Elizabeth Landry (my middle name, Elizabeth, honors her) and her first spouse, Wilson
Moseley; they married in Louisiana at the dawn of the "Roaring Twenties." For whatever reason, their union did not go the
distance. She remarried and was living with her new husband
in Chicago by the 1930s.

Subsequently, Daddy was raised primarily by his grandmother,
Lucy Borden, aka "Mama Lu"—the youngest of three daughters
that our Civil War hero, Andrew Day, had with his second wife,
Dolley.

Many of my father's people wound up in New Orleans, and
these entertainers eventually migrated to Chicago. There is no
shortage of fascinating lore about their adventures.

Grandpa Wilson was said to have played piano for the infamous Al Capone at a popular Chitown hotel on Roosevelt Road.
When the "Bugs" Moran gang of bootleggers raided the place,
my relative was spared in the ensuing shootout only because the
piano protected him from the whizzing bullets.

Supposedly, as a reward for keeping quiet, one of Grandpa's
brothers, Rufus, was given a lifetime job. It could all be a family
legend, except that many years later, I ran into my uncle who
was operating an elevator at a downtown Chicago building. He
did not dispute the story.

The men in Daddy's clan weren't the only musicians. His
mother was a trained opera singer. My grandmother, whom we
called "Mama Liz," was also an entrepreneur; after leaving the
South, at one point, she owned a neighborhood grocery store.
During my childhood, she introduced me to the concept of

business. I helped out behind the counter as she provided goods to the community.

Mama Liz's family had a bloodline that we believe goes back to North Africa, where they were Muslims. She was a Black nationalist who would become an acolyte of Marcus Garvey and a follower of the Honorable Elijah Mohammed and the Nation of Islam. She once took me to hear him speak at the mosque in Chicago.

Years later, in 1972, I was part of a political entourage who attended the National Black Political Convention, a historic three-day gathering of Black leaders in Gary, Indiana, that received widespread attention. There were thousands of people in attendance, and to my surprise, one of them was my grandmother. I was seated on bleachers in the gymnasium when I spotted this stout little woman slowly moving through the crowd. I ran over.

"Mama Liz!" I said, hugging her tightly. "What are you doing here?"

"I'm here to be with my people!" she said. I laughed. My grandmother was always hell on wheels.

Although my father did not grow up in the same household as his mother, he had plenty of companionship. His grandmother's full house included her husband, a slew of sons, and extended relations. One of Daddy's uncles was Francois Moseley, a jazz musician who had his own band, Francois Moseley's Louisiana Stompers, and later hit stages as Frankie Franko & His Louisianians.

In the late 1920s and early 1930s, the Louisianians booked engagements at nightclubs in Chicago.

In addition to their live act, the band even had a recording contract with the record label Melotone. Two of their songs, "Somebody Stole My Gal" and "Golden Lily Blues" were on wax and played on the radio.

I grew up hearing stories about my relatives, and my siblings and I were able to meet some of them in the flesh during trips that we took each summer to the Deep South.

I have vivid childhood memories of boarding a train at the station in Chicago and heading to Alabama. My mother packed us a lunch of fried chicken, hard-boiled eggs, and fruit, ample provisions for the lengthy trip.

As we journeyed further south, the states were still segregated. I saw firsthand the "colored" and "whites" signs, symbols of a racial hierarchy that was codified under Jim Crow.

The tensions of the times aside, the farm was a sanctuary for my family. God's handiwork adorned the land, which to my young mind, seemed to stretch as far as the eye could see.

Sweet birdsong awakened us each morning. Cornstalks torpedoed the vast sky. Chickens ran amok, squawking, and spotted cows grazed.

I remember a forest thick with trees—elm, cedar, and loblolly pine—and the most beautiful clearing where I loved to plop down on the grass and gaze up at the sky. There was a pond, spring fed, filled with fish.

My great-grandmother, Ollie, was the matriarch and steward of the farm. She was affectionately known as "Mother Dear"— which Southern accents rounded to Muh-Dear. I actually knew her, even though we entered the world in different centuries.

When Ollie was born in 1876, slavery in America had ended just eleven years earlier with the 13th Amendment to the Constitution.

I came along in the 1940s, in the shadow of WWII.

By some stroke of the universe, our lives overlapped. My great-grandmother was in her seventies and eighties during my childhood.

What a divine gift she was to me and every member of our family. Ollie made an indelible impression on me, and imparted countless lessons that guide me to this day.

She was a remarkable woman. If the men in my bloodline were distinguished by their sense of duty, the women in my clan were known for being smart, strong, and highly capable.

I can still picture Mother Dear's shotgun-style house, at the end of a long, winding dirt road. Set back a ways from that was the outhouse; there was no indoor plumbing or a bathroom in those days.

Indoors, my great-grandmother's kitchen had a potbellied stove where she cooked food on a wood chip fire. There was one bedroom, where she kept an antique wooden storage chest. She opened it from time to time, revealing to me a Bible, handmade quilts, and heirlooms that were sacred treasures.

First thing in the morning, the sun blazing over the vast fields, Mother Dear got to work "driving" a mule and plow. That old mule had nothing on my great-grandmother.

As the beast tilled straight rows in the rich earth, Ollie would use planting methods practiced by Indigenous and African cultures. This knowledge had been passed down to her.

First, she would drop a fish scrap into the earth, then deposit a seed and completely cover it with soil. The fish acted as a type of fertilizer. Sometimes she used a mixture of herbs to purify the soil. Under the broiling sun, she repeated the process again and again. Given the acreage of the farm, the arduous work took hours on end.

Fortunately, Ollie and the family did not have to labor in the proverbial vineyards alone. My relatives shared the land with tenant farmers whose backbreaking labor was crucial to the seasonal harvests. I recall the rows of rickety shacks where multiple families lived.

Bushels of corn were picked by hand. Fresh pecans would be harvested, then gathered into fifty-pound sacks and hoisted onto wagons to be sold at the market. Livestock had to be bred and fed.

Ollie knew the contours of the land, and intimately understood Mother Nature's rhythms. I remember her foraging for mushrooms in the forest. She regularly traversed the farm on horseback to survey the crops and orchards. And, she collected rents.

In my mind's eye, I still see her galloping across the fields, the long full skirt she wore billowing behind her. She always toted a pistol in her apron pocket.

Her rides were sometimes a matter of life or death. In addition to being a farmer, my great-grandmother was a midwife and healer, respected for her knowledge of traditional remedies.

Mother Dear delivered babies, and in later years obtained mid-wifery credentials. She also treated whatever ailed family members, tenants, and neighbors. She was kind and caring, and the relationships she maintained were of mutual trust. There was a sense of interdependence and community.

One instance of her benevolence was the mysterious stranger who was given the nickname "Chicken." He was discovered beaten and bloodied, lying on the side of a dirt road near the farm. His tongue had been cut out, in what folks whispered was a racially motivated act of revenge.

My great-grandmother took that poor man in, never thinking twice. She tended his wounds, fed him, and prayed him back to life. For all intents and purposes, our family adopted him.

"Chicken" became a valued farmhand and a beloved "cousin" who lived out the rest of his days on the farm. Mother Dear's acts of kindness instilled in me at an early age that people can and should help each other, because, "There but for the grace of God, go I."

Ollie was not only generous, she was fearless. Hers was an era when Black Americans, and women, had zero rights. Daily indignities, intimidation, and the threat of violence loomed constantly.

One night, the Klan rode onto the family homestead, torches ablaze. My great-grandmother hurriedly grabbed her long rifle and ran outside.

Ollie fired a warning shot into the air, yelling at the intruders to git back where they came from. The men were menacing, but Mother Dear stood her ground. Eventually, the night riders departed, the thunderous sound of clacking hoofs reverberating in their wake. For the time being, at least, trouble was averted.

Yet my great-grandmother and her loved ones knew they were not safe in the volatile South. Any type of slight, real or imagined, one false look, could set in motion dire consequences. Lynchings had become far too common. That, along with lagging economic opportunities, seemed to offer folks no reprieve from the repression. So, my people and millions of others like us left.

WELCOME TO THE
NEIGHBORHOOD

Mother and Daddy were believers in the shining promise of the American Dream.

My folks' dream was moving our family into a house we could call our own. They worked their fingers to the bone to achieve their mutual goal. Armed with high school diplomas—a major accomplishment in their day—plus some college, they entered the job market and began their respective careers in earnest.

Instead of practicing law, Daddy found a career in law enforcement. He joined the police force and became one of Chicago's finest.

ChiTown has a long history of "Black men in blue." The first, James Shelton, was appointed back in 1871. Still, their numbers were still relatively small when my father joined the force as a foot patrolman. He felt a sense of duty and relished the opportunity to serve the community. His half brother, my Uncle Burton, was also a cop and together they formed the beginnings of a family dynasty. Years later, my youngest brother, Joseph, Daddy's namesake, would proudly follow in their footsteps on the force.

Meanwhile, Mother's aim of becoming a nurse proved elusive, but she did launch a career in the health care field. She trained to become a medical technician and spent her days in the lab at one of Chicago's major hospitals.

Mother was in the vanguard as one of the few Black women in the role, and she excelled at her job. She understood science and was observant of what the doctors and nurses did. According to family lore, one time a physician with whom she worked came to work inebriated. She talked him through surgery, and even assisted at one point, helping him save a patient's life.

As my parents worked long hours, scrimped and saved, their due diligence paid off.

When I was about six or seven years old, they purchased a house in Chatham, a neighborhood on Chicago's South Side. It was squarely within the city limits but had the feel of a suburban utopia.

Our brick bungalow was roomy enough for a young, growing family. The house had four bedrooms, two baths, a living and dining room, and a kitchen. We looked out onto a manicured front lawn and there was a backyard where we children could run, jump, and play.

We even had a housekeeper. Miss Mary, a nice older Southern lady, helped out with meal preparation and babysitting because of my parents' dueling, grueling work schedules.

In those early years, life on South Prairie Avenue was a peaceful paradise.

We kids would climb the mulberry trees and pick berries. We pitched tents in the backyard and rode bicycles. We lingered outside on the curb until after the sun had gone down. It was blissful.

When the Moseleys first moved in to our new home, the

neighborhood was integrated. There were people who looked like us, along with a smattering of white families.

The majority of our neighbors were working-class folks. There were also Black professionals—teachers, doctors, and such—who were solidly middle class.

The melding of all these groups in a single community was a societal transformation that had been a long time coming.

Neighborhoods like ours had undergone dramatic demographic shifts. Segregation had previously kept these enclaves off-limits to Black families, but after decades of pressure, these communities had finally started to open up. Naturally, not everyone was happy about it.

In 1937, Carl Hansberry—a Black businessman and the father of acclaimed playwright Lorraine Hansberry—purchased a home for his family in one of Chicago's white neighborhoods. It would become the basis for her famous play, *A Raisin in the Sun*.

Mr. Hansberry had sidestepped the local property association, which had a restrictive covenant that specified no members of the "colored" race could move in.

Some of the white families filed a lawsuit, and Mr. Hansberry countersued, represented by NAACP lawyers. The case made the rounds through Illinois courts, before eventually reaching the highest court in the land. In 1940, the Supreme Court issued a favorable ruling that invalidated the restrictive covenant; it would set the stage for a landmark case nearly a decade later, *Shelley v. Kraemer*, that legally ended housing discrimination.

The Hansberry case was not an isolated issue of housing discrimination in Chicago. In the 1940s there had been a series of race riots sparked by housing. Amid a post-WWII housing shortage, Black veterans sought to live in temporary units that already housed white vets and their families. But neighborhood resistance was virulent and violent—a sad outcome for those who had served our country.

Of course, I knew none of this as a child. It wasn't until I entered law school in the late '60s, that I began to study key legal rulings in the battle for civil rights.

As we settled into domesticity in our new neighborhood, it seemed picture-perfect. Neighbors greeted each other with "good morning." Children played outside with no sense of danger. No one hesitated to help each other, and there was a sense of community.

Yet even in that urban idyll, even after the legal gains, prejudice crept in. Soon after we moved in to our new house, it became abundantly clear that some of our neighbors considered habitation near African Americans intolerable.

On one side of us, there was a young family much like ours, except they happened to be white. They had a little girl who was the exact same age as me.

We immediately gravitated toward each other. I was delighted to have a friend. Our respective bedroom windows faced the other, and we would look out, wave, and talk. We gleefully frolicked outside, playing hopscotch and other games.

Her mother did not seem to mind us playing together, nor did my parents. Mother was generally relaxed about her children playing outdoors, and she would dismiss any concerns with "You'll eat a peck of dirt before you die!"

Unfortunately, our next-door neighbor's father was not quite so easygoing about his daughter. All you-know-what broke loose when he discovered that we were playmates.

He was angry—make that furious. He loudly forbade his daughter to have any further contact with me. To ensure that his little one understood, he gave her a spanking. The sound of her crying echoed into our yard.

The matter might have ended there, were it not for two little girls determined to play together with their dolls in peace.

The next time my new friend and I ventured outside, we embraced each other and whispered in childlike language about the nonsense that grown-ups had saddled us with. In our own way, we would push back.

We were both pupils at Martha M. Ruggles Elementary, a public school on Chicago's South Side located a short walk from our block. I was actually one of the earliest Black children to integrate its classrooms, a result of the landmark *Brown v. Board of Education* case.

In the 1954 decision, the Supreme Court determined that segregation in public schools was "inherently unequal" and unconstitutional. I never had to run a gauntlet of hate to enter the schoolhouse the way many brave Black Southern youth were forced to do. But, on multiple occasions, rocks were thrown through the window of my classroom, and the teacher would yell for us to "duck and cover" under our desks. Meanwhile, the decision directly impacted me—and my neighbor.

As Black and white children began attending school together across the country, some of us were forming friendships in defiance of the color line.

Two little girls concocted a scheme.

When she left for school each morning, I would leave around the same time. We would walk on separate sides of the street, pretending to ignore the other. Once we were far enough from the prying eyes of adults, we would meet up and proceed the rest of the way together. Our plan worked! We clasped hands and practically skipped into the school building together.

We pulled this off a few times until grown-up affairs intervened once again. One day, I saw a moving van parked outside their house. It had been sold, and our neighbors left soon after, without so much as a friendly wave as their car pulled away. I never saw my playmate again.

I was confused and sad. Ours was a sweet, innocent friendship. Somehow, even as a child, I recognized that our different skin tones should not have precluded us from learning and playing together.

My parents may have discussed the matter among themselves, but I do not recall either of them saying anything to me. Children were seen and not heard, and we knew better than to ask about what they called "grown folks' business."

Perhaps my mother and father had no words to explain such heady concepts as racism to a child, or white flight, which was sweeping our neighborhood and countless communities across the country.

The good news was that incremental progress was being made. In 1947, Jackie Robinson broke the color barrier in Major League Baseball. The following year, President Truman signed an executive order desegregating the armed forces.

A societal transformation was underway. Change was swirling around the Moseleys, too.

Many people in my parents' generation did not have friendships or intimate relationships with anyone of another race or creed.

My family's experience, however, was quite the opposite, influenced by Daddy's showbiz background and our family's progressive politics.

Throughout his life, my father was what was known back then as a "race" man—someone dedicated to bettering the conditions of their race—as well as a reformer and activist. He never hesitated to speak up in favor of civil rights, union and labor causes, and equality for working-class and poor people. He would declare: "That's the way you get your blessings."

Meanwhile, my mother's family was equally open-minded. She was fond of saying, "It doesn't matter whether you came to this country on the *Mayflower* or on a slave ship, we're all in the same boat now."

My parents had friends across a broad spectrum of humanity. Our house was often filled with all manner of people: Black, white, Asian, Native American, Hispanic. One of my mother's best friends was a Polish woman. One of my "uncles" was Japanese;

another was Jewish. And the musicians whom Daddy jammed with were every color of the rainbow.

Mother's glamorous older sister, Auntie Darrel, had gotten hitched to a white man—Uncle Norman—before interracial marriages became legal in the 1960s. She loved men of any race and was also rumored to have dated a big-time Chicago mobster. My point is, I was exposed early in life to a wide range of people who offered me a different perspective on race relations, a picture of what a diverse nation and world could be.

My parents' friends and associates were an eclectic mix of musicians, artists, intellectuals, ordinary folks, and movers and shakers.

They converged harmoniously in our home when my parents threw house parties from time to time. I knew Charlie "Bird" Parker, Thelonious Monk, Gene Ammons, and my aunt dated Dexter Gordon at one point. Occasionally, a few of Hollywood's stars and starlets were among our guests.

I was very young, but those splendid celebrations still figure in my mind.

My siblings and I relished watching the guests arrive in their finest attire, and seeing them mingle, dance, and sip cocktails.

I remember one sparkling gathering when I was about five years old. My parents had already tucked me and John in with our favorite bedtime rhyme:

To bed, to bed, you sleepy head.
Let's wait a minute, said Slow.
Let's open the pot, said Greedy Gut, and we'll eat before we go.

But I was wide awake and determined to join the festivities.

I was not a mischievous child, per se, but I was precocious, inquisitive, and prone to getting into things as a result of my curiosity.

48 CAROL MOSELEY BRAUN

As the eldest, I was also the ringleader, and my little brother obediently followed whatever his big sister told him to do.

That evening, during the soiree, we snuck into my parents' bedroom, where my mother had laid out jewelry and cosmetics on her dressing table. There was a jar of fade cream, advertised in those days as vanishing cream, which I'd seen my mother rub on her face before bedtime. I decided to use the "vanishing cream" to our advantage.

"Let's put this on and go to the party!" I told John. "We'll be invisible and they won't know we're there."

In my mind, the plan was foolproof.

We made a grand entrance, streaking through the crowd naked as jaybirds and smeared from head to toe in creamy goop.

The guests laughed and clapped at our antics. Our parents were not amused, however, and after we had worn out our welcome, we were ushered back to our rooms and put to bed. That night is one of my fondest childhood memories.

I learned as a little girl to hold on tightly to the good times, lest the beautiful memories scatter like dust in the wind.

HOME IS WHERE THE HEART (AND FIGHTING) IS

Daddy sat down at the baby grand piano in our living room, slowly flipping the sheet music with his sturdy brown hands.

Seemingly in a trance, he began to play soft, gentle notes. As his fingers danced across the ebony and ivory keys, the achingly lovely strains of "Clair de Lune" wafted through our house.

We were his captive audience. My mother, my siblings, and I sat scattered around the room, gazing up as he played. Yet the expression about music having "charms to soothe the savage breast" certainly did not apply to his impromptu performance. With each arpeggio, with every chord of the music rising and falling in succession, the collective mood in our home shifted through phases of tension, anxiety, and ultimately, fear.

As a little girl, I trembled each time Daddy performed Debussy's famous piece, because I knew from experience what was coming next. The same hands that so skillfully played the piano, would soon inflict another brutal beating upon us.

★ ★ ★

If the old adage that "opposites attract" is true, my parents' marriage was a test case.

My mother and father could not have been more different.

Mother was a homebody, "fireside and slippers," as she termed it. One of her favorite pastimes was sewing, and occasionally she made our clothes. She enjoyed baking, and homemade pies were her specialty.

Daddy did not want to sit at home. He had come up in a showbiz family, and while he was not someone who drank or partied excessively, he enjoyed dressing up and going out on the town from time to time.

My parents also had different approaches when it came to religion and spirituality.

Mother's family were practicing Catholics, and we were raised in the faith. Mass was part of our Sunday routine at the parish not far from our home. As a child, I met many men and women of the cloth, including a Black priest, and a few Black nuns, who were rare and made a positive impression on me.

My father was more of a spiritual seeker. He wanted to expose his children to the spectrum of religious practices and doctrines.

He drove us around to churches of different denominations, and we also visited synagogues, mosques, and temples. The amalgamation of those early spiritual experiences shaped me, and together with my Catholic upbringing and adoration of the Father, Son, and Holy Spirit, laid the foundation for my strong faith.

They may not have seen eye to eye on religion, but there was one thing that Mother and Daddy could agree upon. My parents constantly drilled the idea of education, education, education into our heads. They stressed the formal pursuit of knowledge not only as a means for self-advancement, but racial progress, and uplifting the broader community, nation, and world.

They told us with education we could achieve anything.

Mother was my first role model and taught me to "do the best job you can where you're planted." This was her ethos, which eventually became mine, that whatever you do is a reflection of who you are, so it is imperative to do the best job possible.

Daddy had a similar philosophy. He introduced me to the concept of ambition, and at an early age conveyed to me that women need not place limits on themselves.

In my day, it was still uncommon to see Black lawyers, or women practicing law, and Black women lawyers were veritable unicorns. Daddy was the first person who told me I should become a lawyer. I suppose having a lawyer for a daughter was the next best thing to being one himself. He truly believed in me.

My father's encouragement was one of the many contradictions of his complicated, mercurial personality. He could be a loving advocate one minute, and an absolute monster the next.

It felt as if we were living with a madman. We were pummeled. Chased. Beaten with belts.

My youngest siblings were largely spared, but John and I were not. As the eldest, I was often singled out. I remember once when I forgot to do the dishes, my father soaked a wet rope in the bathtub, then whipped me. He could not only be cruel, but sadistic.

The fighting in our house typically followed a pattern. Something would set Daddy off.

He would yell at my mother, and she would yell back, their voices carrying through the house and crashing against the walls.

Sometimes they traded barbs, and the insults would end there. At other times, he used intimidation, such as waving his police revolver.

In fact, Daddy's wrath led to him losing his job on the force. The story goes that one day in the precinct, he expressed interest in a leadership position. A white officer laughed and told him that a N—cop, would never be promoted.

Woe to the fool who crossed my father. He beat his colleague up, badly. We don't know if the incident was the first time he'd acted violently on the job. No matter: he was fired.

My father losing that steady, well-paying position only added to the tensions in our household.

It's not that he was lazy. My father did everything under the sun after that—from working at a major automotive company, to selling life insurance, and trying various entrepreneurial ventures.

But he was not one to kowtow to authority. Daddy did not hesitate to tell white supervisors to kiss his black ass. In an era where "colored" and "Negro" men were routinely emasculated in public, his defiance took courage. On some level, I think Mother understood, and even admired his courage—that he was standing up for himself in the face of blatant racism.

But understanding only goes so far, especially when there are mouths to feed.

While Daddy cycled through jobs, my mother worked her butt off, hoping that our father might tuck tail and become a bit humbler in the workplace.

Mother had a tireless work ethic. To supplement her salary, she would often accept "on call" jobs wherever the hospital needed extra staff, sometimes juggling up to three shifts on any given day.

Her sacrifices made it difficult to reconcile Daddy's periodic unemployment, especially when economic realities were at stake: a mortgage, car payments, and most importantly, four small children.

But my father's pride got in the way, time and time again.

With Daddy being fired or quitting jobs left and right, Mother's income often carried the household budget.

That reality seemed to embolden my mother during their arguments. She would sometimes goad him. I remember during one shouting match she yelled, "You've had fifteen jobs in sixteen years!" The zinger was rooted in truth, but it bruised his ego. He stalked out of the room.

Mother could hold her own with verbal jabs, and sometimes dominate, but she was no match for a former pugilist.

She was unable to defend herself against Daddy's blows. One time, he hit her across the face with such force that it nearly put her eye out.

I am sure that the neighbors heard her screams, and ours, and noticed the bruises. But in those days, domestic violence was considered a dirty secret. It was something that happened more often than people realized or cared to admit. Yet it was considered a private matter. People kept it to themselves and didn't acknowledge it publicly. And even among relatives and friends, there was a reluctance to interfere.

Back then, women had little to no resources, or ability to fight back, and even now, too many women struggle under the oppression of domestic abuse. I recall that after one episode, my mother called the police. Things had gotten so bad she had no choice. But when the officers arrived and learned that Daddy was a fellow cop, they looked out for him, and that was that. They left and the abuser remained, ruling the roost. No one protected us.

The violence in our house did not happen daily or weekly, yet it was as constant as the four seasons. We lived on edge, anticipating the next piano concerto that would precede the hell.

Despite the tumult in our home, I do have some happy childhood memories.

Daddy loved to travel, and once school was out, the entire family would embark on road trips across the country. We would pile into the car and set off for adventure. My father enjoyed outdoor pursuits such as fishing and hunting, and we went camping, angling, and visited the national parks.

The Moseleys embarked on exciting road trips to the Grand Canyon and Petrified Forest National Park in Arizona. We once drove all the way out west to Sequoia National Park in California to see the magnificent canopy of trees.

One vacation stands out. We were staying at a Michigan resort, one that I recall my parents saying exclusively catered to
"our people." I was playing with some of the kids who were
fellow guests and bragged that I could drive a car.

My father had a new Buick. By some stroke of luck, he had
left the keys in the ignition. Egged on by my peers, I managed
to start the vehicle and get it in gear.

But when my passengers—all children, mind you—spied my
father walking up the hill, they panicked. A few jumped out
while the car was moving, yelling as they bailed. I was distracted
by their shrieks and the prospect of my father catching me. I ac-
celerated and crashed straight into a tree. For a few minutes, I sat
there, trembling. I was shaken, but thank God, no one was hurt.

My father raced over. To my astonishment, he did not yell or
spank me. He seemed relieved that his daughter—although not
his new car—was intact.

I realize now that before our trips, Daddy must have consulted
the "Green Book"—an indispensable guide for Black people at
that time about where they could find friendly lodging and dining, as well as guidance on which travel routes to safely take.

Back then there was always a level of uncertainty, and of danger, when traveling while Black.

Still, we enjoyed our time together on the open road, savor-
ing Mother Nature, exploring America's tourist attractions, and
making new friends.

While the vacations our family took were welcome respites,
when we returned home, reality smacked us in the face. Literally.

On the open road, Daddy seemed happy and free. Back in
his own castle, however, the king's bullying and brutish behavior would return.

Something had to give. As the violence continued, my poor
mother essentially had a nervous breakdown.

At one point, she lost the ability to walk or move. Lying in
bed, she barely spoke.

One of our neighbors was a psychiatrist, probably the only Black man we knew in the profession. He came over to see Mother as her condition worsened. His diagnosis was that her paralysis was a psychological reaction caused by stress from prolonged abuse.

Honestly, we didn't know if she would make it. By the grace of God, she mustered her strength and recovered in a few weeks. Her condition had been incredibly frightening for all of us. Even Daddy, who was the reason for her distress, seemed frightened.

In retrospect, I believe my father suffered from deep psychological issues himself, although they were never identified or addressed. Sadly, his behavior became more extreme.

One snowy Christmas Eve, my siblings and I were happily helping Mother trim the tree, eagerly awaiting Santa's arrival and the presents Jolly Old Saint Nick might bring.

My father had just come home from a night of carousing with our Great-uncle Rufus, one of his father's brothers.

Daddy was drunk—three sheets to the wind. He told my mother to pack up so we could all drive to his mother's house in Gary, Indiana, which was hundreds of miles away. My mother was incredulous. The idea of our family getting on the road with him drunk behind the wheel was preposterous.

My mother told him as much, and my father became belligerent. He left the room and stumbled toward the spot where he kept his stash of weapons.

My mother looked at us children with fear in her eyes. She knew we had to get out of there. Mother hurriedly slipped our coats over our pajamas, and we bolted out of the house. Mother had one of my younger siblings—then a baby—in her arms.

We knew my father would come after us, so we began crisscrossing through the neighborhood backyards, crawling over and under fences in the snow. We were headed to the bus stop on King Drive. Mother said we would seek refuge at her mother's house across town.

We crouched together behind a tavern on the corner of the

street, near the bus stop. Mother held us close as we huddled, shivering, in the frigid cold. Paralyzed by fear, we did not dare utter a word or even cry.

By that time, Daddy had gotten into his car—in a drunken rage—and had set out trying to find us. We heard him bellowing out the car window as he slowly drove through the icy streets.

As he got closer, we spied a long-barreled shotgun hanging out of the driver's side window. We were terrified. But we remained hidden, waiting for the bus.

After what seemed like an eternity, we spotted the bus pulling up. We ran across the snow, all holding hands. Mother was clutching the baby tightly. Impossibly, we reached the vehicle and were able to board safely. In the mayhem, I dropped my new baby doll, an early Christmas present I had managed to grab as we fled our home. We could not risk going back to get the doll. I was heartbroken.

The bus ride to my grandmother's house was tense. As the bus navigated through the city's icy streets, I half expected to see Daddy pull up alongside the vehicle, hollering at us to get off and come home. Eventually, we arrived at my grandmother's house and practically fell inside when she opened the door. To our great surprise, Daddy was there. He had passed out on the couch. Whether he remembered all that transpired was unclear. The next day, he did not apologize and nothing further was said. Everyone was traumatized, but we tried to have a somewhat normal Christmas.

Life would change after that fateful holiday. Mother was fed up and began contemplating divorce. I never ever played with dolls again. And to this day, I cringe whenever I hear "Clair de Lune."

BUCKET OF BLOOD

After one too many epic battles, my parents were divorcing. Our family of six was shattered and scattered like the wind.

Their acrimonious split, while long overdue, had far-reaching repercussions. For starters, we lost the house.

My parents had fought bitterly during the divorce proceedings about the property. As a married couple, their combined salaries had enabled them to jointly pay the mortgage, something neither one could afford independently. Each furious with the other, they stubbornly refused to make any payments. The impasse stretched on and on until, finally, the bank foreclosed. Our little piece of the American Dream was gone.

First, we lost the house...then we lost Daddy. My father decided to take off, inexplicably, for California. Given his ties to labor causes and entertainment, perhaps he had contacts there.

I do not recall Daddy saying goodbye before leaving Chicago. Perhaps he did, and it's buried deep within my psyche, but something of that magnitude tends to stay with you. Whether there was a fatherly farewell or not, his departure was gut-wrenching.

Mother was shell-shocked. It was one thing for their marriage to implode, but Daddy's decision to move across the country was another. To our mother, it felt almost as if he'd abandoned his own flesh and blood.

My poor mother. She faced the daunting prospect of raising her young'uns solo at a time when she was crushed emotionally, and financially vulnerable.

Mind you, this was the 1950s. Mother was fortunate to have a paraprofessional position at the hospital, yet salaries for working women paled in comparison to those of men.

Moreover, my mother was dealing with the social mores of the era. Women without husbands faced a certain stigma, unfairly, as did single mothers. A Black single mother was often subject to even harsher stereotypes and judgments.

All of this undoubtedly weighed on Mother as she navigated the new realities of her life, and that of her children.

The most pressing concern was that we needed a roof over our heads. I remember my mother circling FOR RENT ads in the newspaper, then driving around to different places, practically begging landlords to rent to us.

Time after time, she was turned away. The explanations given to her were sometimes vague. At other times, the rejection was blatantly expressed: "Ma'am, you have too many children."

Mother could ignore the ignorant comments, but the truth of the matter was that raising four children on one income, without any type of public assistance, was untenable. So, she made a heartbreaking decision, one that would result in another fissure in our already troubled family.

Marsha and Joey, the two youngest siblings, would be sent out of state to stay with "Mama Liz." She lived in Indiana with her second husband. Their home was hundreds of miles away.

We older children—my brother John and I—would remain with Mother and move in with our grandmother, Edna Sr., across town.

Mother agonized about breaking up our household, but she truly felt there was no other choice. I think she reasoned that, at least, everyone would be safe with relatives. That was true, but it did not make the ordeal any less wrenching.

The day dawned for my siblings to leave us.

Mother tried to be strong. In tough times, she could be stoic, so histrionics in front of her brood were out of the question. Still, anguish clouded her pretty face as she gently kissed and squeezed the little ones. We children were bawling uncontrollably, not knowing when we would see or speak with our siblings again.

Remember, we did not have social media, mobile phones, and ride shares in those days. Even with a car, the prospect of regular visits with loved ones who lived hundreds of miles away was daunting.

Practically overnight, it seemed, our family unit was broken— again. Mother was without two of her precious children, and we were without our beloved siblings.

My mother did not have the luxury of wallowing in misery. She had always been a pragmatist, and someone who pushed forward no matter what.

Mother dried her tears, packed up our belongings, and readied me and John to move with her to Grandmother's house.

Crammed into the back seat of her car, sandwiched between my brother and a heap of boxes, I moped and stared out the window. No one said much during the drive. At each traffic light, however, I noticed that the landscape was shifting.

Gone were the tidy houses and leafy, picturesque blocks, replaced by an environment of overcrowded slums and decaying buildings.

When we pulled up to my grandmother's house, though, I breathed a sigh of relief.

The three-story nineteenth-century Victorian house she owned was situated on a street that was an oasis in the midst of grim surroundings. Its period architecture featured a turret and stained-glass windows.

The two Ednas—mother and daughter—were happy to see each other. They embraced, as we sullenly lugged in our suitcases. "Welcome home!" my grandmother said in her sweet Southern drawl, wrapping her arms around me and my brother. Her warmth was contagious, and I managed a slight smile.

Grandmother's place might have been the perfect landing for us, except for one tiny matter that my mother neglected to mention beforehand. Our new homestead was a boarding house. The backstory is that Edna Sr.—by this time divorced from my grandfather, the WWI war hero—had begun taking in boarders to help pay the mortgage. In retrospect, I admire her business savvy. At the time, it was one more seismic shock.

I closed my eyes and wished that when I opened them, we would be back on South Prairie Avenue.

Certainly, our old home was far from the picture of domestic tranquility. Yet, we had some good times in that house, too. My parents loved me and my siblings, that much we knew for certain. And, before Daddy's demons took hold, my mother and father loved each other.

Children crave love and stability. I had the former, but the latter was gone. I was too young to fully understand the dysfunction that swirled around me. I did realize that our world, my world, had turned upside down.

My folks had divorced. My father had flown the coop. My baby siblings had been shipped off.

We had transitioned from a middle-class existence—complete with a four-bedroom home, a dog, rabbits, and a housekeeper—to a boarding house with a bunch of strangers on the wrong side of town. Worse yet, I no longer had my own bedroom.

Mother, ever the optimist, seemed determined to make the best of our imperfect circumstances. She transitioned from being the mistress of her own manor, to being back under her mother's roof, in a truly communal living situation. Our family lived on the first floor, while grandmother's tenants occupied a series of apartments (folks called them kitchenettes back then) on the upper levels. The good news was that we formed bonds with the residents of the boarding house. They became our extended family, and my "uncles" and "aunties" looked out for us. Many a day, the women in the house were surrogate "mamas" while my own mother worked.

It was crowded. There was scant privacy. But I never heard Mother utter a word of complaint, not once. We dared not complain either. The mantra about children being seen and not heard overrode any gripes.

We settled in. One day, not long after our move, I ventured outside and heard some of the neighbors talking. Apparently, our new neighborhood had quite the reputation. Locals simply referred to it as "Bucket of Blood." If that sounds foreboding, well, it was.

Up until our move, I had been relatively sheltered. Unfortunately, I had experienced domestic violence and discrimination at an early age, but I never had real exposure to economic deprivation, lack, and hopelessness.

The Black people in my old world were so-called "strivers" and upwardly mobile. I didn't know a thing about crime, vice, and crushing poverty.

I had no idea that fifteen people could live in a one-bedroom tenement house, with roaches crawling on the walls. I'd never seen hustlers and "ladies of the evening" hanging out on the corners. I'd never heard gunshots echoing through the night. Yet all that—and more—was reality in our newfound neighborhood. As we became part of the community, my eyes were opened.

I will never forget the time when a young mother came tearing out of a nearby apartment building, and her voice was frantic. "A rat bit my baby! A rat bit my baby!" she said, crying and cradling the infant.

Between the mama screaming, her baby wailing, and people hollering for help, near panic ensued. I was just a teenager, but someone needed to take charge.

"We need to get help!" I said. Someone told me that Cook County Hospital was the closest facility that would treat Black people.

I did not want the mother to go there alone, so we made our way there together. She was seated on the floor in the hallway, as the baby wailed. We waited for hours and hours before anyone on staff would admit and attend to this ailing little baby.

I can still remember my rage building, as I tried in vain to process how something like this could happen in a civilized society. "This is not right!" I kept repeating. "It's not supposed to be this hard to see a doctor!"

After waiting nearly all day, someone finally came out and called the mother's name. The baby was treated and, miraculously, was in decent health. The mother thanked me profusely as we exited the hospital. This emergency had ended well, but the entire episode left me shaken.

Even before that infant could walk or talk, poverty had left its mark—literally—in the form of a rat bite.

I credit that time in my life, in large part, with motivating me to enter public service.

The hideous things that I witnessed that day, and overall, in my community, demanded answers.

The human suffering that I saw all around me lit a fire in my heart. Public office eventually became my vehicle to try and change things.

That entire period in my life was difficult. I was grappling with teenage angst, magnified by my father's absence.

I was receiving adult attention from the wrong types. The

local pimp, "Tee-Bone," had taken a liking to me. He began offering me rides home from school.

Seated in his Cadillac, I wondered if this smooth sweet talker was simply being nice, or if he was trying to recruit me for his stable of women. One time, when we got to my grandmother's house, he leaned in close. "I can take care of you if you ever need anything," he said, his smile revealing shiny gold teeth.

"Um, okay," I replied nervously. I practically leapt out of the front seat and bolted into the house.

I was starting to understand that young women who lived in Bucket of Blood were at risk of growing up way too fast.

One day, I was walking around Lake Michigan with a few new girlfriends when one of them casually asked me, "You got any kids?" I was taken aback.

I was about fourteen or fifteen years old at the time, and told her so. "You mean to tell me you ain't got a man at your age? And no kids?" she asked incredulously.

The other girls nodded their heads in agreement and snickered.

That night at home, I looked in the mirror and wondered if there was something wrong with me. I did not have a man. I did not have children.

It sounds unbelievable now, but my self-esteem was suffering because I was a Goody Two–shoes who was trying to do the right things: study hard, respect my elders, and so on.

By this time, I was enrolled at Parker High School. Parker was predominately Black, and while there was a white school that was closer, technically, I was not in that district. I wound up taking three transit buses each day across town. Most days, I barely arrived on time.

Yet I made the most of my educational opportunities. I managed to become an honors student, a cheerleader, and I was well-liked by my teachers. Still, I felt like an outsider—a feeling that has followed me all my life.

Although I had steered clear of boys up to that point, I decided it was time for me to get a boyfriend. There were a few nice guys in my classes, and one of them noticed me. We began talking during recess. The word "date" was not even in my vocabulary, but my classmate seemed to have a handle on how to ask a girl out. "Can I come over after school?" he asked.

"Sure!" I said.

We chatted some more, and when he learned that I lived so far from school, he suggested we take the bus to my house together instead of him coming over on his own.

That made sense to me, and we agreed to have our first date the next day. I was incredibly excited. The next morning as I readied for school, I took extra time styling my hair, and applied Vaseline on my lips to make 'em shine. I put on a cute outfit.

After the school bell rang to dismiss everyone that day, I spotted my future beau in the schoolyard. He sauntered over to me with all the teenage male bravado he could manage. "Ready to go?" he asked.

I smiled. "Yes, ready."

The bus ride took a while but was otherwise uneventful. I was nervous, and my classmate seemed suddenly shy. When we reached my stop, we got off and started walking the few short blocks to my grandmother's house, making small talk.

As I approached our block, I saw my mother on the porch. She was vigorously shaking out a large rug. Something other than dust seemed to be flying out of the fibers.

"Hi, Carol. Hello, young man," she said, acknowledging me and my friend. I gave her a wan smile, and tried to hurry past her, lest she begin asking questions about my budding romance. You don't do that with Southern mamas, though. She smiled and asked his name, age, and family history. Pretty soon, she would have us hitched!

Once the question and answer session was over, we came inside. To my dismay, our normally pristine home was in an absolute disarray. And there was a very odd chemical smell.

Apparently, my mother had decided to use one of those cockroach bombs that fumigates and draws the insects out of their hiding places. Creepy black critters were scurrying all over the place—in the house, on the porch, and even out on the lawn.

While Mother looked pleased with her handiwork, I was mortified. So was my date. He was gracious enough to remain silent, but I could tell from his facial expression that he was horrified. Our first date ended before it began.

The next day at school, he barely said hello. I was just praying that he hadn't told anyone that Carol Moseley was living in a roach motel. Needless to say, we never went out again. So much for the birds and bees; the cockroaches did me in.

My quest for teenage romance would have to wait. My reproductive system was rebelling, even before I had time to think about what to do with a boy.

I had always been something of a sickly child. As a toddler, I somehow contracted tuberculosis, a bacterial infection that affects the lungs.

In my day, TB, as it was called, was very serious and potentially deadly. Mother blamed herself, thinking that somehow the germs she brought home from her hospital job were to blame.

I was hospitalized for several days, slipping in and out of consciousness, as my parents and relatives held a prayer vigil by my bedside.

It sounds incredible, but I had a near-death experience while in the hospital.

I remember walking toward what appeared to be a shack or cabin. The sun was shining, and I was wearing a white dress. A soothing voice kept telling me, "Stay awake, don't go to sleep." I don't recall much else, but when I awakened several hours later my fever had broken. I was elated to be able to go home with my mother and father. Looking back, I felt an inexplicable sense of peace. I now know it was the presence of a Higher Power, and I believed that the Creator saved my life.

This go round, I was a teen who was terribly ill. I had started my menstrual cycle around age twelve, and my menses had always been very painful and accompanied by heavy bleeding. Each month, I would skip school for at least a day or so. I would lie in bed, cramped and feeling the chills, popping aspirin as blood soaked through my bedsheets.

My family had become so used to my monthly trauma, that no one paid me any mind when I took to my bed one afternoon after school. But when one of my mother's friends came over that night, she inquired about me. Mother said I had been in bed all day, and her friend popped upstairs to check on me. She took one look at me and said, "Edna, this girl needs to see a doctor!"

Mother looked ashen. She loaded me in her car, and we rushed to the ER. I was doubled over with pain and barely able to walk. The team admitted me immediately. The doctors said that I was hemorrhaging blood by the minute. Had I remained at home, I likely would have died.

After a week or so recuperating, I was able to return to school. I was able to catch up on my missed coursework, which was a relief. I was a good student, and had been selected for a gifted and talented program off campus. I planned to go to college. Several of my teachers had already told me that I had "potential."

It was hard to focus on my studies, however, because that period of my life felt so unbearable.

As soon as I was old enough, I got myself a part-time job. I was a cashier after school, and I would work five or six hours, then hurry home to face a long to-do list.

I felt like Cinderella. My mother was working all the time, leaving me with far too many adult responsibilities. I was cooking meals, cleaning, and trying to keep an eye on my two youngest siblings who thankfully had come back to us from Indiana.

Marsha was super smart and bookish. Daddy had sent her a set of Biblical encyclopedias, and she would read them and other books for hours. Years later, she would receive a scholarship to attend Yale University, graduate cum laude, and go on to earn a law degree from Harvard. Joey, the baby of the bunch, was equally special: serious and detail-oriented, traits that would serve him well in his future career as a police officer turned detective. They were good children, but I could tell they did not like me bossing them around, nor meting out discipline.

The one who really needed to be corralled was John. The eldest son was acting out, beginning to experiment with alcohol and skipping school.

One day, I came home and John was kicked back on the couch. He had on new clothes and was sporting a brand-new gold watch which he waved in my direction. "Look what Auntie Darrel gave me," he boasted.

It wasn't his birthday or anything like that, and I was perplexed by the gifts. John explained that our mother's sister wanted to encourage him to remain in school.

I don't know what came over me, but I lost it.

Here I was studying hard, helping around the house, and babysitting my siblings. No one said thank you, no one gave me a gift.

I stomped upstairs and dialed one of my friends on the phone, asking if I could come over for a few days. She agreed. I threw a few items into my book bag and left, slamming the door.

I did not call it running away, but that is what it amounted to. I was tired of being the good girl. I felt the need to get away from all the mess that had been happening in my family for years.

I came back home eventually, but whenever something upset me I left for a few days. I wound up running away again several times. My mother was beside herself, fretting and taking my rebellion personally.

I loved Mother, I loved my siblings. I knew, however, that I was too young for all the responsibilities that had been laid at my feet.

By senior year, I had begun applying to colleges. I remember watching some of my peers navigate the process with input from their parents', but I did the legwork basically on my own sans assistance.

I graduated as the class salutatorian. It was a jubilant moment when I walked across that stage, and my loved ones were there cheering me on.

I had received a partial scholarship to the University of Illinois Urbana-Champaign, about a two-hour drive from Chicago. I could not wait to enter a new environment.

I will never regret my time living in Bucket of Blood. I had seen the world through a different lens, and while it was not always pretty, the people and experiences therein offered me a greater perspective on life.

Now it was time to spread my wings and fly.

MARCHING WITH A KING

"Don't go down there, Carol," my mother warned me, her voice a mixture of fear and anger. "You'll get yourself killed!"

I nodded my head but said nothing, hoping my mother would interpret my silence as an implicit agreement not to go. I already knew, however, that I planned to disobey her. I was headed to a civil rights protest in Chicago led by Dr. Martin Luther King Jr.

It was the summer of 1966. I was nineteen years old. The fight for equality had been ignited across the Deep South in places like Georgia, Mississippi, and my mother's native Alabama. I knew why my mother was so afraid to let me go to the protest; her life had been permanently scarred by racism and unchecked violence. Her older sister had been killed years earlier in Union Springs, Alabama—run over by a truck—a heinous crime that ultimately led to the family migrating to Chicago. Mother lived with that trauma every day, and now her worst fears were being reignited all over again.

In spite of my mother's admonition, I was not deterred. I couldn't escape news of the protests, even if I tried. My peers had been talking nonstop about the Movement, and there had been nonstop press coverage about Dr. King bringing his message to my hometown.

I wanted to be part of freedom's cause, and felt my participation was the right thing to do, if not the only thing to do. All of my life, I'd been raised by my family to help somebody along the way. Marching with Dr. King seemed the best way to put those teachings into practice. My mother was not at all political, but my father had a heart for social justice. I'd inherited that.

King and fellow leaders of the Southern Christian Leadership Conference had come to the Midwest at the request of the Chicago Freedom Movement. Their mission was to push for improved living conditions for Negroes, many of whom were concentrated in slums and public housing across the city. Dr. King even moved with his family into a dilapidated apartment, which was overrun with vermin, to bring attention to the decrepit conditions many Black Chicagoans were forced to live in.

That hot August morning, I dropped my mother off at the hospital where she worked and assured her that I would be back later to pick her up, as usual. Once she was out of eyesight, I drove the short distance to Marquette Park which was right on the southwest side of town. The park was located in a rough, working-class white neighborhood where Negroes knew not to venture.

As I pulled up to the park, I was astonished by the size of the crowd. There were hundreds of people all crammed together, the heat and hostility rising up through the air. Even more astonishing, though, was the viciousness of the mob that met the marchers. Men, women, and children alike were standing around the park, screaming all kinds of nasty obscenities, their faces animated with rage. Suddenly I understood why my mother was so afraid of me being in the midst of people who harbored such hatred in their hearts.

I made my way through the rabid crowd toward the demonstration. The veteran civil rights marchers organized us in a line, so that we were basically walking down the street in pairs of two. My marching partner was an older white male, probably in his thirties. While I don't remember his name, I will always remember his reassuring calm. He seemed to be a veteran civil rights protestor because he remained poised and levelheaded throughout the entire march. I was thankful to him because my heart was practically beating out of my chest, and with good reason.

Shortly after we began marching, the mob began throwing rocks, bottles, and bricks at us.

They were spitting and yelling all kinds of awful things. No one was safe. There was a group of nuns marching alongside us, and the crowds hurled insults and obscenities their way, too. "Sister, which one of these N—s are you going to sleep with tonight?" Some even called these sisters of the cloth "bitches." It was simply horrific. Dr. King later told the press, "I've been in many demonstrations all across the South, but I can say that I have never seen—even in Mississippi and Alabama—mobs as hostile and as hate-filled as I've seen here in Chicago."

I was very upset, as you can imagine, having never been exposed to any of this. I had come to the march determined to stand up for equality and freedom, and even though I knew there were some who might oppose us, I was not fully prepared for the ugliness I witnessed that day. My marching partner coached me through it all, telling me what to do, what not to do, and how to avoid getting rattled. Which was good, because I was trying desperately not to be scared.

We marched to the middle of the park, and I noticed that people were starting to congregate and form what appeared to be a human shield. I deduced that the veteran marchers had protocols for Dr. King's protection. Women and children stood on the inside of the developing circle, with the men forming the outside barrier. As a young woman, the veteran marchers probably thought I was a child or something close to that, so I was moved to the inside.

It all happened so quickly.

I suddenly found myself within arm's distance of the famous minister, who, just years earlier had delivered his dream of racial harmony to a global audience. I was close enough to touch this American hero. So close, in fact, that I could see the beads of sweat on his brown skin, see his soulful and penetrating eyes.

Dr. King was like the calm in the eye of a hurricane. All around us, there was mayhem. At some point as the crowd was hurling objects, the reverend was hit, struck in the back of his head by a rock. He stumbled a bit and fell to one knee. I saw him, crouched down in an almost Jesus-like way. His face was beatific. He took a few minutes to compose himself and rose again to his feet. I was amazed how composed and unflappable he was through it all—he didn't let the violence touch his spirit.

Truthfully, a part of me wanted to pick up something and throw it right back. But Dr. King's adherence to the principles of nonviolence impressed me. There was chaos all around, but he appeared serene in the midst of it.

When I was born in the 1940s, the Civil Rights Movement had not yet fully bloomed, though the seeds had been planted.

As a child, I saw the Movement unfolding before my eyes, pushing the envelope about the "place" of Black people in society. My father was a member of the National Association for the Advancement of Colored People (NAACP), the nation's oldest civil rights group, which was leading the charge to dismantle legal segregation. The NAACP aggressively employed a litigation strategy in the courts, led by brilliant Black lawyers, including some of my heroes, Constance Baker Motley and Thurgood Marshall, the future Supreme Court justice. He and his legal team had successfully argued a series of landmark cases, among them, *Brown v. Board of Education of Topeka* in 1954.

Brown, a momentous Supreme Court decision that I would later study in law school, ruled that separating public schoolchildren in Kansas—or anywhere else—on the basis of race was unconstitutional. It signaled the end of legalized racial segregation in public schools nationwide, overruling the "separate but equal" doctrine set forth in the 1896 *Plessy v. Ferguson* case.

In May 1955, the high court released another decision, sometimes referred to as *Brown II*. States were instructed to commence their desegregation plans "with all deliberate speed."

Thus, states began the process of integrating their school systems. This made me what was known as a "Brown baby." I was about seven years old when I integrated my local elementary school, which had previously been all white. To be clear, this was no "Little Rock Nine" situation. I never had to brave an angry mob or run a gauntlet to reach the schoolhouse door, but there were challenges. There were frequent skirmishes and name-calling in the schoolyard, which may have been discriminatory in nature, or may have simply been the normalized bullying that many students encounter. However, I wound up fighting a lot. And, I remember my embarrassment when one of my white teachers placed me in the "dummy" row in the back of the classroom, a result of what was then my undiagnosed dyslexia. As a little Black girl integrating a white school, I was not given the attention I needed at that time.

By the time I reached high school, my classmates were mostly Black. There, I was surrounded by a community of students that all looked like me. I didn't have to worry about the exhausting injustices of racism on a daily basis. But once I left the school grounds or ventured outside of my neighborhood, certain parts of Chicago were not safe.

On one particular afternoon, I caught the bus to the downtown shopping district to look for new school clothes. It wasn't unusual for me to move about on my own because my parents' divorce forced me to become self-sufficient.

After I finished shopping, I stepped into a luncheonette to get a cup of coffee. The eatery had a counter with stools, so I sat down with my packages, preparing to order. Immediately, I sensed that something was wrong. It felt as if people were staring at me, and they were. I slowly looked around and noticed that I was the only Black patron in the place. I sat there for a while, waiting to be served. But the waitresses ignored me, and the other customers around me either looked away uncomfortably or shot me dirty looks.

Taking a page from that of countless freedom fighters, I decided then and there that I would stand up for what was right. There is an old Negro spiritual, "I Shall Not Be Moved," which dates back to the days of slavery. Inspired by Biblical scripture, it speaks of one trusting in the Lord and being like "a tree planted by the waters," steadfast and unmoving. Centuries later, that spiritual morphed into a popular song called "We Shall Not Be Moved" that was used during labor protests in the 1930s, and later, during the Civil Rights Movement. I knew this song, and it gave me strength that day. I decided that I would not be moved.

I launched an impromptu, one-woman sit-in, just like students were doing all around the country in that era. I was familiar with this type of direct action, which dominated the news. One in particular captured the public's attention. In the winter of 1960, four Black college students from North Carolina Agricultural and Technical College entered a F.W. Woolworth five and dime in Greensboro, North Carolina.

The A & T students purchased their items before sitting at the lunch counter reserved for white customers. When a waitress asked them to leave, they politely refused. For whatever reason, they were not arrested. But they also weren't served. The four students remained seated for nearly an hour until closing time.

The following morning, about two dozen new students arrived at the same Woolworth's and sat down at the counter. They would not be moved. Day three led to more coordinated peaceful protests. As their actions gained national media coverage, the mayor and city officials scrambled to find a resolution. By the summer of 1960, the Woolworth's lunch counter had been desegregated. The spark these young people lit—which would inspire my protest a few years later—turned into a flame. In the months that followed, thousands of students and people, representing many races, religions, and creeds, participated in sit-ins in cities and towns in the South and beyond. That day at the luncheonette, I did not have any of my peers with me, nor were there any reinforcements coming. I probably should have been scared, but I was just so outraged. Outraged that no one would serve me, let alone look at me. Outraged that I might be asked to leave, just because of the color of my skin. So I sat there. I would not be moved. About a half hour passed. I would not be moved. Finally, a waitress came over, and begrudgingly took my order. When she brought the coffee back to me, of course, I did not dare to drink it. Who knows what in the world was in that cup? However, I politely put my quarter down on the counter to pay for the beverage, and I left. I was shaken by the experience, and given my mother's experiences with racial discrimination, I didn't tell her what had happened. But I was proud of myself. In my own small way, I had taken a firm stand for justice and equality.

The luncheonette incident was not my only brush with racism as a young person. My high school, Parker High School, opened in 1901 on Chicago's South Side. It was named for Francis W. Parker, a military colonel, leading to our school nickname: The Colonels. Our colors were green and white, and the official school song was clearly penned for the once all-white student body that became predominantly Black:

Green for the tall straight pine trees
White for the fine ideal of youth
The glorious colors of Parker
The emblem of spirit and truth

I was a cheerleader, an activity generally associated with popular girls, although I was never really part of the "in" crowd. Yet I had made the cheering squad, and there was something about donning our cute little uniforms that made me feel as if I fit in.

One year, Parker's football team played a game against South Shore, the white high school across town. Chicago is a city built on ethnic diversity: Irish, Italian, Lithuanian, Polish, German, Puerto Rican, and more—all coexisting—but African Americans and whites did not live in the same neighborhoods, attend the same schools, or churches; nor socialize, ever.

However, the adults in charge saw fit to bring kids together who were normally separated, through athletics. The football game was a big deal, and we traveled to the South Shore side to play. I remember crowds of cheering fans, the bright lights of the stadium, and the excitement as the game began. We cheerleaders tumbled and did cartwheels in our outfits, and I was proud to root for my school. Our cheers and chants must have done the trick because Parker went on to win the game over South Shore. It was a moment of jubilation and celebration, which quickly turned to mayhem.

Shortly after our win was secured, a mini riot broke out, led by the South Shore side. The next thing I knew, we cheerleaders were being chased through the streets by the players on the opposing team, and possibly folks from the neighborhood who joined them. They were hollering out, yelling obscenities, threatening to beat us to smithereens. We could tell they weren't kidding.

In that neighborhood, we could not blend in, and with my cheerleading uniform on, it felt as if I had a scarlet letter on my back. I ran as fast as my legs could carry me, never looking back for fear of what would happen if they caught me. I didn't know where I was running, I just ran. Wanting to get off the streets, I ducked into a building—one of those multifamily units that were prevalent then in Chicago—and I hid. I was alone, very frightened, and defenseless. I stayed there for maybe twenty minutes or so before peeking out to make sure the coast was clear. I made a run for it. Eventually, I safely made it home, but the sheer terror of being chased by an angry mob would help fuel my desire to build a more equitable society.

The Civil Rights Movement stretched on throughout the 1960s, and we moved the needle toward ending segregation and uplifting the cause of freedom.

Growing up, my experiences on the cheering squad and at the luncheonette counter helped to shape who I was, and the public servant that I would become.

Yet it was my time marching with Dr. King that left the biggest impact. Watching him, it was the power of his actions and civil disobedience which convinced me that nonviolence is always the righteous path. I was aware of more militant groups, including the Black Panthers. I had friends, including Bobby Rush, who joined the Panthers years before he became a congressman. Other friends used terms like "pigs" and worse, but as the relative of police officers, I didn't feel comfortable with that language. I did not harbor ill against law enforcement. And I did not hate white people or anyone else.

Dr. King's words, and his unwavering bravery on the day of the march, even in the face of violence and possible death, changed my life. It convinced me of the morality of peace, of sisterhood and brotherhood, and of always striving to make the world a better place. These are the ideals that have carried me throughout my life, then and now.

There's a well-known story in the Bible that speaks of a woman who pushed through the crowd to reach Jesus, touching the hem of His garment in hopes of being healed. On that day in my hometown, the good Lord gave me a glimpse of one of His earthly messengers, by bringing me close to Dr. King. And just like that believer eons ago, I, too, was healed.

COLLEGE AND THE COW

I was determined to become the first person in my family to earn a college degree. I had a partial scholarship, a blessing for which I was thankful. That, coupled with my savings from various jobs, had enabled me to cobble together enough to cover tuition and expenses.

I was bound for academic adventure at the University of Illinois Urbana-Champaign. The school was located about 140 miles southwest of Chicago in the historic "twin" cities of Urbana and Champaign in central Illinois.

I had embarked upon the two-and-a-half-hour trip "downstate"—as we locals fondly refer to that neck of the woods—via train. I was traveling on my own.

By this time, I was highly independent. My family was supportive, naturally, of my collegiate ambitions, yet blissfully unaware of the details. By necessity, I had become self-sufficient and accustomed to handling my own affairs.

As the train rattled past rolling hills and fields of tall prairie grass, my head was in the clouds, evoking lyrics from a popular folk song, "The Ballad of Casey Jones":

Gonna ride that train to the end of the line
There's ridges and bridges, and hills to climb
Got a head of steam and ahead of time.
Ahead of time, ahead of time...

I spent the journey napping, nibbling on a bag lunch, and pondering what my future might look like as a college student.

After thinking about majoring in art history, and hearing everyone rail against the idea, I decided to major in premed, with the aim of becoming a doctor. The goal was a lofty one, certainly, but my parents had drilled into the Moseley children that we could achieve most anything with education, hard work, and tenacity. I viewed college as my ticket to ride.

As the train pulled into the depot, I tried to collect myself before disembarking. I had packed light.

I lugged my suitcase to the exit. A few taxicabs were lined up outside the station. I climbed in and made small talk with the driver until we pulled up to the sprawling campus, with its mix of stately historic and modern buildings.

My new collegiate home awaited. I was filled with giddy anticipation about this next chapter of my life.

I was entering college in the 1960s, an era marked by social upheaval and cultural change. Civil rights marches. Antiwar protests. The rise of feminism, and hippies espousing "peace and love."

The University of Illinois is a state school with deep roots in the Prairie State. Founded in the 1870s as a public land grant institution for working people, none other than Abraham Lincoln had lobbied for the school during his career as a young Illinois lawyer. By the 1920s, the university was being touted as what one leader called "an oasis of intellectuality in a desert of fertility."

Fast forward to the twenty-first century, and the university is one of the largest state schools in the nation. Its academic system boasts multiple campuses, and an enrollment north of fifty thousand students who hail from across the country and around the world.

Six decades ago, however, the environs were decidedly less diverse. In a sea of students, women and students of color were barely represented. Black student enrollment, in particular, was very low.

As I moved around, I just did not see many people who looked like me, be it fellow students or instructors. I was the only Black girl in my entire dormitory—unless I somehow missed someone else.

There had been early Black students at the university, pioneers who paved the way for my generation of scholars. Jonathan Rogan first integrated the student body in 1887; he stuck it out for a year. Three years later, William Walter Smith would become the university's first Black graduate, and he later completed a second degree in engineering.

There were also early Black women graduates. Maudelle Brown Bousfield earned her mathematics degree with honors in 1906 and went on to become the first Black principal in the Chicago public school system.

Certainly, there were high-achieving Black students during my era, including scholar-athletes on the school's football and basketball teams. But I didn't know any of them. If only I had become acquainted with these fellow degree aspirants.

My freshman year had barely begun, and already I was lonely. I tried to fit in and make friends, and some of my peers were nice to me. Yet I felt like an outsider, an ache that was all too familiar.

I longed for companionship. Eventually I found it, albeit in an entirely unexpected way.

My dorm looked out over a wide grassy field. One day, I noticed a herd of cows grazing. The next thing I knew, one of them had wandered up to my window, which was on the first floor. At that moment, I was stupefied.

I was face-to-face with this bovine, who mooed loudly. If you have ever seen a cow close up, needless to say these animals are huge. A mature Holstein, for instance, can weigh anywhere from 1,500 to 1,700 pounds.

However, as someone who'd spent summers on my great-grandmother's farm, the cow did not frighten me. I had seen my share of livestock. Looking into the eyes of this gentle giant, I felt a compassionate connection with one of God's creatures.

It's hilarious looking back, but that cow and I became fast friends. I quickly learned that my bovine buddy was ravenous. I began racing back from class and feeding her my leftover food—especially apples—from the cafeteria. At this rate, the cow was getting more out of my daily meal plan than I was.

That cow's presence was a mystery to me. Why did she pick my window in the first place? Did she understand when I smiled and spoke in soothing tones to her? I later learned that the university has an agriculture school with a global reputation. Possibly, the herd was connected all those years ago to its curriculum.

Whatever the case, that sweet cow kept me sane at a time when I was trying to cope with a series of challenges.

I was away from home for the first time and missed my loved ones. Our family dynamic had its complexities, but we dearly loved each other.

I was in an environment where I felt no sense of camaraderie. Moreover, I was starting to question if I was safe.

One semester, one of my roommates invited me to come and spend the weekend at her house.

I was thrilled that someone finally wanted to include me in

their social activities. The fact that my roommate was white never crossed my mind.

Before I could respond and tell her that I looked forward to the slumber party, she told me, "My father will defend you regardless."

I wasn't sure what to make of that remark. I remember thinking, "Why are you saying this to me? Why would your father have to defend me?" Her tone was reassuring, but I was confused by her words.

Turns out that there was a sundown law in her Illinois town. Essentially, this meant that no Black people could be caught in the community after dark. As the daughter of Black Southerners, I immediately understood the unspoken and hidden dangers.

"Thank you very much," I said, making it clear that I was declining the invitation. "I will probably go home this weekend."

My sense of feeling like a fish out of water did not go away. Meanwhile, I was struggling in some of my classes. When I decided to pursue the science and premed track, I really had not thought the matter through.

I wanted to become a doctor in order to help people. I'd always earned good grades in my science classes. However, I had little to no aptitude for higher-level classes such as biology and chemistry. I also knew from experience that I lacked the constitution for the gorier aspects of medicine.

Back in high school, I had volunteered as a "candy striper" at my mother's hospital. We wore red-and-white-striped pinafores and lent a hand wherever the hospital needed us.

My very first day, I observed a surgical procedure that involved ample amounts of blood. I took one look and fainted. When I came to, a small crowd had gathered around me. I was embarrassed beyond belief! They did not let me go, but I was promptly transferred to the medical records department.

I was clearly in the wrong major. But so-so grades were not my only concern.

Out of the blue, I wound up contracting mono, which college students in my day called "the kissing disease."

I had not kissed any guys on campus or off. Yet I had a sore throat, a fever, and felt lethargic. The campus doctor who diagnosed me explained that I would need to be quarantined, and my recovery would take several weeks.

I curled up under the covers in the infirmary's single bed feeling absolutely miserable. Besides my health, I was extremely worried about missing classes and coursework that would need to be made up.

I felt overwhelmed. At some point, someone arranged for me to call my mother. She seemed surprised yet happy to hear from me. As I began talking, however, she heard the desperation in my voice. "What's wrong, Carol?" she asked, sounding alarmed. "Are you alright?"

"No, Mother," I said, trying not to burst into tears. "I'm sick. I am coming home."

I took the train back home to Chicago. I was on bed rest for several weeks.

My education was up in the air. I could get an excused absence from classes due to illness, but if I stayed out too long, I would have to officially withdraw from school.

A spate of conflicting thoughts ran through my head. I truly desired a college education. Yet I was a first-generation student dealing with academic demands and social isolation with scant support. The prospect of returning to campus filled me with anxiety.

I felt additional pressure because I wanted to make my family proud of me. Both of my parents had started college but were unable to finish. I wanted to earn a four-year degree for myself—and for them.

As the weeks flew by, I felt better. Yet time was running out for me to either head back to school or remain in Chicago. I did not want to be perceived as a quitter, nor did I want to return to a place where I had been unhappy.

Quit or persevere. Give up or stick it out.

I was mulling over this major decision on my own, one that ostensibly could impact the rest of my life.

I finally convinced myself that college was no longer a possibility for me. I was sad but resigned. In the blink of an eye, I was a college dropout.

I come from generations of women who have always possessed a strong work ethic.

I knew immediately that after dropping out of college, my first order of business was to find a full-time job.

My salary would be used, as it had been for years, to help my family.

I'd first began working around age fifteen or so, as a checkout girl at a local grocery store. Every time I got paid, my mother would take the money and use it to help defray the household bills.

I was a de facto breadwinner.

The good news was that I quickly secured a position—my first "real" job. I was hired by the Chicago Housing Authority, created in the 1930s as an outgrowth of President Franklin D. Roosevelt's sweeping New Deal initiative.

Chicago got its first public housing projects under the New Deal, and CHA managed these properties owned and operated by the federal government.

My title was lengthy—Community and Tenant Relations Aide—and the job entailed providing residents with information and assisting them with accessing available resources for their families.

In my first few weeks, I wore a business suit and went door to door with a clipboard. I noticed that most heads of household were Black mothers, many of them young and about the same age as me. Some of the tenants listened patiently to my spiel, but others made it abundantly clear they had no time or interest.

Fortunately, I was being paid well. In fact, my salary was probably comparable to or higher than what my mother made. Still, I was not sure if the job was fulfilling. I had left college, and my entire future loomed. But to what end? It was a confusing time for me.

Meanwhile, I was dealing with several workplace dilemmas. For starters, one of my managers, did not treat me very well. She spoke to me in harsh tones and frequently made unprofessional demands. I was told to run her errands. One time she even made me go out to her car in the rain to retrieve her stinky shoes.

That was not my only problem at work. Another supervisor, a man, kept asking me out.

I was a young woman and inexperienced. I had no sense of the rules, and such terms as "sexual harassment" were not yet part of the broader lexicon.

The next time he asked me for a date, I relented, albeit reluctantly. I agreed mostly to get him off my back. I should have known better.

We went to a nightclub. To my surprise, I sort of enjoyed myself. But I was tired afterward and planned to call it a night. He begged me to have a nightcap. He scribbled down an address to this Chicago high rise, which I figured was his apartment.

I got there and rang the doorbell. A woman answered. This struck me as odd.

She looked me up and down, and said my date was in the bathroom. I heard water running. While I waited, the woman offered me a drink. After a few minutes, my co-worker emerged from the bathroom. Well, this fool was naked! His privates were fully exposed and standing at attention. He glided over to the couch where I was sitting. "Hey, baby," he whispered in my ear. "Why don't we have a threesome?"

I was stunned, and my head was spinning—literally. That

cocktail I had been offered earlier had possibly been spiked. I had only taken a sip or two, but I was dizzy and disoriented.

I was seated near a window. We were on a higher floor of the building, but I pushed it open anyway and gulped in fresh air. I had to get out of there fast. I rose, shakily, and hurried toward the door.

He started to come after me. I wasn't about to stick around and see what else was in store. "Get out of my way, you creep!" I said, pushing past him. He shrank back, jilted. The woman just glared at me.

My hands were trembling as I managed to open the door, dash to the elevator, and bang on the down button. Safely in the lobby, I rushed out into the night.

I was shaken and furious. The next morning at work, he passed my desk and acted as if nothing had happened. But one of the other supervisors, an older man who had been kind and something of a mentor to me, noticed my unease.

I explained what went down and told him I regretted going out with that hound dog in the first place. The older supervisor listened and nodded. He assured me that I had no cause for shame.

Soon after, the two men went into an office and closed the door. I recall hearing some raised voices.

I am not sure whether any disciplinary action was taken. I do know the younger boss did not ask me out again, nor did he give me any further trouble.

I tried to focus on my job, making site visits and doing all that I could to improve the lives of residents in public housing. One afternoon, I was at my desk when the female supervisor called. "They're rioting at the projects!" she yelled into the phone. "Grab a hard hat and get over there!"

I had no idea on that April day in 1968, that Dr. King had been assassinated. I got in my car and raced over to one of Chicago's larger housing complexes. Indeed, there was pandemonium. People in the area were running, screaming. The *pop, pop, pop* of gunfire and smoke from trash can fires permeated the air.

I was trying to make sense of it all, when someone shouted, "They killed Dr. King!"

"No! No, that can't be!" I cried out.

As bullets whizzed over my head, I crouched down and ran for cover, eventually finding shelter behind a massive smoke-stack. I slumped to the ground, my hard hat on, as the tears fell. I sat there for what felt like hours, just rocking back and forth and crying.

The tensions and protests raged on across the city, but eventually calmed down in the housing complex. I made my way home, feeling empty.

I will never, ever forget that day. Not long after, I submitted my resignation. It was time for me to return to college and complete my education. In my own small way, I was honoring Dr. King.

I'd slowly gotten over the disillusionment of my early college experience, and my fervor for higher education returned with a vengeance.

Some of my friends had selected Ivy League or Seven Sisters colleges. I had neither the finances, nor the necessary guidance to navigate getting into such schools.

I decided to re-enroll at the University of Illinois. For my second go-round, I would be attending classes right in my hometown.

The University of Illinois at Chicago Circle—dubbed "Circle" for short—opened its doors to students in early 1965.

The school was championed by Richard J. Daley, the city's legendary, longtime mayor. Mayor Daley had fixed his mind on creating a new public university, and whatever this shrewd and powerful politician wanted, he usually got.

"Circle's" urban campus straddled two immigrant neighborhoods—Little Italy and Greektown—and the university's name was a nod to a nearby freeway loop.

Apparently, that gave Walter Netsch, a renowned Chicago architect (whom I would come to know many years later), ample inspiration. He designed the buildings in concentric circles, with visually stunning results. Everyone was buzzing about the new campus, and I was lucky enough to be one of its inaugural students.

Based on my prior college experience at Urbana-Champaign, I thought more carefully about declaring my major.

I'd been thinking about studying art history. But everyone I mentioned it to nixed that idea. "You'll never make a living!" I was told.

I thought of my upbringing around my father's friends and associates, many of them civil rights and labor advocates who discussed politics and engaged in activism. My choice was influenced by that milieu: I would major in political science.

I had a vastly different, very positive college experience at the "Circle."

The lively campus bustled with students of every race, color, and creed, many of them first-generation scholars like myself. I had my first Black professor, a prim and proper gentleman who pushed and encouraged me. Being in his classroom expanded my mind and outlook on life.

Besides a robust curriculum, UIC offered every kind of extracurricular club and organization imaginable—from athletics to chess to fraternities and sororities. The only thing it did not have, at that time, was a dormitory.

I lived in a small apartment near campus, with a roommate. We did not become close, but living with her taught me the value of getting along with people of different backgrounds.

Once again, I had been fortunate to receive a partial scholarship. I assumed a full course load of classes and landed a job at the US Post Office. I was sorting third class mail, and filling those heavy mailbags was arduous, dirty work. I came home covered with dust that got in my ears, nose, and hair.

When I was not working, my peers and I hung out in the student union after class—or for some, in lieu of class—studying, playing cards, and debating issues of the day.

I did not have a specific clique. I tried to mingle and be friendly with everyone. I relished meeting people from different backgrounds, cultures, and all walks of life.

Given the seismic shifts that shaped the '60s, ideological debates on campus were frequent, loud, and intense.

You might find students in the Chicano Movement pontificating in both Spanish and English about liberation, or fiery speeches espousing Black Power from students who were Black Panthers.

Feminists burned their bras and demanded equal rights for women, and gay students were beginning to openly embrace their identities.

It was a heady and exhilarating time.

Even as a young adult, I stood in solidarity with the ideals of peace, justice, and equality. Human dignity. Unity. Working to make our nation and world a better place for all.

I participated in my share of rallies, protests, and organizing. I took part in boycotts organized by Operation Breadbasket.

In the early '60s, Dr. King and his organization, the Southern Christian Leadership Conference (SCLC), had launched the economic empowerment program. Its thrust was getting businesses to hire Black employees, treat customers respectfully, and promote community-owned goods and services.

Jesse Jackson, then a theology student, had been asked by Dr. King to lead the campaign, which had a slogan: "Keep a slice of the bread in your community."

I was also part of efforts to feed children via the Panthers' community breakfast program.

I personally drew the line at violence, bigotry, and illegal activity. I am the proud descendant of US veterans and hail from a law enforcement family; you were not gonna catch me doing things like torching the American flag or getting in the face of police officers as some did.

That said, beyond such serious endeavors, I had fun. I was finally attracting attention from the opposite sex. I was invited to parties and asked out on dates. I was even selected to participate in the Miss Kappa Alpha Psi, Inc. pageant, an event sponsored by the historic Black Greek letter organization for men. I did not win, but it was nice to be among other young women and men who were smart and go-getters.

Most importantly, I got my first taste of running for a political office as a college student.

One day, a classmate was chatting me up about a new political organization on campus. It was called the Action Party and they needed a treasurer. "You should run, Carol!" my friend urged me.

I had no idea whatsoever what running for office entailed. I do not recall our party platform, nor my campaign speech, beyond promising to empower students. We may have put up a few posters. Yet somehow I won.

Little did I know at the time, it would set the stage for a future career in politics on the national and international stage.

In 1969, I was a senior preparing to graduate. I was thrilled, as was my entire family.

By this time, Daddy was back in our lives. He had returned from the West Coast a changed man: kinder, gentler, and contrite about the sins of the past. Mother forgave him. We all did.

My father was still pushing me to go to law school. Now that I had a degree in political science, he urged me to seize the opportunities that most Black men or women of his generation did not have.

I had no idea what I might do with my life. But as always, fate and serendipity stepped in with an answer.

LOVE AND LAWYERING

I aspired to use my undergrad degree to become an art historian. The thing is, I didn't know a single person who could help me enter that profession.

My father was a frustrated would-be lawyer. He had always dreamed of being an attorney, but in his era, Black barristers were few and far between.

So, Daddy kept pressing me. I understood that he was just looking out for my best interests. He encouraged me to pursue law, believing that the vocation would enable me to make a good living and do good for people.

One day, while walking down the street, I had a chance encounter that I now view as divine intervention. It was one of many serendipitous moments over the course of my life that have shifted my direction.

I ran into this friend of mine. I fell into lockstep with him, and we started chatting about this and that. We spoke of Mother Nature's beauty and of butterflies. He explained that butterfly comes from an Old English word, "butterfleoge," and that some people used to call butterflies "flutterbys."

I laughed and laughed. It was a delightful conversation. At some point, I got around to asking him where he was going.

My pal was headed over to the University of Chicago Law School, which was in the neighborhood.

"Oh, why are you going there?" I asked.

"I plan to take the LSAT," he said, referring to the Law School Admission Test by its acronym.

"What's the LSAT?" I asked. He explained that it was a standardized test used for entry to law school. *Hmm*, I thought to myself.

"I think I'll do that, too," I told him.

We reached the campus, and I followed my friend inside the law school building. There was a table with pamphlets and information, and we both signed up to take the LSAT. The test was being administered on the same campus in a few weeks.

I thanked him and went on my way. I did not dare tell anyone else.

The day dawned for me to sit for the exam. I was on pins and needles. Needless to say, the LSAT is extremely rigorous, what with its reading comprehension, analytical reasoning, and mind-bending multiple-choice questions.

Meanwhile, there was some type of protest happening on campus at the same time as the exam. I had participated in my share of civil rights marches and women's rallies and have always considered free speech and peaceful assembly a vital part of our democracy. Amid the loud chants, I tried my best to focus. A few hours later, the proctor signaled that we should wrap up. Between the test itself and the din outside, I was mentally spent. I felt certain that I had blown it.

I was a nervous wreck until my test scores came in the mail. To my astonishment, I had actually performed pretty well. "Thank you, Lord," I said.

Once again, my financial circumstances and having no one to hold my hand during the process dictated my decision not to apply to multiple law schools. When I sent my application off to the University of Chicago and was accepted, that sealed the deal for me. "I'll go there," I told my family. Everybody was happy for me. Daddy, especially, was over the moon.

I entered the University of Chicago's law school in 1969, part of a cohort that made history in terms of its diversity.

I recall that my class had eight Black students, a first. I believe that there were also a record number of women, ten, in the school at that time.

The law school, which opened its doors in 1902, boasts a long tradition of admitting women and students of color.

Sophonisba Breckinridge, who was in the university's inaugural class, became the first woman graduate in 1904.

More than a decade later, Earl Dickerson of Mississippi, became the school's first Black juris doctorate graduate in 1920. A WWII veteran, alderman, and businessman who was active in civil rights causes, he distinguished himself in legal circles by winning *Hansberry v. Lee*, the 1940s Supreme Court case that challenged Chicago's racially restrictive housing covenants.

While women, and increasingly, students of color matriculated at the law school, early on, there would typically be no more than one or two individuals representing "minority" groups in each class.

My class broke that mold. In doing so, we attracted our share of attention, and some might say, fanfare.

In a student body previously filled with all men, it was not surprising that there was curiosity about women law students. And Black students being in the class was a novelty, as well.

For Black women like me, the scrutiny and intrigue seemed to be magnified. When I walked into my classes, heads would turn. I encountered stares, smiles, and a few looks that I could not quite decipher.

I understood the fascination, to some extent, but I had more pressing matters on my mind as a first-year law student. I was trying to grasp incredibly complex legal material and keep up with the copious reading required for all of my law classes.

I had always been a good student. Yet, it required me working twice as hard as my peers. Reading, in particular, took a gargantuan effort on my part.

During law school, I finally learned the root cause of my struggles. One of my professors suggested that I might have dyslexia, a language disorder.

Dyslexia is not a disease, nor is it a reflection of one's intelligence. Experts say it is a neurobiological condition that is genetic.

I was evaluated and formally diagnosed with dyslexia. Some people might have found the news upsetting, but for me, it came as a relief.

Decades ago, neurodiversity was not on most people's radar. For years, I had been grappling unwittingly with this condition that no one—from my parents to teachers—recognized, understood, or even knew existed.

I had made it all this way, and to law school. I thought back to elementary and high school and realized that my education had always been fraught with some difficulty or another.

I can vividly remember being teased in kindergarten. My parents had sent me to Henry Horner Elementary, a public school, when I was just four years old. I was smaller in stature than the other children and not mature enough emotionally to be with the five year olds. The kids would taunt me and call me a "baby."

I'd cry so much during recess that my teacher—a kind young woman named Miss Church—would bring me inside and try to comfort me. As I bawled, she would gently rock me in her arms, and sing lullabies until I calmed down.

Another stop on my school journey was St. Dorothy's. We children were baptized Catholic, and Mother wanted us to have a religious-centered education. Yet Daddy's up-and-down work history meant that they could not always afford the tuition. So my parents would pull me in and out of parochial school, depending on their financial situation.

At Ruggles Elementary, my second public school, I experienced my first awareness of being treated differently.

One of my teachers—who wasn't sweet like Miss Church—took one look at my skin tone and assigned me to sit in what she cruelly called the "dummy row."

Even at that tender age, I bristled at the label. I recall feeling ashamed and hurt by the manner in which I was being prejudged.

I was determined not to let anyone pigeonhole me. I developed my own strategies and employed coping mechanisms to compensate for my learning difficulties.

The one I remember the most is using a ruler to keep my eyes focused on the text I was reading. This helped tremendously, as I was able to keep up with the materials as assigned. In addition to the ruler trick, I discovered that I sometimes needed to read the material more than once, so as not to miss anything.

I refused to be labeled inferior and worked to prove my teacher wrong. When the semester ended, my test scores and performance in class had elevated me to a chair in the "smart" row. I had overcome by dint of hard work, determination, and stubbornness. Being in the "smart row" was a vindication of my abilities and my first recollection of fighting for myself.

Now I was in law school and the sheer volume and demands of my courses felt like a déjà vu of third grade. I knew from experience that I would have to work twice as hard, persevere, and not let anyone's opinion of my intellect deter me.

All of my classes were difficult, but I was extremely worried about one of them.

I was struggling with tax law. I was down in the dumps about it, and complaining to anyone who would listen. One of my classmates heard my lament and said, "Oh, you should go talk to Michael Braun. I think he'd be interested in tutoring you."

Michael was a 2L, in his second year. I had seen him around, and he struck me as a nice guy. He was smart and had been invited to join our school's law review, the prestigious legal journal.

I caught up with him one day after class. I dispensed with formalities. "I am in danger of failing tax," I said. "Please, can you help me?" Michael agreed and didn't waste any time scheduling a study session.

"Can you meet me this evening?" he said.

"Yes!" I agreed. That's how the two of us started studying together.

I immediately felt comfortable around Michael, although our backgrounds could not have been more different. As we got to know each other, I learned that he had grown up in a family of WASPs, who were conservative Republicans.

He listened attentively as I told him about my clan, who were Democrats with liberal political views. We delved into the explosive racial politics of the day, and from what I could glean, he did not have a prejudiced bone in his body. He treated everyone respectfully, which impressed me.

Things were strictly platonic with Michael, because there is nothing romantic about tax law. We became friends, and he began coming over to my apartment regularly to study.

I had moved to Hyde Park, a multicultural neighborhood of parks, museums, and coffee shops that was home to University of Chicago.

This was my second college apartment, following my first humble abode as an undergrad. For law school, I opted not to cohabitate with a roommate. I had a cute little bachelorette pad, in a nice building with pleasant neighbors of varying ages and backgrounds.

One of them was a kind elderly Jewish woman, whom I would

come to learn was a Holocaust survivor. One day, she opened up about her horrific experiences in a Nazi concentration camp and the loss of her loved ones. It was sobering to hear her first-hand reflections, which have stayed with me ever since.

The true stories that my neighbor shared made my complaints about tax law—or anything else—seem trivial. That said, I had to pass this class. I had come this far by faith and was not about to flunk out of law school.

My professor had a reputation as a preeminent lawyer in the tax field, and I knew better than to go into one of his lectures unprepared.

Michael quizzed me on concepts and legal terms. Once we finished our studies, we talked and relaxed. Sometimes I made him a bite to eat.

I noticed a shift in our relationship. Our study sessions had progressed to flirting. I thought Michael was handsome, and he seemed to find me attractive.

I recall one time when he started tickling me. We were on the couch, and I was giggling and trying to catch my breath. Out of the blue, I burped. Loudly. I was mortified, but he just laughed it off. I knew then that this guy was special.

Michael's calm disposition appealed to me after growing up in a household with an abusive father.

The more traumatic aspects of my childhood impacted the way I navigated life.

I try to be kind, and I tend to empathize with the under-dog. On the other hand, my experiences toughened me. I don't go around picking fights, but I will defend myself if necessary.

One afternoon, Michael came over to study. By this time, we were smitten. When I heard him outside, I flung open the door, greeting him with a big hug.

We sat down on the couch and cracked open our thick text-books. I happened to look out the window, which had a view of the gangway. What I saw caused me to do a double take.

There, in broad daylight, was a thief riding off with my bicycle!

During law school, I did not own a car. I rode my bike to campus, which was a few blocks from my apartment. Cycling was my primary means of transportation unless I took the bus. Given my tight class schedule, hopping on my bike was easier.

I normally left my bicycle in the vestibule of my building. I rushed downstairs. The culprit hadn't gotten very far down the street, so I yelled out, "Stop, that's my bike!"

I ran back inside and to my bedroom. When I returned to the living room, Michael looked at me as if I had three heads. "What are you doing with that gun?!" he hollered.

"I'm gonna shoot the idiot who stole my bike!" I hollered back.

My boyfriend had no idea that I was a gun owner. Perhaps he had forgotten I was the daughter of a former cop who sometimes took his kids on hunting trips. Daddy was actually the one who taught me how to shoot, reasoning that I should know how to protect myself.

Constitutional Law was one of my first classes, so I understood the Second Amendment. I had a license, and my pistol was registered. That said, I am sure my boyfriend did not expect his girlfriend to exact vigilante justice.

I was furious about the theft. I stood there clutching my "piece," trying to decide if I was going to chase after the culprit, who by that time was long gone with my two wheels.

I was pacing and waving my gun wildly, until Michael sat me down and talked some sense into me. He gently reassured me that I could always get a new bicycle. Finally, I simmered down.

Needless to say, in all the excitement, we did not get any studying done.

The good news is that I survived tax law. At the end of the semester, I squeaked by just enough to pass, thanks to my own due diligence and Michael's patient tutelage. He got an A in the course. We were proud of each other and celebrated with a kiss.

When our lips met, I felt butterflies.

There's a line that Shakespeare penned in the play *King Lear* which goes something like this: "So we'll live, and pray, and sing, and tell old tales, and laugh at gilded butterflies."

I had butterflies. Or maybe they were flutterbys like my other friend had mentioned.

Whatever the case, things were becoming more serious with Michael Braun.

I continued to apply myself in law school with study sessions, long hours at the library, and engaging in class debates with my peers.

Passing tax law showed me that belief in myself and perseverance could turn situations around in my favor.

Over the years, that approach has helped me go far. We don't always get everything that we want in this life, but if we don't give up, work diligently, and do right, I believe the Lord will reward us with what our hearts desire if it is in His will.

Learning that I had dyslexia turned out to be a blessing, because it taught me perseverance, patience, and determination. While there might have been other ways to get those lessons, I credit dyslexia for teaching them to me.

There were myriad lessons—academic and otherwise—in law school. Looking back, I really appreciate how important those years were.

Although I was spending a good deal of time with Michael, I was also forming friendships with other students. As I did in undergrad, I moved between groups. When the Black law students got together, however, it felt like family. We were each other's cheerleaders, sounding boards, and support system. We started talking about making our informal gatherings an official organization.

The blueprint already existed at New York University School of Law. In 1968, student visionaries founded what would become the Black Allied Law Students Association, known as BALSA.

Chapters with similar missions and variations on the name soon spread across the country. I met the students from the NYU charter chapter, and thought it was important to establish one on our Chicago campus.

Today, the Earl B. Dickerson chapter of the Black Law Students Association (BLSA) honors the early twentieth-century pioneer who earned his JD at our school. It's gratifying to know that I had a hand in ensuring that future lawyers have an organization that seeks to nurture their professional advancement and a spirit of camaraderie.

Not everyone at the law school seemed to understand our collective purpose. One of my women professors—a well-known legal theoretician—called me into her office for a discussion about it.

"You have to understand, Carol. You are, first, a University of Chicago law student, and then you are a woman, and then you are Negro," she told me.

I replied respectfully, "No, professor. It's just the opposite." She was taken aback, but I proceeded with my argument, as any good law student would. "The world sees me as Black first, and then as a woman, and then they get to the law school.

"My education is the last point of reference for my identity," I continued. "And that's not because I would have it that way. The truth is, this is the way the world sees me, and that is what I have to react to every single day."

My professor's expression made it clear that she did not take kindly to my response. However, I think she appreciated that I was giving her my honest perspective of society at that time.

The meeting of minds with fellow Black students was one of many developments happening in my world during law school.

My budding interest in politics had been stoked as an undergraduate and was further elevated when various candidates visited the law school to engage with students.

One of those who impressed me was Richard "Dick" Newhouse, a onetime journalist with the *Chicago Defender* who later earned his JD at University of Chicago.

Newhouse, a Southern gent originally from Kentucky, had run in 1968 for the Illinois Senate, and won a seat. Now he was campaigning for reelection; somehow, I found time to join the team as a volunteer.

Through Dick's people, I was recommended to work on the campaign of Harold Washington, at the time, a budding political star who was serving in the Illinois House of Representatives. I volunteered because I'd heard good things about him, although we hadn't yet met in person.

Harold's career took off. He would later ascend to Congress, and then go on to become the first Black mayor of Chicago in 1983. Along the way, we became political allies and friends. I trace those early networking connections—and many more that would follow—back to the law school.

My courtship with Michael had steadily progressed. We had gone from being study buddies, to falling in love.

Ahead of the winter semester break, Michael asked me to come home with him to New Jersey to meet his family.

By that time, we had both told our parents that we were in an interracial relationship. I think we both were hoping—perhaps, somewhat naively—that it would not be an issue.

When we pulled into the driveway of his childhood home after a long drive, Michael's father was warm and welcoming. His mother, however, made it clear that she was none too thrilled with my presence.

She gave me the once-over, her eyes traveling from my blouse and blue jeans, to my full-length fur coat, which I wore to deal with Chicago's brutal winters. She rolled her eyes as if to say,

"Who is this gauche young woman?" I steeled myself for what was going to be a long weekend.

Our sleeping arrangements were the first hurdle. Michael's parents had told him in advance that we would bunk in separate bedrooms since we were not married. I just didn't realize how separate.

Apparently, I was being dispatched to his sister's house a few miles away. To make sure I understood, his mother had neatly folded some bed linens and left them out for me.

I was offended by her lack of hospitality. "I don't have to deal with this!" I told Michael. "I'm leaving. I can spend the holidays with my own family."

Michael pleaded and convinced me to stay, and I did so, only because I realized that he was caught between a rock and a hard place. He was a dutiful son who loved his mother. But I was his girlfriend, and he had professed love to me, too. We had begun talking about a future together.

Dinner that evening was uncomfortable. At some point, the topic turned to interracial marriages. "How would the children be raised?" his mother asked.

"Well, they would be Black of course," I said sarcastically.

Mrs. Braun gave me a look, while his father tried to change the subject. It was Michael's elderly grandmother who lightened the mood.

"You're pretty," she said. "You remind me of a little colored girl that I grew up with," she added.

Her use of the word "colored" was archaic, of course, but at least she was trying to give me a compliment. "Thank you," I said, smiling.

When it was time to head back to Chicago and school, we packed up the car and Michael's family came outside to see us off. His mother gave me a hug, one of those quick back pats.

Michael had announced to his folks that he intended to ask for my hand in marriage. We already knew how Mrs. Braun felt. Meanwhile, my father had previously voiced his disapproval when we first started dating.

It's fruitless to try to quench the fire of two young people in love. We focused on law school and each other.

Michael was a year ahead of me, and before we knew it, it was time for him to graduate. His parents and sister came down for the ceremony, and his mother and I were cordial to each other. She seemed resigned to the relationship.

Michael passed the bar exam on his first go-round, and entertained multiple offers from blue chip law firms. Instead, he chose a small boutique firm where he would have some autonomy and earn a handsome salary.

We scouted for a place together and landed on the city's North Side. Although we spent the bulk of our time there, I kept my apartment.

My third year of law school was a haze of finals and prepping for the forthcoming bar exam. I graduated, not at the top of my class, but not at the bottom either. I was simply glad to be finished. It had been an exhilarating ride. I had achieved my dream—and that of my father—but I was ready for the next chapter.

Michael and I never formally announced our engagement, nor did we throw a party or anything like that. And as a young couple starting out, we did not want to spend a heap of money on our nuptials.

We considered getting married in church, then city hall, and finally decided to tie the knot at our new apartment.

We were grateful to be surrounded by our respective families. The Brauns and the Moseleys had made peace with our love, and it was a lovely ceremony.

There was only one interruption, and it wasn't someone objecting to our union. It came when my sister Marsha's huge Afro hairstyle nearly caught fire when she got too close to all of the flickering candles.

Michael told me that I looked beautiful. I certainly felt happy.

I was wearing a designer dress that came from Marshall Field's, one of Chicago's famous department stores. The day I went to pick it up from alterations, the saleswoman had remarked, "What a beautiful dress! Is this for your lady?" I was baffled.

"Your lady, ma'am," she repeated.

Ahhhh. She thought I was a maid picking up a garment for a socialite. Bless her heart, as my mother would say.

I paid for the dress in cash and headed toward the exit with my package. Little did she know, I was the lady.

WORKING GIRL

Life was happily chugging along.

Michael and I had settled into domestic bliss as newlyweds. And not only was my husband practicing law, I was newly employed in the legal profession.

I had landed my first position at a small Chicago law firm located in Streeterville, on the Near North Side.

This was the early 1970s, and Judson Miner and Allison Davis were young, talented lawyers who hung out their shingle in the community.

I had first met Mr. Davis when he visited the law school. I'd already had professional overtures from one of the big downtown firms, but talking with him convinced me to reject that initial offer and pivot.

Early on, the firm specialized in civil rights law and community development. This approach coincided with my desire to utilize law to lend a helping hand to people. Equally appealing to me was seeing that the firm was integrated.

Judd was Jewish, and Allison was the son and namesake of the first Black tenured professor at the University of Chicago. An integrated business partnership was rare back then in the legal profession, or most places for that matter. It was not long before Charles Barnhill joined the team. They would later expand the team, although I only recall three partners during my time there.

I appreciated the tutelage of these more experienced attorneys. For me to possess a law degree was an accomplishment I'd never imagined for myself. I'd studied assiduously for three years and was eager to finally practice.

Alas, it took longer than anticipated. While my husband had passed the bar exam on his first go-round, I was not so lucky. Failing the test was not only frustrating, it made me question whether I had the right stuff to be a lawyer.

I remember sulking around about it. My law school pals tried to reassure me that the pass rate for first-time takers is low. Years later, I read that one in five people must repeat the exam again, but back then, I had no idea. My confidence was shaken.

I had to pass the bar, or my legal career would be over before it started. I threw myself into jurisprudence. Rising extra early. Staying up and studying into the wee hours. Every spare minute, my nose was buried in a casebook or *Black's Law Dictionary*.

Months later, I sat for the exam a second time. Afterward, I got to know the postal carrier well because I was waiting by the mailbox every single day. When the results finally arrived, I tore open the envelope. I scanned the letter. Success! I was elated, and frankly, relieved. I was officially licensed to practice law in the state of Illinois.

In that era, a mere 3 percent of lawyers were women, and women of color were woefully underrepresented. Still, women in the legal profession were opening doors, and making our presence felt despite gender barriers.

I was ready to make my mark. I had inherited a stellar work ethic from my mother and generations of formidable women in my family. I was also lucky to have professional role models in Chicago.

I think fondly of trailblazing lawyers like Jewel Lafontant, who was this elegant, dynamic movie star–ish figure from a prominent African American family.

A third-generation attorney, her father co-founded the National Bar Association, and her grandfather was a lawyer and hotelier, who had been falsely accused during the Tulsa, Oklahoma, race riot of 1921. He fled to Chicago, and his son's legal acumen saved him from extradition. The family fought to clear his name, and eventually an apology was issued.

Jewel became the first Black woman to graduate from the University of Chicago Law School and went on to have a groundbreaking career.

She served under several Presidents. Dwight Eisenhower appointed her an Assistant United States Attorney. Richard Nixon tapped her as the country's first woman US Deputy Solicitor General. Later, George H.W. Bush made her US ambassador-at-large and coordinator of refugee affairs.

The ambassador, whom I'd met during my college years, was phenomenal. She was someone for young women like me to look up to and say, "I want to be like that when I grow up." Years later, I would benefit from the campaign expertise and loyal friendship of her son, John W. Rogers, Jr. The financial guru founded Ariel Investments, an asset management firm headquartered in Chicago that has global reach.

Edith Sampson was another phenomenal pioneer in law whom I met along the way. In 1962, she became the first Black woman in Illinois to be elected a judge on the Chicago Municipal Court.

Daddy was the one who took me to meet her when I was a youngster. We also visited Anna Langford, a lawyer who would later be elected Chicago's first Black alderwoman.

I smile thinking about Judge Sampson because she did not suffer fools gladly. Her personality was no-nonsense, almost gruff.

One of her favorite sayings was "I talk from my heart and let the law take care of itself."

Another role model in my young life was Arnita Young-Boswell. She was a social worker, educator, and activist. Her brother was Whitney Young Jr., the civil rights titan who headed the National Urban League during the 1960s and early '70s.

Young-Boswell led a life of service in her own right. During WWII, she was an American Red Cross worker who lent her skills to soldiers. Later, she became the first national director of Project Head Start, the federal program launched in the 1950s to provide preschool children from low-income families with comprehensive support.

I got to know this exceptional woman because she would host teas and whatnot, and extend invites to young ladies in the community. I recall going with my girlfriends to visit her lovely home, where she'd provide counsel about education and life.

I wish I'd listened more carefully, but the fact is she took us under her wing and provided much-needed direction.

These extraordinary women were mentors, although we may not have used such a formal term back then. As my journey continued, I would meet numerous individuals—women and men alike, of different races and backgrounds—who were positive influences.

Most of these special human beings have gone home to God, but in their own ways, each helped inculcate in me the values of public service. I think of the Bible verse, Luke 12:48, "For unto whomsoever much is given, of him shall be much required..."

Among the law firm's tiny staff of lawyers, I recall being the only woman back then. At work, inside the townhouse the partners had purchased and renovated, they were taking on important legal cases, giving the office an air of purpose and excitement.

The only thing was, as a young, newly minted lawyer, I was not litigating any of those big cases.

I was a junior associate, and as is normal in any profession, I had to pay my dues. That is what I was doing. My days consisted of legal research, writing briefs, and performing administrative tasks. I made pots of coffee from time to time.

Mind you, I was not mistreated in any way. The partners were good to me. I was listening, learning, and absorbing the minutiae of the law with every case the firm handled.

My daily schedule was full, but not so busy that I could not take a lunch break. One day, I made a discovery that opened a whole new world to me.

Right in the neighborhood was a French restaurant. I wandered in one day.

The ambiance was posh, the epitome of fine dining. White tablecloths, china, crystal stemware, and fresh flowers adorned the space.

A maître d' welcomed patrons with a flourish. "Bonjour," he said, greeting me graciously. I'd grown up with Mother speaking conversational French to us, and I knew a few phrases from school.

"Bonjour, monsieur," I replied, smiling.

I perused the menu of haute cuisine. Hors d'oeuvres, bouillabaisse, and truffles beckoned. When my courses arrived, I tucked into the fare and sipped a glass of wine. I felt transported to a magical world, one that was nouveau and magnificent. Or, as the French would say, magnifique!

That dining experience turned this Midwest girl into a Francophile. Although I delight in Americana, I came to adore all things French: the cuisine, fashion, and their spirit of joie de vivre, a phrase that loosely translates into an enjoyment of life.

Back in the office, I continued to absorb the inner workings of the legal profession. I suppose some people in my position would have been content, but deep down was a yearning to do more. I sought to blaze trails as my mentors and role models had done.

I made the tough decision to leave the firm that had taken a

chance on a young novice lawyer. Before tendering my resignation, I thanked the partners for helping me to develop invaluable skills and inspiring me to use the law to address injustice,
empower communities, and so much more.

Over the years, the firm where I launched my legal career has
expanded and flourished. They have offices in several cities, and
boast a lengthy list of distinguished alumni, from federal judges
to a US president. A young, brilliant, Harvard-educated lawyer named Barack Obama was an associate there, just as I was
years earlier. Later, he too, would serve Illinois as a state legislator and US senator before making history in the White House.

It was time to ponder my next steps. The times were chang-
ing, and it felt as if the world was my oyster. Around this time,
Nina Simone had recorded a hit song called "To Be Young,
Gifted and Black," which became an anthem in certain circles.
I felt that same sense of possibility.

I had broken the cardinal rule of never quitting one position
without another one lined up. So, I started job hunting.

Michael kept saying to me that we could live off his law earn-
ings and I did not have to work. I was accustomed to earning
my own money. Moreover, I wanted to use my law degree in
service to the greater good.

One summer day, we went to the beach along Lake Michigan. I took a dip, while Michael laid his towel on the sand and
began sunning himself.

After a while, I emerged from the water. I was toweling off,
when I noticed a man off in the distance waving to me. He
began walking my way.

At first, I wondered if he was flirting because these were my
curvy beach bunny days. However, my husband was right next
to me, so there was no harm in being friendly.

The guy turned out to be someone that we both knew from

our legal circle. We were all making small talk. At some point, I may have joked about being an out of work lawyer.

What he said next was one of those moments of serendipity that have followed me all my life. "They're hiring at the US Attorney's Office," he told me. "You should apply."

I thanked him for the job lead and "The Man Upstairs" for the timing. God had supplied my needs, once again.

I followed up about the position. It did not take long before I heard back. They wanted me to come in for an interview. I dressed in my most conservative suit and high heels and headed to the federal office building in downtown Chicago.

At that time, James Robert Thompson was the US Attorney for the Northern District of Illinois. Appointed by Richard Nixon, he was a so-called "Rockefeller" Republican. He had a reputation for being nonpartisan, and principled, someone who upheld the letter of the law.

Jim was one of the people who interviewed me during that pivotal meeting decades ago. I was fairly nervous. Among the range of questions I remember being asked was whether I had anything in my background that might prove embarrassing to me or the office. I thought for a moment. "Yes," I said, haltingly.

Prior to me and Michael getting married, we had lived together for a bit. In those days, cohabitating was called "shacking up" or worse, "living in sin." Our living situation did not go over well with either of our parents, but it was something that plenty of young couples in our generation of "free love" did.

I shared that personal story and waited for a reaction. One of the interviewers appeared visibly relieved and smiled at me. "Oh, that's fine," he said quickly.

Not much time elapsed before the office contacted me to say I'd been hired. I was thrilled. I'd landed a plum position as an Assistant United States Attorney for the Northern District. I was twenty-six years old and would be making a salary that was more money than anyone in my family ever had.

I shared the good news with Michael, and we celebrated. Mother offered congratulations, as did my siblings. They were all happy for me.

The only person who was less than enthused? Daddy. "You'll be nothing but a government paper pusher, Carol," he said.

My father meant well. He envisioned me as the next Constance Baker Motley, who'd been hired by Thurgood Marshall as the first woman attorney at the NAACP, where she handled civil rights cases. The trailblazer went on to make history when President Lyndon B. Johnson elevated her to a federal judgeship, the first Black woman ever to serve in that capacity.

My father may have been an armchair lawyer, but his words did not come out of a vacuum. He was keenly aware—as was I—of the Black community's painful history with the justice system.

My parents and grandparents had Southern roots, and among the reasons they and millions of other families had fled during the Great Migration was a sense of witnessing and experiencing injustice day in, day out, and feeling that they had little to no official recourse. No one to protect them. No one to speak up for their rights. That sense of indignity fueled the Civil Rights Movement.

So, I did not get upset with Daddy. When I explained to him that I would be one of a handful of Black women in my role as a prosecutor, he softened some. He seemed to be proud of me.

I was sworn in, taking a solemn oath to uphold the Constitution.

I liked Jim right away, and we got on well during my tenure. He assigned me to the Civil Division, and from time to time I handled criminal and appellate cases. I could not have asked for better legal training.

An older gentleman headed the division and was my immediate boss. He was seasoned and very knowledgeable. Looking back, I was fortunate to learn the ropes from him.

I'd come from a small firm, and almost overnight had joined

an office with dozens of attorneys, paralegals, investigators, and other staffers. I'd gained valuable experience in my prior position, but this was a whole new ball game with a sizable learning curve.

For starters, the Department of Justice had policies and procedures that had to be followed to a T. I learned this immediately, albeit not in the way I might have wanted to.

My supervisor was a stickler for process.

I recall one occasion when we were sitting in my office discussing a case. I mentioned that I'd taken a file home.

He hit the roof. "Under no circumstances can you do that, Carol!" he said, reminding me of our strict rules.

"I had not thought of that at all," I said apologetically, assuring him that it would never happen again.

"This is unforgivable," he said, before stalking out of the room.

I went home that evening, fretting about "Filegate." I wondered if I would face disciplinary action, or even be fired. By the next day, however, my boss had moved on. He had likely made a calculation that his rebuke had chastened me. And he was right. I understood that the way I handled each case had to be above reproach.

I came along at an interesting time. Chicagoland had a centuries-long reputation for cronyism and corruption, and in that era, our office made headlines for major indictments.

I was not directly involved in those cases, although some of my senior colleagues were.

Still, my plate was full. I handled some criminal prosecutions, and discovered it was not my cup of tea. I also did appellate work, helping to write a brief on the first Racketeering and Organized Crime (aka RICO) case in Illinois. Yet I preferred the civil cases which really schooled me in the structure and operation of the law, as well as policy issues.

I got to third chair the lawsuit that the American Medical

Association filed related to health care reforms under Jimmy Carter's administration. I read every dot and tilde, as we say, of the health care laws. It gave me insight into how health care was developed and structured, and helped to shape my views. I was also involved with some environmental law cases. And, there were a variety of housing, health care, and poverty cases, all of which I got an opportunity to try in court. Lawyers in our office got great trial experience because we were in court every day. It developed my skills, and an appreciation for legal issues in ways that I don't think I could've gotten otherwise.

I understood our charge and sought to perform my duties with integrity. That said, I experienced mixed emotions depending upon the backstories of tough cases and their outcomes.

I remember litigating one case in which a businessman who had been convicted of a white-collar crime violated the terms of his parole. He had committed a second offense, and the government's position was that he should be returned to prison.

During courtroom arguments, his wife and son, a little boy who looked to be about five years old, were present for the entire trial. When the verdict was reached, the man was found guilty. My eyes landed on his son, who just bawled as the bailiff escorted his father out in handcuffs. I left the courtroom that day feeling like an absolutely horrible person. That man had done wrong, yes, but I'd contributed to the breakup of a family. We'd won, but to me, the victory felt hollow.

I tried a couple of cases of that ilk, in which my prosecutorial responsibilities clashed with my inner moral compass. It was tough. And there were times when I felt compelled to speak up.

Case in point: the mother of Black Panther Fred Hampton was suing the government for her son's untimely death. I was asked to join the team of prosecutors who would fight the lawsuit.

I told my higher-ups there was no way in hell that I was doing this. First, I knew Fred. In my college days, he'd come over to my campus to see mutual friends and all of us hung out. We were idealistic young people, kids really, who talked about saving the world. So, certainly the case would have posed an ethical and moral conflict. Perhaps they felt a Black attorney would make the optics look better. I got some pushback, but I stood my ground. Mrs. Hampton prevailed, and I avoided a case that would have been soul crushing.

Conversely, there were cases that appealed to me. One in particular involved housing policy, and homeowners who had experienced unfair practices that led to foreclosures.

We won this case, and the outcome helped countless Americans, not only in Chicago, but in communities nationwide. It was gratifying to use my skills as a lawyer to do good, and I left the courtroom that day feeling a sense of satisfaction.

I knew from my own family's experience how hard people work, scrimp, and save to purchase homes, a tangible symbol of the American Dream.

Working on that case reminded me of my family's latter days in Bucket of Blood. My dear grandmother Edna Sr. had died of cancer while we lived there. Her passing left us not only grief-stricken but homeless after an unexpected family feud arose over her house.

At the center of the dispute was my mother, and her older sister, Auntie Darrel. The sisters had always been very close despite distinctly different personalities.

Mother was salt of the earth, Auntie Darrel was wild as the wind. She was sexy, fashionable, and fun-loving.

Auntie was a medical technician who'd actually helped bring my mother into the field. She worked hard and played equally hard.

Whether at a nightclub, dolled up to the nines, or zipping round town in a convertible, a leopard print scarf wrapped around her hair, my aunt attracted attention.

Men fell at her feet. She had been married multiple times and had a bunch of boyfriends in between. Mother had always ob-

served her sister's lifestyle with a mix of admiration and bemuse-
ment, but never judgment. They loved each other.

No one knows exactly what transpired, but somehow in the
midst of grieving their beloved mother, the two of them fell out.

From what I could gather, my aunt co-owned the house with
my grandmother and planned to sell the property after her death.

Auntie Darrel had given the boarders notice to vacate the
premises. Then she surprised all of us by giving notice to her
own sister.

Understandably, Mother balked at leaving, and they went back
and forth for weeks. Then Auntie Darrel took it to the mat: she
had the gas, electricity, and even the water turned off.

My mother was beside herself. She was gainfully employed
but securing an affordable place to live for herself and children
had already proven a dicey proposition. Following my parents'
divorce, the house had been our refuge. Now it was a source
of sibling conflict.

My mother refused to leave, my aunt refused to budge, and
the situation became bleaker with each passing day.

I remember taking an empty pail and going to a neighbor's
house, asking them to fill it with water for us to drink and
bathe. The power was out, so we huddled together under blan-
kets at night trying desperately to stay warm. The refrigerator
was empty—it could not stay cold without electricity. We ate
food that would not spoil. A neighbor sometimes brought over
hot soup.

How it had come to this was a mystery. We all adored Auntie
Darrel. I tried to understand what would make someone treat
their sister, nieces, and nephews—or any human being—in such
a manner. There seemed to be no solution to the impasse.

In what was an ironic reversal of fortunes, we would later find
a place, renting from one of the families who formerly lived in
grandmother Edna's boarding house. They were good people,
and we were grateful.

Still, Mother did not give up. She worked double shifts, and kept saving her pennies, until she was finally able to make a down payment on another house in West Chesterfield, a middle-class Black neighborhood of brick duplexes that's been referred to as "The Black Gold Coast" and "the mink ghetto."

I'll never forget the look on my mother's face when the Realtor handed her the keys. She nearly jumped for joy.

Back at the US Attorney's office, I was working extremely hard. People in high places were taking notice.

In 1975, I won the attorney general's Special Achievement Award. It was a prestigious honor, and definitely a feather in my cap. Actually, I almost missed this opportunity. I learned by happenstance that one could submit cases on which they'd worked for consideration, and applied at the last minute.

I barely made the deadline. But it worked out. The recognition gave me a sense of professional validation. It made me feel that my marathon hours, and outsized efforts were not in vain.

My job came with a generous benefits package, including vacation days. But with such a rigorous caseload, taking any time off seemed counterproductive. I talked to Michael, and he agreed that some R & R was in order for both of us. We traveled to an outdoor lakefront destination and enjoyed couple time. We were simply happy to be together and not in a courtroom.

When I returned to work, a surprise was awaiting me. Because of my big award, I was being, ahem, rewarded with a major new case that was dumped in my lap—dump being the operative word. My desk was already piled with folders and every file cabinet was full. While I was out, someone had dragged boxes and boxes of new files into my office. The materials were unorganized, and it would take days and days to review it all. I was quite distraught.

"Somebody's doing this to mess with me," I said out loud. I am not someone who cries easily, but I shed a few tears that day.

There were other frustrations. I learned firsthand that having a big-time job would not shield me from awful stereotypes about Black women.

One winter evening, while working late on a case that had an upcoming trial, I made my way downstairs to catch a taxi outside of my office.

It was very cold, as Chicago is that time of year, so I had on a long fur coat covering my business suit and dressy boots. My hope was that I could quickly hail a cab and get home after a long, full day.

After a few minutes of standing near the curb, a police squad car pulled up in front of me, and the officer on the passenger side leaned out and yelled, "Hey, you, give up that corner!"

I was always respectful of the police, given my family history in law enforcement. But I had no idea what he was referring to, and looked around, perplexed. The cruiser then pulled off as I continued to wait for a taxi.

Unfortunately, several cabs passed me by, which was not un-common.

As I continued to wait in the frigid temperatures, the squad car circled back, drove around the block, and pulled up again to the curb. "I told you to give up that corner!" the same of-ficer yelled out.

This time, I surmised what the heck was happening. The of-ficer assumed that a Black woman dressed up and waiting on a street corner was a prostitute looking for johns. I was livid.

Fuming, but trying to think clearly, I considered pulling my US Attorney's badge out of my purse and giving him a piece of my mind. I knew, however, that any type of altercation could lead to a confrontation and my arrest.

I was pondering all of this when a taxicab finally stopped for me. I had to make a split-second decision: make a point and possibly find myself in hot water or leave peacefully. I chose to go home.

As someone whose father, brother, and uncle all proudly

served on the police force, I have the utmost respect for those officers who perform the tough job of maintaining public safety, while mindful of courtesy and civil liberties.

Sadly, that officer made assumptions about me, and about my humanity. Black women have been historically sexualized with stereotypes that we are "loose" based on our dress, style, and appearance. Tragically, far too many encounters that Black people have with police in our country have proven life-threatening or even deadly.

It's possible that I dodged a bullet on that corner. It was far more important for me to get home safely than confront an officer who had already branded me a Jezebel. We both had official badges—his as a cop, mine as a US Attorney—but clearly my race and gender had left me vulnerable that day to street corner injustice.

Around my third year of serving in the office of the US Attorney in Chicago, I started to contemplate moving on. The job was fulfilling. I was being of service to our nation, and trying to uphold the credo of liberty and justice for all. However, the pace was grueling. I was tired, tired, tired.

There was another reason for my fatigue, one that gave me an even more important reason to step back: I was expecting.

Michael was ecstatic, tenderly doting on me. For years, he'd reminded me that I didn't have to work. Now, with a baby coming, he urged me to resign.

I had not decided what to do—take maternity leave or give my notice. Whatever the case, I was determined to finish up my cases and not leave my colleagues in a lurch.

One morning I had a scheduled court appearance, and the judge called me and opposing counsel up to the bench. I was quite far along by that time, and visibly showing. I waddled to the front of the courtroom. He took one look at my girth, and quipped: "Bailiff, go get some hot water. She's gonna pop!"

Well, that convinced me: it was time to exit. I had performed my duties faithfully. Some of my colleagues had become friends, and I kept in touch with them over the years, including James Thompson. He became one of the longest running governors in Illinois history. Upon his death in 2020, I joined a throng of mourners at his services.

I'd had a great run in the US Attorney's Office. But now it was time for this legal eagle to head home, feather my nest, and prepare for the arrival of a chick. Goodbye legal briefs, hello diapers.

A BABY AND BOBOLINKS

Our baby arrived on a bright summer's day, a plump eight-pounder with penetrating eyes and a dark thatch of hair. We decided to name him Matthew, which means "gift of God." Indeed, he was a divine present, a tiny miracle.

I immediately fell head over heels in love with our son, as did Michael, and we remain so to this very day. Our hearts were full, our family complete.

I settled into the role of wife, homemaker, and new mom. The domestic bliss that had often slipped through my fingers during childhood was finally mine.

I spent my days tending to the baby, decorating, and making our home comfortable. I shopped at the market, pored over cookbooks, and prepared gourmet meals. I played hostess at dinner parties where we invited our circle of friends from the worlds of academia and law.

When the weather was nice, I would take Matt outside for fresh air. I wanted to introduce our son, a fourth-generation Chicagoan, to the rich, storied history of our hometown.

Chicago is a great American city. Settled in the 1700s by Jean Baptiste Point du Sable, an explorer and trader born in what is now Haiti, it was formally incorporated in 1837.

Carl Sandburg's iconic poem "Chicago" so eloquently details our Midwest bona fides, a place "proud to be Hog Butcher, Tool maker, Stacker of Wheat, Player with Railroads and Freight Handler to the Nation."

Chicago is a city of neighborhoods, many of them founded by generations of immigrants and migrants whose unique contributions comprise America's marvelous melting pot.

We lived in Hyde Park, a vibrant, cultured community on the South Side. With its mix of university students and professors, affluent families, and its diversity, including interracial households like ours, the neighborhood bustled with artistic, intellectual, and social activity.

I dressed the baby for his city tour. Michael had gussied up our son's baby carriage, inspired by the lyrics of the '70s hit song "Be Thankful for What You Got." The chorus was catchy: *"Diamond in the back, sunroof top..."* My husband had cut out a diamond shape in the fabric and inserted clear plastic to customize the carriage. Baby Matt was rolling and strolling in style.

We regularly visited Jackson Park, about two blocks from our home. Named for President Andrew Jackson, the park was designed in the nineteenth century by Frederick Law Olmsted, the acclaimed architect behind New York City's Central Park.

Olmsted had begun working on his vision for Jackson Park when the Great Chicago Fire of 1871 gutted the city; it would be well over a decade before he completed the project. The result is a picturesque masterpiece spanning more than five hundred acres, complete with stunning views of Lake Michigan, a museum, gardens, and recreational areas for the public to enjoy.

One day, I was happily pushing the baby along in his chariot when we happened upon a scene that compelled me to stop. A group of protestors, mostly women, were chanting and carrying signs. "Save the bobolinks!" they shouted repeatedly.

I listened to those assembled, neighbors who were community advocates, bird watchers, and conservationists. They were upset that park district officials had proposed building a golf driving range smack dab in the nesting habitat of a bird called the bobolink.

The bobolink is a small songbird that is lovely to hear and behold. The males have black and white feathers with a gold nape; females are ochre colored with dark stripes. While many birds build their nests in trees, bobolinks nest on the ground, favoring grassy fields. That, the activists argued, made the birds particularly vulnerable.

As a new mother, it tugged at my heartstrings to think of mama birds, papa birds, and sweet little baby birds having their wings clipped in any way. This seemed to me a worthy environmental issue, and the passion of these concerned citizens struck a chord with me. That evening over dinner, I told Michael that I was joining the fight to protect the bobolinks!

By this time, I had participated in my share of demonstrations inspired by Dr. King's model of nonviolence. Besides my earlier protests, I braved hostile, rock-throwing crowds to help integrate Rainbow Beach, a public stretch along Lake Michigan in South Shore. The beach was named to honor World War I heroes, the army's 42nd Infantry, nicknamed the "Rainbow Division." These heroes of many races—symbolized by the colors of a rainbow—valiantly liberated Nazi concentration camps during the war. Sadly, the beach was not welcoming to bathers of all racial backgrounds. It took NAACP youth-led freedom "wade-ins" and other direct action before the tide began to change.

I'd even forfeited a job following one particular protest. I was working at my after-school cashier job when I noticed people carrying signs and chanting "Don't Shop Here!" outside the supermarket. The group was part of "Operation Breadbasket."

That day outside the grocery store, one of the activists was a woman named Rev. Willie Barrow. The petite firebrand told me my employer was selling rotten meat, which did not surprise me at all. I quit on the spot, grabbed a picket sign, and joined the demonstration.

Now I was back in the fray, chanting outdoors, and toting a sign that read "Park District No, Bobolinks Yes." Baby Matt was with me, as always, dozing in his snazzy stroller.

Some might have pooh-poohed us for raising a ruckus about a bird. Yet as someone who spent childhood summers on a farm, I understood how conservation of the bobolinks' habitat was integral to a larger natural ecosystem.

Mind you, I have no issue with the game of golf itself, or any sport being played in designated public spaces. Jackson Park has a popular golf course that's been around since the late 1800s, and we were not trying to interrupt anyone's tee time. Our concern was that the addition of a driving range might disturb the bobolinks, and the hundreds of other bird species in the park.

All of the activists knew that when it came to parks or any other municipal decisions, the buck stopped at city hall.

ChiTown has become infamous over the centuries for its rough and tumble politics. Rightfully or wrongfully, there's long been a reputation of cronyism, nepotism, and assorted wheeling and dealing.

When I was growing up, what was known in politics as "The Machine" dictated certain realities in our city: Who held office, who got jobs, who won contracts. What got started, or what got stopped. And so on.

There's a story that Chicagoans of a certain age, especially, have heard and sometimes tell.

Back in 1948, a young law student stopped by the headquarters of a Chicago ward committeeman to inquire about volunteering on the gubernatorial campaign of Adlai Stevenson. His name was Abner Mikva, and I'd later meet and admire this prominent figure in law and politics.

"Who sent you?" the committee boss barked.

"Nobody sent me," the young man replied.

The committeeman shot back, "We don't want nobody that nobody sent."

That line sort of aptly sums up The Machine. The thing is, depending upon your perspective, their outsized influence was beneficial, or it was heavy-handed and detrimental.

My father had his own run-in with The Machine back in the day.

Daddy was always independent-minded politically. As an activist, he worked behind the scenes in civil rights, labor and union organizing, and essentially thought Machine politics was antithetical to good government. In the '60s, he worked on the campaign of an impressive early Black candidate named Charlie Chew, a fellow WWII veteran who at the time, was anti-Machine. At this point, my father was in his entrepreneurial phase, selling real estate with a business partner. Within days, a city inspector paid them a visit and shut down the business. Daddy was furious about the strong-arm tactics, but there was nothing he could do. Many years later, I would work with Mr. Chew in my state legislative career.

In the meantime, it seems my father's activism had rubbed off on me.

We kept pressing about the bobolinks, but it became clear, to use a golf term, that the "birdies" and not the birds would win this round. Reluctantly, we packed up our picket signs and went home.

The golf driving range was completed in the late '70s; it has provided countless Chicagoans recreation and relaxation.

In the early '80s, Bobolink Meadow, named after the songbird, was designated in Jackson Park as a protected area.

★ ★ ★

The upside of the bobolink flap was that I got to know my neighbors and make new friends.

One of them was Kathryn Clement. Kay, as she was known, was a force in the local community and beyond.

Active in Democratic politics, she'd been involved in numerous local and national campaigns, from those of former Illinois governor Adlai Stevenson II, to John F. Kennedy. She was also a preservationist and proud "tree hugger."

Months after the bobolink protests, I ran into Kay while pushing the baby's chariot down the street. I did not know it then, but God had orchestrated yet another serendipitous moment of me being in the right place at the right time.

Kay stopped to say hello, and we exchanged pleasantries. She mentioned that the state representative from our district, Robert "Bob" Mann, intended to retire. "Have you ever considered running for office?" she asked. "I believe you'd be good at it."

I was flattered, but politely demurred. "Oh no. I've got my hands full with the baby."

Kay was persistent. "Well, there's going to be a community meeting and this will be on the agenda," she said. "Why don't you come along with me?"

I agreed to go, mostly out of curiosity. I attended the meeting, where the dialogue centered around this suddenly open seat in the state legislature.

As people went back and forth, my name was tossed out as a potential candidate. This was a bit surprising, since I had not expressed an iota of interest in the seat.

I was sitting there processing all this. Then, a man whom I did not know, stood up and looked directly at me.

"Don't run, you can't possibly win," he began. "The Blacks won't vote for you because you're not part of The Machine, the whites won't vote for you because you're Black, and nobody's going to vote for you because you're a woman."

I was taken aback by his diatribe, especially since it was quite premature.

The truth is, I had never really thought of running for elective office. Sure, I'd been treasurer with the Action Party, but that was back in college.

I had, however, volunteered for multiple political campaigns, Democrats and Republicans alike.

One candidate was Charles "Chuck" Percy, a Republican who ran successfully for the US Senate in 1966. Apart from Percy's election, I stumped for Jim Thompson, my old boss in the US Attorney's Office, when he ran for governor. He made history in the statehouse by serving four consecutive terms.

Early on, I had campaigned for Democrats, too, writing speeches for state senator Dick Newhouse, and going door-to-door canvassing for future mayor Harold Washington during his state Representative days.

Still, I'd never considered a career in politics for myself. Yet when that man got up on his soapbox, something inside me began to shift.

First, I was a grown woman, one who came of age during the Women's Liberation Movement. I did not like being told what to do.

Second, that man did not know anything about me, nor my credentials. Third: How dare he or anyone assume that I could not win? It felt like a challenge.

The meeting wrapped up and I went home. I needed time to ponder the prospect of elected office. A key concern for me was how the community would fare, because we were losing a very good representative.

As I weighed my options, the political maneuvering began. Different factions started showing up at my house to talk with me about the race.

One group claimed that because the neighborhood was integrated, a Black person couldn't get elected. Moreover, if I ran for office, they told me, it would mess things up for the independent Democrats who'd been fighting The Machine forever.

The political advice didn't end there. Another group stopped by, telling me that bottom line, a Black person could not get elected to this particular seat.

On and on came the parade of unsolicited feedback.

When the last group left our house, Michael turned to me and said, "Well, they said the wrong thing, didn't they?" I looked at my husband and smiled. "They sure did."

I was ready to shout, "Sign me up, folks!" and get in the game. However, a major decision such as running for office would affect our young family. I needed Michael's buy-in.

Thankfully, he was on board, and even put his money where his mouth was to the tune of $10,000. The money I borrowed from my husband would jump-start my campaign for state representative in the 24th District.

My life experiences were shaped by the political upheaval and social progress of the sixties and seventies. As a college student, I had ample experience participating in civic and community affairs.

Yet I was a political novice in terms of professional campaigns. I admitted as much to the women who'd encouraged me to toss my hat into the ring. And they essentially said, "That's fine. You can learn."

Kay played a pivotal role and became my campaign manager. We'd meet up with other homemakers from the neighborhood at her Hyde Park mansion to strategize. We dubbed our sessions the "kitchen campaign."

Officially, we called ourselves the Coalition Crusade for Good Government. My supporters and I envisioned a new brand of politics, one that was nonracial, inclusive, and which would bring all kinds of people together. My campaign literature detailed that philosophy as well, and how we could build coalitions that fostered unity.

The field was crowded—at least ten people were running. Two of us were women. I was the only Black woman.

Mine was a grassroots campaign. I did it the old-school way. I went door-to-door and met voters. I must've knocked on thousands of doors in my district. I went to coffee sips, houses of worship, and attended debates where I introduced myself and presented my platform.

I spent a good deal of time just engaging with people, asking folks what their needs and concerns were. When I was out on the campaign trail, sometimes with the campaign team and volunteers, people seemed to react favorably to our message.

I remember meeting voters at the bus stop on 57th and Lake Park around six in the morning. It was one of those frigid Chicago days. I had on a heavy coat, and Kay, who'd accompanied me, had brought along these husky boots and a big hat for me. I put those on, and just stood there for hours, shaking hands with people as they boarded the different buses. A woman came up to me. "Honey," she said, "if you want the job this bad to stand out in the cold, I'm gonna vote for you."

My family also pitched in on the campaign trail. Daddy was especially enthusiastic.

My father took to the streets in a green station wagon plastered with my campaign posters and bumper stickers, and he was not shy about soliciting votes.

"Lift up the needy! Down with the greedy!" he shouted out the windows. "Vote Carol Moseley Braun!"

We solicited donations and held a few fundraisers that generated contributions from community members. Despite not having a hefty war chest and no prior name recognition, I felt encouraged. I sensed momentum, and apparently, someone else noticed it, too.

One evening, I learned firsthand just how dirty politics could be. We were up late stuffing envelopes at my tiny campaign headquarters. All of a sudden, a brick came crashing through the window. "What the hell!?" I yelled, ducking for cover as glass shattered in every direction.

Once the shock wore off, some of us ran outside, and looked up and down the street. There was no sign of whoever did this, but clearly they wanted to intimidate me and send a message. Well, it was received. Loud and clear. I knew, however, that no threat was going to stop me from forging ahead with our campaign and the greater democratic process. If anything, it only made me more determined.

When I first ran for the Illinois General Assembly, we had multimember districts and a system of cumulative voting. This type of proportional representation had been in place for a century dating back to the 1870s.

Each voter had three votes, which they could cast for their candidates of choice in the primary and general elections. Voters could give one candidate all three votes, or they could divide them up among the candidates.

In theory, the process was intended to ensure that each district had representatives of both the majority and minority parties.

The outcome might yield two Democrats and one Republican, or two Republicans and one Democrat. Or a mix of Independents, Democrats, and Republicans.

The cumulative voting system was abolished in the '80s, but before that happened, we hoped it would help me win one of the three slots.

Election day dawned. I stuck to my normal routine: making breakfast and getting the baby fed, bathed, and dressed. This was Matt's first election, and even though he was far too young to vote, I wanted him with me and Michael as we did our civic duty.

The entire family was praying for me, and I was cautiously optimistic. I'd made my pitch to voters, done the legwork, and had amassed a vocal group of supporters, among them, the lawmaker who'd retired. Now it was time to see what the good people of Illinois, who lived in my district, had to say about my candidacy.

Once the polls closed, my family, the "kitchen campaign," and I waited. Results began to trickle in from the elections board, and the early results gave me hope. As the evening wore on, I had a solid lead that held. Then came the greatest news of all: I'd won handily! We were all jumping up and down and celebrating. Given the large field, there were plenty of candidates who were not happy about the outcome.

The Machine saw an upset. The incumbent that they reportedly backed lost in a tight finish.

When all the votes were tallied, I emerged as the top vote getter. Bernard Epton, a Republican who had already served a few terms, won reelection. Barbara Flynn Currie, the other woman in the race, rounded out the top three. It's funny now, but Barbara and I started out in the race as fierce competitors. However, we came to respect each other. Decades later, she made history in the legislature as the state's first woman majority leader.

It was thrilling to see women's representation statewide in that election. In fact, more women than ever before were elected to the Illinois General Assembly during that cycle. The press started calling it the "Year of the Woman." I had no idea back then, but it would not be my last.

Certainly, this woman was elated. I'd won my first election and could scarcely believe it. My first foray into elective politics had resulted in a victory that naysayers predicted could never happen.

In short order, I'd gone from being a federal prosecutor, to a stay-at-home mom, to running successfully for state office. I'm romanticizing it, perhaps, but the journey began with a little bird.

That night in bed, I was exhausted from campaigning. Michael kissed me tenderly, and told me how proud he was of me. For some time, he'd sensed that I was bored at home, and just wasn't going to stay put. "Thanks, honey. Love you," I murmured, before drifting off.

The next morning, fully awake, I let my husband know that I'd actually enjoyed my brief time as a homemaker. However, he was right about one thing: I was not going to stay in one place.

Next stop, the Illinois General Assembly.

SPRINGFIELD

It was early January, 1979. I had risen before dawn to make the three-hour drive from Chicago to Springfield, the state capital in central Illinois.

Awash in American history, the city is known for being the birthplace of Abraham Lincoln, and the seat of state government since the 1830s.

Once inside the state Capitol building, I walked briskly to the House of Representatives' chamber, and took my seat. The space was striking, with carved dark woodwork, luminous chandeliers, and ceilings adorned with murals and artwork.

Springfield was brimming with people: lawmakers, lobbyists, bystanders. The 81st General Assembly of the State of Illinois was convening, and I was being sworn in to elected office for the very first time. My loved ones and supporters were seated with fellow guests in the gallery. Baby Matt was so cute, all dressed up in a tiny little suit for my big day.

The ceremony unfolded with the requisite pomp and pageantry, the press corps scribbling notes, and paperwork.

"Your attention please," the provisional clerk announced. "The members-elect will find oaths on the desks, oaths of office. Kindly sign on the red line as provided for signature. The pages will come up and down the aisles and pick them up."

I quickly signed the document and glanced around. The House has since downsized, but in my class of legislators there were a whopping 177 members. It was thrilling to see my new colleagues who hailed from every corner of the great Prairie State, all duly elected to serve.

Soon after, a gentleman strode to the podium and offered salutations. His tone was warm.

"I am pleased to meet, to greet the members-elect and their families on this occasion," said Alan J. Dixon, at that time, the Illinois secretary of state.

Little did I know it then, but the universe was winking at me yet again: a decade or so later, Mr. Dixon and I would be matched up in a three-way primary race for the US Senate.

That day, however, Secretary Dixon was faithfully executing his duties in accordance with the state constitution. He later introduced the chief justice of the Illinois Supreme Court, who administered the oath of office.

I stood, proudly, and raised my right hand.

"I solemnly swear to support the Constitution of the United States, and that of the State of Illinois," I said. Furthermore, I promised to "faithfully discharge my duties" to the "best of my ability."

As I recited those words, reflecting upon their meaning, the gravity of my new legislative position began to sink in.

Earlier, a pastor had delivered a powerful invocation. His prayer echoed through the chamber with a spiritual message that seemed tailor-made for me and all who hold office.

O Lord, the people of Illinois with trustful confidence have chosen those who are now gathered here to be their primary benefactors in state government. A government that daily affects their lives and the lives of their children.

Give, O Lord, these legislators a sense of destiny and high purpose, give them an awareness of the solemn powers they are being given over the lives of others. Open their ears to all the people, especially the weak and the poor and give them a share of glory and a vision of Your kingdom that they may dare to do great and good things. Amen.

As a newly minted member, I was now in good company. President Lincoln had once served in the Illinois House. John W.E. Thomas, the state's first Black legislator, was elected in 1876.

The first woman to serve in this legislative body was Lottie Holman O'Neill in 1922; she was elected two years after the Nineteenth Amendment was ratified, giving women the right to vote. State representative Floy Clements broke additional barriers in 1958, paving the way for future Black women lawmakers like me.

I thought of the good people of Illinois, and the good people in my district, which encompassed parts of Hyde Park, South Shore, Woodlawn, and Kenwood, to name a few neighborhoods. Its demographic ranged from the working class, to wealthy denizens, to college students, and to families in public housing.

I was elected to represent them all, and as the preacher said, to be one of their "primary benefactors in state government." Through responsive constituent service and policies that benefited people socially, economically, and otherwise, that is what I intended to do.

I was a freshman lawmaker, one of approximately thirty newcomers. I wasted no time in terms of bringing forth legislation.

Among the first measures I sponsored was a bill to provide a cost of living increase to public assistance recipients. I'd seen poverty up close while living in Bucket of Blood, and later, during my tenant outreach job with the Chicago Housing Authority.

I visited the offices of each and every member, both Democrats and Republicans, to speak with them personally about my legislation. I'd come prepared with a folder that had data and information showing how the bill might impact their district.

I was able to sit down with quite a few colleagues, although not everyone was available. Still, the ones I met with must have listened: the bill passed the House. I was absolutely giddy.

Following the vote, an older member who was known to be an arch conservative, came over to my desk. I'd met him during my visits to push the measure, and we'd had a pleasant conversation.

"Miss Brauns," he said, adding an *s* to my last name, "I almost voted for your bill."

I sensed a "but" was coming. "I did not vote for it," he confirmed.

"But I want you to know, you're the second-nicest colored lady I ever met," he said, cheerfully. "The first one took care of my family for years."

The gentleman had no idea that his word choice was offensive. However, I could tell he meant no harm with his outdated semantics.

Besides, it was far too early in my tenure to make unnecessary political enemies. "Thank you for sitting down with me," I told him. "I hope we can find common ground on future legislation."

I was slowly learning the ropes in Springfield, but I quickly surmised that political allies were necessary for one's success.

There were spoken and unspoken rules. To wit, while I'd had beginner's luck with my public aid bill in the House, it did not pass the Senate. And it seemed I'd unwittingly breached protocol. No one had explained to me that for certain bills, one typically went to leadership first to get their buy-in, and then to fellow members.

I needed mentorship from astute insiders who understood the legislative process and the larger political landscape.

I was eager to build effective coalitions with my peers. I decided to join a few groups, among them the Illinois Legislative Black Caucus and the Illinois House Democratic Women's Caucus.

The Women's Caucus was small (at the time, the legislature was about 13 percent female) and filled with smart, impassioned women leaders who embodied public service. The term "women's issues" is sometimes derided, but we were determined to address issues and challenges intrinsic to women, and advance legislative policies that helped elevate their needs, along with those of children and families.

The state's Black Caucus was founded in 1967. The lawmakers advanced the legislative interests of Black Americans and sought to ensure they were equitably represented in the General Assembly.

We addressed a wealth of issues: education, housing, health, employment, and minority business development were among those on our agenda.

The Black legislators tended to be tight-knit. So much so, that multiple members sat near each other on the House floor. The seats were playfully dubbed "Catfish Row," from the fictitious enclave inhabited by Porgy, Bess, and company on the page, stage, and screen; that in turn, was based on the historic community of "Cabbage Row" in Charleston, South Carolina.

I didn't sit on Catfish Row, but I did form valuable alliances, and later became part of the Black Caucus's leadership—meeting up with Daddy's old political friend, state senator Charlie Chew. I formed lasting friendships with him and many other lawmakers. One of my closest colleagues was Ethel Skyles Alexander, a fellow House member who was elected the same year as me.

Because Springfield was several hours from Chicago, I sometimes carpooled with fellow lawmakers. At other times, I used our per diem for lodging in town during the session. Ethel was my roommate, and we became fast friends.

Ethel was a second-generation representative, the daughter of Charles Skyles, a pioneering Black lawmaker who served in the 1940s.

Some twenty years my senior, she was deeply knowledgeable. I've often said that I knew government, but I learned politics from Ethel. She served in the state senate, as well, before retiring in the early 1990s. Ethel, who was deeply religious, lived to the ripe, old age of ninety-one. I still miss her dearly.

Another woman who befriended me in Springfield was Billie Paige. She was not a lawmaker, but an influential player as a top lobbyist, one of the first Black women partners at a major lobbying firm. Billie was brilliant and bold. Down the line, she would play an integral role in my US Senate campaign. Billie too, has passed on, as have so many VIPs from my life. I cherish her memory.

While I found natural affinity with some of the women and Black stakeholders in Springfield, my network was not insular.

I made a point of being friendly with all of my colleagues. I got to know and collaborated with legislators in my own party and across the aisle, and of varying backgrounds.

One of my seatmates was John P. Daley, a scion of Chicago's powerful political dynasty. He was very nice to me. We liked each other as people, whatever the politics. He was a bit more low-key than his legendary father, Richard J. Daley, and brother, Richard M. Daley, both of whom were Chicago's longest-serving mayors. John was a Democratic committeeman and a savvy legislator, and I relied upon his experience to help put out a lot of the fires that, frankly, were always burning in the legislature.

I entered the General Assembly as an unabashed liberal and champion of civil and human rights. I focused on sponsoring and supporting legislation centered around women and families; eradicating poverty; health care access (I proposed universal health care before the issue gained widespread national attention); and educational initiatives.

Indeed, education was one of my priorities as a lawmaker. I sponsored bills to boost education funding, introduced legislation to increase teacher salaries, and worked aggressively on education reform.

I was the chief sponsor of the Urban School Improvement Act, landmark legislation that established parent councils in Chicago public schools. These councils were designed to give families greater input over the inner workings of their children's schools.

I also played a legislative role in helping to create the Chicago High School for Agricultural Sciences, the only school of its kind in the Midwest and the second in the country. In 1986, the General Assembly passed a measure to revitalize agricultural education in our state; funds were incorporated into the Illinois State Board of Education budget. Given my family's farming roots, it was special to see a high school with this hands-on, unique curriculum, come to fruition.

I championed other legislative measures that, while constituent driven, resonated with me because of my own life experiences.

Never forgetting my mother's pain, and my own trauma, I sponsored measures to protect domestic violence survivors. I also worked to secure tenants' rights, remembering how landlords would not rent to my mother and her children post-divorce. I sponsored some of the state's early set-aside programs for women and "minorities," (the term we used back then) and was an early advocate for LGBTQ rights.

Early on, I was among those leading the call about divesting from South Africa during apartheid.

A few terms in, I began moving up the leadership ladder. Speaker Michael Madigan named me assistant majority leader, the first Black person and woman in the post in state history. Some of the old-timers didn't appreciate me stepping ahead of them, but simply put, that was politics.

When Harold Washington was elected Chicago's first Black mayor in 1983, he made me his floor leader. It meant articulating the city's priorities to fellow members and coordinating appropriate legislative strategies.

The years passed. I was juggling marriage and motherhood, and extremely long hours. I sought reelection and was gratified when my constituents allowed me the privilege of returning to Springfield.

Not every victory was mine. I fought for years to abolish the death penalty and proposed a moratorium. Data showed the penalty was often racist in its application, disproportionately impacting Black and Hispanic Americans.

Moreover, as a Christian, the moral questions of being "judge and jury" to another human did not sit well with me. I remember having lengthy emotional conversations and fierce debates with colleagues.

Alas, my years-long quest to get a moratorium bill to the finish line never happened during my tenure. I was long gone from the legislature when Illinois finally abolished the death penalty; Governor Pat Quinn signed that legislation in 2011.

There were other battles that I took on with more success, but ample controversy.

In the '80s, I decided to sue my own party, specifically Illinois Democratic party leaders, around reapportionment. The process, based on census data and done every decade, determines how many seats each state receives in Congress.

In our state, there'd been a tradition whereby the party representatives would pull a piece of paper out of Abraham Lincoln's hat—no joke. And that would determine who gets the right to draw the lines if there is a tie. So the Democrats got the favor of the hat that year and drew the maps. And those maps choppily configured the districts of Hispanic voters—and our city at the time had two sizable Mexican American and Puerto

Rican neighborhoods—in a way that would eliminate Hispanic representation.

Moreover, Black voters had been gerrymandered into the minimum number of districts in which they could have a voting majority. It was wrong, and while me and other state lawmakers tried to stop it in the legislature, we were outvoted. *Crosby v. State Board of Elections* became a landmark case, and it was a slugfest. What most people didn't know was that the lawsuit originated following a conversation I'd had with the man who became a key plaintiff, Bruce Crosby. I ran into him on the street, and he started complaining to me about the redistricting map. "This is just a travesty that the lines would be drawn that way. Can't you do something about it, Representative?" he asked.

"You know we tried to fight it," I replied. "That map seems carved in stone."

His face fell in disappointment at my response.

"Well, somebody could file a lawsuit," I countered. He said, "Well, you're a lawyer, aren't you?" And so it went.

I drew up the lawsuit on my dining room table, and then I filed the case just to make it public record. I reached out to a friend at one of the mega law firms, hoping they could take this on pro bono. And they said, "No. This is too much of a political hot potato." I was crushed. I was on the verge of tears walking out of their office when I later ran into Tom Sullivan, a former US Attorney. At the time, he was in private practice with one of Chicago's major law firms. And we began chatting about the case. He said it sounded really interesting, and asked me to send him the files. Well, he and his colleagues took off running, with the condition that I remain in the legal loop. Dick Newhouse was among those who were integrally involved as well. Eventually, there was a consolidated lawsuit with several plaintiffs and legal defense groups involved.

I do not recommend suing a legislative redistricting commission led by one's own political party. It is an extremely difficult proposition, especially while still in office. My own district, which abutted Lake Michigan, had not been dramatically re-drawn. However, to me the lawsuit was not about my own self-interest, but larger principles of democracy.

I worked harder on this lawsuit than any other in my life. People in the community helped with things like the computer programming. The testimony in the nine-day trial, complete with two-hundred plus exhibits, was revealing, and sometimes baffling. Some Democrats who were called as some of the two-dozen witnesses knew the party leadership was mistreating its historically loyal voters, but would not acknowledge it on the stand. Perhaps the powers that be were counting on no one un-derstanding the inanity of what had been done until it was too late for the maps to be changed.

But they got a surprise: we won. And we made history be-cause it was the first time a reapportionment case had been won in the North; the Voting Rights Act Provision had been lim-ited to just the Southern states. But this case extended the VRA for the first time.

I made no small number of enemies, and was even threat-ened with banishment from the party. Still, I had to do what I believed was right. The really great news was that the case gave rise to the first Hispanic district ever in Illinois, and additional Black districts.

I had considered leaving the legislature. I had garnered a string of "best legislator" awards. There were also kudos from groups that I'd worked to help: the Chicago Firefighters Union, the Illinois Women's Political Caucus, the Chicago Board of Education, the Illinois Association of Realtors, and the Illinois Council of Sheriffs, to name a few.

But I was exhausted. I was driving three hundred miles back and forth. I was trying to ensure Matthew had all that he needed from his mother. And I was seeing cracks in my marriage, which alarmed me.

After ten years in the Illinois General Assembly, it seemed time to move on to my next opportunity.

When I left the House, my colleagues introduced a resolution that recognized me as "the conscience of the House." It was an absolute honor. Years later, I would recall this vote of confidence from my peers, especially as the twists and turns of national "poli-tricks" tossed me around like a rag doll.

I also left with an amended birth certificate. My first attempt to fix it came during my time as a young lawyer working in the US Attorney's office.

I visited vital records and approached one of the clerks. Document in hand, I stated my case. She looked at me skeptically. "But this is a white woman's birth certificate," she said.

"No," I responded. "That is my mother's name, my father's name, and my birth certificate—it's me."

She looked perplexed. "But it says White."

"No, no, no, this is my birth certificate," I countered.

We wound up getting into this lengthy, circular debate. She kept asking, incredulously, "How can you possibly be the person whose birth certificate says White and you're obviously Black?" I kept repeating the truth. Back and forth we went, getting us nowhere. Finally, I told her to forget about it and left, slightly miffed. I was Black as ever in the eyes of the world, but still officially white.

A few years later, when I was elected to the Illinois General Assembly, the matter resurfaced. I needed an official copy of my birth certificate. The governor at the time had nominated a new director of Public Health. We had a statute in Illinois which mandated that the candidate had to be a physician. However, his supporters in the legislature were pushing to change the law so that he could lead the agency. A vote was planned. I went to him and said, "I'll back you on one condition."

He replied, "What's that?"

I said, "You've got to fix my birth certificate." I laid out the whole bizarre situation to him.

He fell out laughing, telling me it was the funniest thing he had ever heard. Later, he became the public health director, and not long after, my birth certificate was corrected. I read it and couldn't help but smile. After all these years, I was finally, officially and indisputably Black.

BROTHER JOHN

The day that my cherubic baby brother arrived home from the hospital, John stole my heart. I am the firstborn child in the Moseley family, and my birth order gave me rank. "Brother," as I called him, was the first son to bless our burgeoning clan. My parents now had a prince and a princess in their domestic kingdom. I had an earth angel by my side.

We were close in age—about eighteen months apart. Immediately, we became inseparable. John was my childhood best friend, confidant, and one of my favorite people in the world.

"Brother," I would chirp after we bounced out of our twin beds each morning, "Let's play!"

"Okay, Bunny!" he would happily reply, using my family nickname.

John would join me in games of hide-and-seek, make-believe, and dutifully sit alongside my baby dolls in our imaginary classroom. As the oldest, I always assigned myself the role of teacher, and he was my star pupil.

Once we attended "real" school, the two of us would walk

together each morning. The short journey was always an adventure. Brother was a rambunctious lad, who would zip up trees, splash in puddles, and good-naturedly chase squirrels. When it snowed, as was common in the Windy City, he would gleefully stick out his tongue to catch the fluttering flakes. He held out both arms and buzzed around pretending to be an airplane. I laughed uproariously at his antics.

Intelligent and equally curious, John was a good student who was well regarded by teachers at school. In the early 1950s, our brown skin made us stand out among our peers in the classroom. Yet Brother made friends easily, thanks to his delightful demeanor, and across racial lines that never really mattered to children anyway. He was warm, friendly, and funny without even trying.

People enjoyed my little brother's company and as I've often said, liked to see him coming. It was the exact opposite reception given to me. I have never really fit in anywhere, and for the life of me, I did not understand the reason why. It was as if I had an invisible sign taped on my back that said "kick me," while John had one that read "hug me." Brother brought sunshine to my days, and sunny skies to everyone around him.

I adored John, but as siblings do, we had our occasional spats. As a big sister there were times when I was embarrassed to be seen in public with my little brother. It didn't help matters that while I was fairly fastidious about my appearance, John was always slightly disheveled, sort of like that *Peanuts* character Pigpen. Mother would dress us neatly for school, but in short order, his clothes were rumpled. His hat was askew. His coat would be flying in the wind.

"You walk on the other side of the street," I would admonish him in my bossy voice. However, my attempts at temporarily disowning Brother proved futile. "That's my sister!" he would gleefully shout to anyone within earshot. John was a free spirit who floated happily through life.

Brother's joie de vivre was a feat in and of itself because our childhood was complicated. The Moseley household was one of love and happiness, intermingled with discord and strife. Our father was demanding and mercurial, and Mother was constantly navigating the tornado that was his temper.

Daddy's shifting moods and the ire that erupted because of them, kept our mother, me, and John constantly on edge. I was just a child, but have linger visceral memories of my parents' arguing. The cacophony of their tense, shrill voices linger.

During our father's rampages, Brother would cower in fear under the piano; if Daddy started coming for him, I would bravely jump in between them and take the licks. Even though we were just children, I instinctively wanted to shield my brother from pain and the harsher realities of life. John was my defender and protector, as well. As someone who has perennially felt the sting of being an outsider, I was no stranger to bullying.

One day in the schoolyard, a group of kids had corralled me into a circle, taunting me and pushing me around. But they had picked on the wrong one. I was scrappy. Then, and throughout my life, I have never been afraid to fight back.

My short arms flailing, my pint-sized legs kicking, I was getting it in with the bullies, or so I thought. Our housekeeper, Miss Mary, who often picked us up from school, witnessed the skirmish and saw that I needed reinforcements.

"John, you better come quick! Your sister is being jumped!" she told him. The next thing I knew, Brother had raced to my rescue, leaping into the fray. We whupped 'em, or at least that was our version of the story while limping home. It was one of many battles that we would face together. Ours was an unspoken pact: we would always have each other's back.

Indeed, until my younger siblings, Marsha and Joe, came along, it was just me and John against the world. Our loving bond remained strong, even as our lives began to sharply diverge with heartbreaking consequences.

★ ★ ★

It was a weekday morning, and my son Matthew and I were doing the off-to-school shuffle. Lunch packed? Check. Homework, check. Uniform ironed, double-check. It was a constant scramble to get my child—and myself—out the door on time.

This wintry day, the trees and sidewalks were blanketed in fresh snow. We Chicagoans often joke about our legendary weather: "Almost winter, winter, still winter, and roadwork."

Matt, excited about tossing a few snowballs before school, had bolted out the door and was headed toward the car.

I'd grabbed my purse and keys, when suddenly, my little boy came barreling back inside our home, frantically jumping up and down. "Mom, come outside!" he said. "Uncle Johnny is sleeping in the car!"

I looked at my son quizzically, trying not to panic. But I was thinking, "What in the world?" I was moving so fast that I didn't stop to put on my coat in the sub-zero temperatures. With Matt leading the way, we headed to the parking lot of our condo building on Hyde Park Boulevard.

Amid the snow-covered vehicles, my car resembled a frozen ice sculpture. I peered through the windows and could make out the contours of a man's face and physique.

My beloved John was sprawled along the back seat. He was visibly shivering. Yet somehow he was sleeping as soundly as if a guest in a five-star hotel.

A flood of emotions washed over me as I gazed at his visage—that of a brilliant, charismatic, and kindhearted man—one who was deep in the throes of addiction.

My heart overflowed with pity. Obviously, Johnny was in terribly bad shape anytime he would trudge on foot across town in a snowstorm to sleep in my car. While my mother provided him periodic lodging—no matter our familial concerns about her enabling his habit—she had lately begun to issue ultimatums about his benders. John repeatedly denied his escalating drug use, but Mother called his bluff.

"Don't BS me, son, I work in a hospital," she would tell him, as he tried to sweet-talk his way out of the cold, hard truth. My mother knew better. Besides her day-to-day experience in a medical lab, her brother, Uncle Tommy, was a musician who had weathered his own battles with dope.

No one in our clan was fooled by what John was not-so-sneakily doing, and we let him know as much while staging countless interventions. "You're killing yourself, Johnny!" I would tell him. Mostly, he ignored my entreaties, but sometimes he listened. I had personally footed the bills for his stints at a methadone clinic and a host of treatment facilities. Still, the cycle of addiction rarely has a straight path. I wrung my hands and we all watched in dismay as John spiraled further down the rabbit hole.

It was gut-wrenching to witness John's predicament, not only because he was my brother, but because he was such a special human being. Everyone loved him—his personality, his heart.

He was an expert chess player and would trash talk me during competitive matches. He fancied himself a singer, and in his youth was part of a corner doo-wop group, a suave crooner, complete with conked hair. My father jokingly called them "fried egg heads."

A good athlete, John played football and was an amateur Golden Gloves boxer, a sport he picked up from Daddy. Brother was witty and funny, and lit up every room that he entered.

Yet at a certain point, his formidable charms had worn thin even with the people who adored him.

John had gotten married, and he was a father. Yet his ongoing drug and alcohol abuse compromised his ability to be fully present for those he loved. He bounced around from place to place.

He had stayed with Mother off and on, but at a certain point, she told him "enough is enough." He was no longer allowed in her home. Without her comfortable abode as a lodging option, sadly, Brother was out on the street.

While pondering what to do, he must've decided that my car was the safest place to lay his weary head.

"John! Johnny! Wake up!" I cried out, my hands trembling as I opened the car door. My brother didn't stir. Matt started sobbing. As shaken as I was, it upset me even more to watch my impressionable young son witness his dear uncle in such a pitiful state. The situation engendered a complex brew of emotions.

The truth is, I felt deep compassion for my beleaguered brother, yet I was angry at the situation that had engulfed him and the entire family. I fully understood that addiction is a disease, not a moral failing, and it's one that people of all stripes wrestle with daily across America.

As a legislator at the state level, and later in Congress, I had advocated for funding and measures to address what was a critical, vexing issue. Policy is one thing. When addiction touches you personally, however, it's a maelstrom that wounds the heart.

John's breaking into my car was not an isolated incident; it was the latest maddening episode as he grasped at the brass ring of sobriety. His inability to get clean was deflating his spirit, and it left the entire family in a tailspin, trying to figure out what to do.

I believe the roots of John's rebellion ran deep. Our loving, but complicated home life, and my parents' contentious divorce had devastated and splintered our household.

Brother and I had relocated with Mother from our safe, suburban-ish home to our grandmother's place in a rough section of the city.

Meanwhile, our two youngest siblings, Marsha and Joey, were dispatched to Indiana, to live with Daddy's people where they felt isolated. Our father had taken off for the West Coast and kept in touch sporadically.

Mother did her best, but she was working practically around the clock. We had some male presence from my uncles. Yet

Brother was navigating the path to manhood largely on his own without a positive role model or a roadmap. It proved disastrous.

John was maybe fifteen years old when he began running with a wild crowd, drinking cheap wine, and hanging out. Brother, who was academically gifted, started skipping school. His troubling behavior further escalated when word filtered to us that he had joined a gang.

In reality he was on the fringes of gang life rather than being a bona fide member. Still, his close association with gangbanging in ChiTown, a metropolis with a notorious history of mob activity, vice, and violence, was frightening and worrisome.

At some point, John had a brief reprieve from street life, when he enlisted in the US Navy. He was following the tradition of our father, a World War II veteran; our grandfather, a "Doughboy" during WWI; and an ancestor who served in the United States Colored Troops during the Civil War.

His joining the military to serve our nation evoked a tremendous sense of family pride.

One afternoon when Mother went to the mailbox, we were overjoyed to find a letter scrawled from John. He had included a photo of himself aboard the massive ship on which he was commissioned. Brother appeared to be the lone Black man among the literal and figurative sea of young men in uniform.

Unfortunately, his stint with Uncle Sam was short-lived. John went AWOL. The circumstances were murky, and he refused to discuss what happened upon his unexpected return home. Always jovial and lighthearted, John now seemed sullen and depressed.

I am not sure if he was doing drugs in the service, or if that had possibly played a role in his self-separation, but he seemed to be slipping down a precipice to doom.

It was difficult to reconcile how John had gone from briefly serving our country to breaking into my car to find shelter during a storm. I suppose he had utilized his street savvy to jimmy the lock, although to be clear, I did not give a rat's patootie about any damages to the vehicle. What left me so bereft was that John could have frozen to death, a stone's throw from my home.

I assumed John was probably high at the time when he trudged across town in a snowstorm. Still, a part of me could not comprehend that if my brother had the presence of mind to bed down in my car, why didn't he just knock on my door and explain his latest predicament? I would not have turned him away.

I understood John's desperation and appreciated his survival instincts. However, I shuddered to think what might have resulted from him breaking into a car. Black men, particularly in certain neighborhoods, do not have the luxury of even looking suspicious. The crime he committed that night might have gotten him arrested, shot, or worse. Still, I knew that his actions had to be viewed through the lens of addiction. He needed my support, not judgment.

John eventually opened his eyes that snowy morn. Miraculously, he was okay. I was not, nor was Matt, who seemed traumatized. I pleaded and pleaded again with my brother to get help, and as he took off to nowhere, a sadness settled in my spirit and lingered there.

In the days that followed, I grappled with what was going on with John, trying my best to comprehend the car incident and what was at the core of his overall struggles. A part of me was mystified how two people raised in the same family environment had turned out so differently. Certainly, we had not had a perfect childhood, but in my mind there were enough happy memories to outweigh the negative ones.

John was vexed, by what I did not know, and his sweet soul seemed tired. He'd started off drinking cheap liquor, then started getting high, smoking reefer, recreationally. Now I watched him sink deeper and deeper into the abyss of heroin addiction.

I tried to carry on with my life and career. At that time, I was serving as a representative in the Illinois General Assembly.

The legislative sessions in Springfield, the Illinois state capital, spanned from January to late spring. My fourteen-hour days were spent introducing legislation, voting on bills, attending committee hearings, and on constituent service.

One day, a male colleague hurried over to my desk. "Carol, may I speak with you for a moment?" he asked. I figured he wanted to discuss a bill, or the latest political happenings.

Then I noticed the expression on his face. He looked positively stricken.

"What's wrong?" I asked.

"There's been some news from back home."

Suddenly, my mind went gray, blue, and black, and hazy images clouded my thoughts like a thick fog. When I finally came to, groggy and disoriented, medics and fellow lawmakers were hovering over me. I had fainted on the floor of the House chamber.

Heaven help me! Brother John was dead.

My youngest brother, Joe, by that time a Chicago detective, had been at his desk in the precinct and took the phone call. On the line was one of his contacts who worked at the city morgue. "A body just came in," she said. The deceased had ID on him. The name was John Moseley. "Any relationship?" she wondered.

Joe was left with the horrific task of identifying his only brother's body. His first thought was to call our Uncle Burton, a veteran on the force who had been promoted to sergeant. Together, they sprang into action, reaching out to colleagues and trying to piece together the puzzle of John's demise.

Brother's body, they learned, was discovered underneath the viaduct on the city's North Side. Word was that he was shooting up in a known drug gallery. As it became clear that John was overdosing, his drug buddies plunged him into a tub of ice, trying in vain to save his life. When he didn't respond, fearing reprisal, they were too scared to seek assistance. Instead, someone dumped his body, half-dressed and left lying like a dog in the street. His belt and shoes were missing.

Joe was left with the torturous task of identifying the corpse, something even his training as a cop could not prepare him for. At one point, in a fit of anguish, he punched his fist through a wall.

Mother, who was recovering from a stroke, absorbed the shock of her eldest son's tragic death about as well as could be expected. Often strong in times of turmoil and the many ebbs and flows of her life, she was not someone who would fall on the floor, nor wail until the breath nearly left her lungs. We siblings could tell, however, that our mother was shattered.

In the dark days that followed, we began to make arrangements. I went all out for Brother's services. His final rites were performed by the same African American undertaker who had prepared the body of Emmitt Till, the young Chicagoan whose abduction and killing in Mississippi decades earlier generated global headlines.

Johnny's homegoing was a blur of tears. I was inconsolable. We all were. As we mutually grieved that day, my brother Joe had passing thoughts of revenge, particularly when some of the so-called friends who chased the dragon with John showed up to the funeral.

Daddy had died about six years before John's untimely passing. Our father had previously returned to Chicago, made amends with my mother and all of us, and married a nice lady. We had several good years with him, attending family gatherings at his new home. Sadly, John's woes interrupted the precious remaining time that father and son might have had together.

John was only thirty-four years old when he passed away in 1986. During his relatively short time on this earth, he had been a son, brother, husband, father, nephew, cousin, and friend to many.

Even as he spiraled, I'd tried to maintain contact with my brother, although we had not spoken on that fateful day. But whenever we talked, we told each other, "I love you." My brother was lost. There was nothing that any of us could do to save him, and God knows I tried.

We mourned Brother for a very long time. As horrible as that period was for me and our family, I put my trust in the Lord. My faith was strengthened through communing with God. In fact, the loss of my brother took me back to some spiritual fundamentals that I had kind of lost along the way. I joined a new church and underwent what can only be described as a transformative spiritual conversion. Seated in the pews, thinking about John, I'd hum one of my favorite spirituals:

> There is a balm in Gilead
> To make the wounded whole
> There is a balm in Gilead
> To heal the sin-sick soul

It's been nearly four decades since Brother slipped away. The pain of losing him will never fade, but at least now I can think of the poignant, loving memories.

I am reminded of John when I drive past certain Chicago neighborhoods and landmarks. I smile remembering our special childhood bond. And my siblings and I often reminisce about him when we get together.

Growing up, I loved to visit the Alabama farm that Mother's people have owned for generations.

The train trip south was not an easy trek owing to segregation. Emmitt Till's death—which occurred when I was eight—was a warning, even to children, to always know your place.

I remember the train station in Montgomery, a city notorious for its Jim Crow laws. The water fountains at the station were hard to miss with their signs designating "colored" and "white."

On one particular trip, my siblings and I were tired and parched. We asked for a drink of water. However, Mother didn't want us drinking from the "colored" water fountains; in her mind it was not worth the indignity. "Children," she told us, "you must wait until we get to your grandmother's house, and we'll get some water there."

That's when John began to throw a temper tantrum, screaming and yelling because he wanted some colored water. He thought it was going to be green, yellow, red, and blue, and spurt from the fountain like a rainbow. "I want some colored water! I want some colored water!" he cried.

Can you imagine? There was Mother, standing in a sweltering hot, segregated train station with her little ones in tow, as one of them threw a fit over "colored" water. He was just an innocent boy, of course, but the incident spoke to the insidiousness of racism and how human beings—even children—were impacted by separations based on skin color.

Years later, the story became part of our family lore. Marsha, Joey, and I would good-naturedly tease Johnny.

We all miss him dearly. As a Christian, I believe Brother John is now finally at rest in the arms of Jesus Christ. And who knows? Perhaps in heaven, there is beautiful, rainbow-colored water.

MARRIAGE AND DIVORCE

When I first ran for a seat in the General Assembly, my husband was my most ardent supporter. By the time I left the legislature a decade later, my lovelorn marriage and broken heart were the stuff of Shakespearean sonnets.

The man I'd fallen for during law school, the father of my only child, and my best friend, was no longer mine. Who he belonged to is another story, but suffice to say, we would no longer be together til death do us part.

The dissolution of our union left me bereft and adrift in a melancholy sea. There was no rage or wrath, only sadness and a longing for what might have been.

Michael was, and is, a good man. During our courtship in law school, he was wonderful. He was a kind, warm, and generous partner. And when our beloved son came along, he was a marvelous father. And yet...

When we were young and in love, our lives were far simpler. As the years progressed, our worlds became more complex due to careers, parenthood, and simply, life. I thought ours was a strong marriage, but as every couple knows, small chinks can begin to dent the armor of lovers.

On some level, I wondered if our breakup was inevitable. Michael came from a stable home, but my domestic situation was fraught. I simply did not have role models for a solid, successful marriage.

My parents had a tumultuous relationship. My grandparents on both sides of the family tree had divorced. My great-grandmother Ollie had three husbands. And Auntie Darrel had so many men that we could barely keep count.

I longed to have a marriage that would give us the proverbial fairy tale of a happy ending. But real life intervened in the form of demanding careers and frenetic schedules: mine in the legislature, Michael, with his own marathon workdays practicing law.

I was immensely grateful for the opportunity to represent the good people of my district, and I pushed myself relentlessly to fulfill those obligations. Sadly, my role as a public servant exacted a steep personal toll on my own hearth and home.

I was spending countless hours commuting between Chicago and Springfield and juggling a host of constituent and legislative demands. During the years that I was back and forth, Michael was forced to take on an inordinate amount of responsibility, from picking up our son from school to domestic duties. He stepped up, admirably, to support my ambitions and our family.

Still, my spouse was a traditionalist. This was a man who originally wanted a stay-at-home wife. The truth is, I could not be the woman he wanted in that regard.

That was not our only marital dilemma. While our core values were similar, in some ways, we were polar opposites.

We're both proud Americans. But I'm a descendant of the Deep South and its people, and I carry with me its culture and history. Michael is the progeny of German American immigrants and shaped by his family's traditions.

I was raised in a household that was loyal to Democratic and liberal politics; his parents were, as he nicely described them, "Nixon" Republicans.

My family's faith practices were an example of religious pluralism: Catholic, Baptist, and Muslim. His people were Protestants.

Most of the time, our different backgrounds were not problematic. But occasionally, there were misunderstandings. During happier times, we'd purchased a vacation home in Wisconsin, a stunning property that overlooked a crystal-blue lake. We fished, hiked, and did skeet shooting; one time I was with the fellas and boasting about my marksmanship; minutes later, I'd accidently shot myself in the foot. But I digress. The lake house was a sanctuary where we welcomed family and friends in the summers and on weekends. To ensure there would be no inadvertent overlap of guests, we kept a running schedule of who was coming and when.

One weekend, I planned to bring some girlfriends up to the lake house. I made sure to inform Michael. I was looking forward to a relaxing respite with just the girls.

I arrived ahead of my friends to get the house in order. When I pulled into the driveway, I noticed several cars and signs of activity. I turned the key, stepped inside, and found the place in a disarray.

In the kitchen, there was food left out on the counter and crumbs that were attracting ants. The floors were streaked with muddy footprints. Towels were strewn here and there.

I hurried outside to the backyard. To my surprise, there was Michael, along with a few of his legal colleagues, and other guests.

My husband was equally surprised yet happy to see me and beckoned me over to say hello to everyone. I greeted them courteously, but inside, I was thinking: "Who are these people? And what are they doing at my vacation home on the same weekend that I have guests coming?"

I did not want to hash out a scheduling dispute with my

spouse in front of everyone, so I politely excused myself and went back inside. I figured we could sort things out privately, and then come up with a viable solution.

In the meantime, I needed to clean up because my friends were still en route. I went to the broom closet and pulled out some cleaning supplies.

I was mopping the floor when a guest from outside—a woman who apparently was dating one of the lawyers—pushed open the back door.

She startled me with her presence and rude demeanor. "We did not know you'd be here," she said. "We were invited to spend the weekend. And I'm not ready to leave."

I had to collect myself. Here this woman was, a stranger to me, acting entitled in the home that I had worked, saved for, and owned with my husband. The unmitigated nerve.

"Excuse me," I countered. "This is *my* house."

She glared at me. I glowered back. I had the heavy mop in one hand, and the bucket nearby at my feet. I was trying to decide whether to put the mop upside her head, along with the dirty, sudsy water.

I was contemplating my next move, when Michael came inside. He quickly assessed from the icy stares and tension in the room that a showdown was brewing. "Carol, please," he said, pulling me aside and whispering that I was overreacting. I did not want to hear it. "I will not be disrespected in my own home!" I told him.

A few minutes passed. I still had the mop in hand, in the strike position. But as a lawyer, I knew I could not assault anyone. I told my husband, "I'm going to the grocery store to stock up for my guests. You need to fix this."

While my husband and I rarely argued or raised our voices— a constant from my childhood that I was relieved to relinquish in marriage—there were times when this girl from Chicago's South Side simply had to speak her piece.

By the time I returned, all the extra cars in the driveway were gone and the backyard chairs were empty. My guests and I went on to have a restful, enjoyable weekend.

There would be episodes of private anguish in our marriage that led to it foundering, then a mutual decision to split. We deeply loved our son and were determined to keep the divorce proceedings civil for his sake. The only thing Michael requested in our settlement was the lake house. I agreed, reluctantly. I miss the good times, and (most) of the memories that were made there.

GOOD DEEDS

I was at a crossroads.

My marriage had ruptured, and I was now a single mother. Our preteen son was bouncing between his divorced parents as we shared custody.

The transition around the split was emotionally taxing on all of us but proved especially devastating for our child.

I recall Matthew saying, "Mom and Dad, I feel like you are on different sides of the street, shooting at each other, and you're hitting me."

His words pierced my heart. As a mother, I did not know which was worse: hearing my child expressing such palpable pain, or the fact that his loving parents bore culpability for an unintentional hurt we could not heal.

Besides the post-divorce heartache, I was feeling restless in my professional life.

At the time, I was still in the Illinois General Assembly and was proud of the reputation I was earning as the "conscience" of that body, fighting for women, families, workers, and those whom the Bible calls "the least of these."

Still, I yearned to do even more as a public servant to help improve people's lives. I was in my late thirties and no longer a political neophyte. I started thinking about higher office.

Back in the '80s, the Land of Lincoln had not yet elected a woman to serve as lieutenant governor. In 1985, I began to seriously explore a run. I reached out to power players and party insiders, announcing my intentions at a Chicago fundraiser that drew supporters, politicos, and media.

Alas, my rocket failed to launch. Essentially, the timing was off. The "establishment"—including some of my allies—did not reject my candidacy outright, but for one reason or another, they did not embrace it either. I lacked the necessary backing to go the distance. I was disappointed, but decided to withdraw before the March 1986 primary. In hindsight, the decision was for the best: that year's political cycle would yield a series of twists, turns, and upsets for Illinois Democrats. Jim Thompson, my former boss, won a historic fourth gubernatorial term, and George Ryan was reelected the state's lieutenant governor.

The good news is that while I did not scale the summit of the lieutenant governor mountaintop, down the line, other Illinois women would successfully make the climb.

Corinne Wood, a Republican, made "her-story" in 1998 when voters elected her lieutenant governor.

Some two decades later, Juliana Stratton became the forty-eighth lieutenant governor of Illinois on a ticket with Governor JB Pritzker. The Democrats' electoral victory made Stratton the first Black woman to hold the second-highest office in Illinois.

Today, according to the Center for American Women and Politics at Rutgers University, at least thirty states have elected women governors, and more than forty states have had women serve as lieutenant governors. There's still work to do in the march for equality, but I cheer the progress made thus far, and the promise of future leadership.

As for me, I began to ponder leaving politics altogether at that point. I hadn't even begun to approach the glass ceiling in my political career, and wondered if moving in another direction was the answer.

I could take my legal and legislative expertise to a law firm, and earn a good salary to support myself and help provide for my son.

I'd basically made up my mind about quitting politics. But a conversation around that time caused me to reconsider.

I'd known Bobby Rush for decades, dating back to his Panther days. We are part of the same generation of Chicagoans and had mutual friends. Our approaches differed, but like me, he has spent a lifetime in the trenches working and fighting for change.

By this time, Bobby was a Chicago alderman, and he would go on to become an Illinois congressman.

"We don't want to lose you in politics," I remember him saying. "You can't leave. It's not time yet."

I appreciated the vote of confidence. And he wasn't the only one who prevailed upon me to reconsider my exit plans.

I'd met Harold Washington long before his historic election as Chicago's first Black mayor in 1983. As a student volunteer, I'd canvassed door-to-door on one of his early campaigns. In Springfield, I had become his trusted floor leader on city legislative issues. Along the way, the city's fifty-first mayor had become both a political mentor and a friend. We used to chuckle about his self-given nickname, "Landslide Washington," referring to his historic 1983 electoral victory by a slim margin.

Harold Washington had shaken up the old boys' network that had long controlled ChiTown with patronage and backdoor politicking. He credited his victory in a field of formidable competitors to a grassroots campaign and multiracial coalitions that pulled myriad groups into the tent. His fitting campaign slogan was, "Let's come together for one city."

Toward the end of his first term, the mayor announced the "Dream Ticket," a diverse slate of Democrats to run for office countywide.

He believed there should be African Americans, whites, Latinos, and Asians as well as gender equality—everybody should be represented in government. That unifying theme has long been my political and personal philosophy.

Mayor Washington personally asked me to join the ticket, and stand for the position of recorder of deeds for Cook County, Illinois.

Cook County is home to Chicago, as well as hundreds of cities, towns, and villages. It's the county seat, and most populous area in the state with more than five million residents.

I was grateful that Mayor Washington saw fit to include me in his vision. Yet I had some hesitations. I was contemplating whether to quit politics, and here I was being asked to jump back into the deep end. It did not escape me, however, that this request was being made at the behest of a groundbreaking leader. How could I refuse? I accepted the invitation to run.

My conversation with Mayor Washington took place somewhere around the fall of 1987. That November, shortly before Thanksgiving, came news that shocked Chicagoans, the state, and nation.

The mayor was working at city hall, when he suddenly keeled over his desk. There were attempts to revive him onsite, and later at the hospital, to no avail. It was later reported that he'd suffered a fatal heart attack.

Harold Washington's death was a staggering loss. The mayor was sixty-five years old, and had just been reelected to a second term. And now, our fearless leader was gone.

I had to win the Cook County election not only for myself, but to honor the memory of a political legend who was in a class by himself.

★ ★ ★

It just so happened that the election was taking place in a presidential election year. Back in 1988, Republican George H.W. Bush, the sitting vice president, was matched against Michael Dukakis, the former governor of Massachusetts.

Republicans had been in power for eight years under President Ronald Reagan. When all was said and done, voters gave the GOP a landslide victory that kept the party in the White House.

Fortunately, our "Dream Ticket" fared better with a full sweep in Cook County.

The good voters of Illinois had seen fit to elect me again, this time to countywide office. I would be Cook County's first Black recorder of deeds, and its first woman elected to a major executive post.

I received nearly a million votes—approximately 225,000 more than my opponent, Alderman Bernie Stone—for which I was grateful.

I was elated to make history, and continue to be of service. Yet, the victory felt bittersweet. Mayor Washington was gone, and the absence of his giant presence left a void.

I thought of him when going to my new office, headquartered in the City Hall-County Building. The neoclassical, twelve-story structure was built in 1911. The hulking edifice, which spans a city block, is where Chicago's mayor, various county officials, and bureaucrats conduct the people's business.

The day of my swearing in, I made my way into the building, eager to make my new role official. Matt was ever by my side. So were my two surviving siblings, Marsha and Joe. Our mother, who had weathered a series of health challenges, had made an especially valiant effort to attend.

John's death seemed to further sap her spirit. She had suffered a stroke, and later, her leg was amputated, which led to her using a wheelchair.

My sister transported Mother safely from the car to the building. But upon arrival, they discovered a problem: it was not fully accessible to the disabled. The stairs proved impossible for my mother to navigate, some door frames could not accommodate her wheelchair, and ramps seemed to be in short supply or nonexistent.

Everyone was upset and flustered. We tried to come up with a last-minute solution, but with time running short before the ceremony began, Marsha and my mother were forced to watch my big day from out in the hallway.

I was incensed. This was happening inside a municipal property where city and county business was transacted, a site that taxpayer dollars helped to build and maintain. Why wasn't a public space of this kind fully accessible?

The irony is that two years later, the Americans with Disabilities Act (ADA) law would be signed by President George Bush with a goal of protecting the civil rights of persons with disabilities. Unfortunately, the revolutionary measure was not in place at the time of my investiture.

As I stood to take the oath of office, my mother and sister were waiting outside, and could not see nor hear the proceedings inside the closed doors of the assembly hall. This was deeply disappointing.

Mother remained sanguine, which was her way. Seeing the quiet fortitude with which she handled the obstacles that had arisen, inspired me. I tried to focus on the meaning of the day.

There's a long, storied history of Black officials serving as the recorder of deeds.

Following the Civil War, President James Garfield appointed Frederick Douglass to the post in the District of Columbia in 1881.

Later, Blanche Bruce—a formerly enslaved man who represented Mississippi in the US Senate from 1875 to 1881—would assume the role. I actually have a vintage deed with his signature on it, which is among my most cherished possessions. Now the good people of Cook County had elected me to serve in this capacity. I whispered a silent prayer, asking the Lord to help me heed my mother's longtime advice: "Do the best job where you are planted."

The countywide office I was inheriting was a critically important part of local government.

We were the record keepers for Cook County. The office was a repository for public records, official documents that ranged from land records to financial filings and transactions, along with a miscellany of data. It was now my responsibility to lead the team who were recording, storing, and maintaining this voluminous cache of information.

I immediately got to work on day one, and started to put my stamp on things. The first order of business: meeting with my new staff of some three hundred civil servants.

I tried to give a pep talk and lay out my expectations. I wanted the team to feel valued, and have a sense of responsibility about their individual and collective roles in making democracy work for everyone. That philosophy has been a core value for me throughout my entire career.

"It's important that we understand that the citizens and tax-payers of Cook County are our customers. In this office, we work for them, not the other way around," I said. "And we have a responsibility to provide the people who come in here courteous service, the same kind service that you yourselves would expect."

In the days, weeks, and months that followed, I set out to do a formal audit and assess the office's operation from top to bottom. I knew from my mother's experience that just as the historic building needed upgrades, I would have to make significant changes to modernize and bring the office into the future.

When I took office in the '80s, the recorder of deeds was stuck in a time warp. The office was drab, dusty, and had vermin. The staff was using antiquated methods to perform tasks—including recording deeds by hand—and there were only a few onsite computers.

As a result, the team was drowning in paperwork. When I arrived, the office had at least eight hundred thousand records on file, and a backlog of some three hundred thousand documents. Talk about bureaucratic red tape.

The glut of paperwork led to delays as the staff struggled to process calls, written requests, and walk-ins. Service was slow and sluggish. I set out to reconfigure our methods in order to serve the public efficiently and effectively.

I had my work cut out for me. Every workday, it seemed, something different cropped up in the office that needed to be addressed.

So, I decided to establish a "blue ribbon" committee to secure outside expertise. The group was made up of thirty or so trusted civic and business leaders who examined and recommended ways to improve the office, as well as new revenue streams.

In the meantime, I started to implement a series of changes, both large and small.

Internally, I instituted a code of ethics. I automated the employee payroll process; previously, the staff stood in line on payday and filed past their supervisor who doled out paychecks.

I streamlined the way our services were delivered. To record a property, the public once had to go through a veritable maze of procedures on several different floors. We changed that so you could visit one counter and get your documents approved, visit a second counter, and then complete the process. I was also supportive of employees' union activity. But my overhaul of the office did not come without some bumps and bruises.

Early on, much to my chagrin, some of the staff refused to listen to me.

I suppose they thought that I was just another politician, who was going to come and go. But for whatever reason, they weren't paying much attention.

I'd tried to foster a positive, productive work environment. I'd said up front that my job was to ensure our office provided excellent service. Indeed, public service was our first obligation.

But with hundreds of workers, not everyone is going to get the message. Some of them appeared to let what I said go in one ear and out the other. Remember that one-liner that the comedian Rodney Dangerfield used to say? "I don't get no respect!"

My name was on the door. I was determined to earn their respect.

I came up with a silly little plan. I went up the street to a five and dime store, and I bought this hand puppet. And the puppet was a balding white guy.

I went to the next staff meeting and said, "Okay, since you won't listen to me, maybe you'll listen to him."

I had the puppet in my hand. I can't do ventriloquism, but I sure tried.

The staff looked shocked at first. But then they laughed. Heartily. I think my point was made, and they got it. Which was, if you're willing to listen to him, then please listen to me, because I'm the boss here.

Fortunately, it did make a difference. As the team began to listen, I was better able to chart our direction.

There was so much more to do. Because insufficient financial resources had plagued the office, I had to make a major push to increase our multimillion-dollar budget.

For that task, I returned to Springfield and testified before some of my former colleagues in the Illinois General Assembly.

We also took another step, asking the legislature to help us repeal what is known as the Torrens system of land registration. Torrens involves government insurance of titles, as well as a separate system of recording property.

For a variety of reasons, the system was roundly criticized. It was not working well in our office. We were able to get law-makers to repeal it, and eventually, shutter that operation.

The ideas on the table included launching satellite offices in other parts of the county, and establishing ways for customers to dial in or use the computer to secure information.

The overhaul of the office was going well. I was pleased with the progress that my team and I had made. I had not taken any time off. I believed the staff could carry on without me for a few days.

I had chosen my destination. I had my plane ticket and was about to head to O'Hare airport when I got an urgent call from one of my senior staffers. "You've got to get over here! Our basements are flooding. There's water everywhere!"

At the time, construction work was underway in Chicago's underground tunnels, which link pedestrians to the business district and public transportation. These passageways lie under what's known as "The Loop," the commercial center of the city with blocks and blocks of stores, offices, restaurants, theatres, and public art.

Somehow during the repairs, crews broke through one of the tunnels and entire portions under The Loop began to flood. This was a massive emergency. Tens of thousands of daily commuters were impacted. The Recorder of Deeds Office kept certain books and records in the sub-basements under the county building. It would have been catastrophic if these valuable records were destroyed or water damaged. Many of these documents were irreplaceable.

I tried not to panic. I had actually prepared my team for emergencies. We regularly conducted fire drills, and a plan was in place to get our records out of the building.

That said, we could not have imagined this particular scenario. My mind was racing as I tried to figure out what to do next.

My suitcase was packed. I had to make a decision: Stay or delegate this to one of my managers?

I will admit that the idea of jumping on a plane and getting the heck out of Dodge was tempting. However, that really was not an option for someone in leadership. I would have to stay put and handle this crisis.

I jumped in my car and sped over to the county building. Emergency vehicles, first responders, officials, and bystanders were everywhere. It was one of those command center kinds of situations.

Some of the staff and I trekked down to the sub-basements. It was dark and dank. Water was gushing and bubbling up everywhere.

I don't know how we did it, but my team sloshed through ankle-deep water and hastily retrieved boxes and boxes of documents and hauled them out. Miraculously, nothing got wet, and we did not lose anything.

Working with first responders, we were able to get the rest of the staff out of the building. Thank God, everyone was safe and sound.

My vacation was canceled. It was just as well. I'd had enough adventure to last me for a while.

In this digital age, where one can easily click on a computer or a smartphone to access public records, it's easy to forget a time when cardboard boxes and file cabinets overflowing with papers was the norm. I have no doubt, however, that my leadership and the efforts of the hundreds of employees under my purview dramatically transformed the Cook County Recorder of Deeds Office. While my critics seized upon everything from certain hiring decisions to placing assets in a minority-owned bank, my tenure was marked by not cronyism and patronage, but, rather, organization and innovation. Our team meticulously recorded more than a million records, and of that, we can be proud.

Today, the recorder of deeds position that Mayor Washington urged me to seek decades ago no longer exists. In 2020, the Cook County Clerk's Office assumed all of its operations and duties. Hopefully, the foundation that we laid decades ago has enabled the public servants who are currently in place to perform their jobs efficiently and effectively for the people. Truly, my tenure marked the end of an era.

HISTORYMAKER
PART ONE

Gliding along Rodeo Drive, I gazed out at the palm trees and posh boutiques of Beverly Hills and pinched myself. The driver pulled up to a luxe hotel, where I was attending a political gala featuring a galaxy of Hollywood stars.

Barbra Streisand. Goldie Hawn. Dionne Warwick. Lily Tomlin. Vanessa Williams. Cybill Shepherd. Patti Austin. These were just some of the talented, smart, and glamorous women in the room.

The year was 1992. Hundreds of movers and shakers from the entertainment firmament had come out for a $500-per-plate fundraiser hosted by the Hollywood Women's Political Committee. The influential PAC was co-founded by Jane Fonda, Streisand, and fellow artists, executives, and creators in 1984. Earlier that year, Geraldine Ferraro made history at the Democratic National Convention as the country's first woman to be a vice presidential nominee on a major party ticket.

Now I was seeking to make history in a bold bid for the US

Senate. In the ballroom were celebrity and VIP donors whose contributions would bolster the coffers of me and other senatorial candidates, all women.

"Women are a majority of this nation," Ms. Streisand told the audience. "It's time we had a place at the table where the life and death decisions of the country, the world, and the planet are made."

Besides myself, multiple candidates took part in the exciting event. Dianne Feinstein, who'd been elected the first woman mayor of San Francisco. Barbara Boxer, at that time, a California congresswoman. And Patty Murray, then a Washington state senator, to name a few.

"Will electing these women to the Senate change anything?" said Ms. Streisand, after calling out our respective names, and the possible committees we might serve on if elected. "You bet it will."

The energy in the ballroom was electric. A Baptist church choir, in tandem with a star-studded chorus, lifted their voices in song. Guests sipped flutes of champagne. Laughter wafted up to the sparkling chandeliers as Ms. Tomlin, the mistress of ceremonies, delivered political punchlines.

Each candidate was given a few minutes to address the tony crowd. When it was my turn for the legendary comic to introduce me, I took a deep breath.

I smoothed my lavender suit and adjusted my long strand of pearls. Then, I stepped up to the podium, where a red, white, and blue image of "Old Glory" shimmered behind me.

"Greetings to Hollywood from the Heartland," my short speech began, as waves of loud applause welcomed me.

"This democracy is alive and well and one involved citizen can make a difference," I said. "The right of women to participate as full and equal citizens in this land is too important to leave to the good ole boys' network. Women will lead the way for change to heal and nurture this country."

I went on to say that every child in our country should have access "to the ladder of opportunity," and emphasized that the "American Dream is still alive."

"This great nation has room for everybody, and in our diversity is strength. And unity," I continued. "When we come together, when we work together, when we build together, we will restore this great nation. We will heal this nation!"

The evening had been exhilarating. The party wound down with a rendition of "America the Beautiful." There was a feminist tweak, however, to the traditional lyrics.

"And crown thy good, with brotherhood, from sea to shining sea," was adjusted to include the word "sisterhood."

The soiree raised nearly $400,000 (the equivalent of about $895,000 today) for our respective campaigns. Little did I know then that I'd meet several of these women again on Capitol Hill.

Growing up in Chicago in the shadow of WWII, I did not dream of becoming a senator. The idea was so far out of the realm of possibility for a woman of my generation, let alone a Black girl.

Yet after finishing college and law school, after my accidental entry into politics led me to the state legislature, I aspired to greater heights. I learned to embrace my own ambition.

I could see myself as a lieutenant governor. I could envision myself in Congress. Even so, the notion of higher political office seemed a pipe dream.

That is, until a series of fortuitous events catapulted me onto the national stage.

Back in 1991, then-president George H.W. Bush selected Clarence Thomas to fill the vacancy of retiring Supreme Court associate justice Thurgood Marshall.

The first Black man to sit on the highest court in the land, Marshall was a liberal lion who'd argued some of the key civil rights cases of our time. Thomas, an arch conservative, opposed affirmative action, and would go on to help overturn *Roe v. Wade*.

Thomas had supporters, yes, but a whole heap of folks were not happy. The nomination set off a firestorm among some women's groups, organized labor, and members of the civil rights community.

As the Senate Judiciary Committee held early confirmation hearings, even the panel could not agree on the nominee. They voted to send his nomination on to the full Senate—sans a favorable recommendation.

Then, came a bombshell: law professor, Anita Hill, accused her former boss of lewd, unwelcome sexual comments when the two were colleagues.

Like millions of Americans, I was glued to the television during the testimony that unfolded like a soap opera on Capitol Hill that summer.

Watching the committee of all-white males asking clumsy, chauvinistic, sometimes sexist questions of Hill—a Black woman and lawyer who could have easily been me—made my blood boil.

It soon became evident that countless women around the country shared my sense of outrage. From Capitol Hill to the streets, women were protesting and speaking out.

I was still in the Recorder of Deeds' Office, starting to wind down my term. I appeared on a few local news programs discussing the Supreme Court and offering my opinions.

Initially, my opposition to the nominee was strictly around his politics. I was also troubled by what seemed to be a blatant move by conservatives and right wingers to shift the Supreme Court away from the legal gains made during the Civil Rights Movement.

As an attorney, I had hoped to see a nominee in the mold of the members of the renowned "Warren Court." In the 1950s and '60s, Chief Justice Earl Warren led the court's liberal wing in a series of groundbreaking rulings. These cases, some argued by Marshall himself, ended segregation in public schools; expanded civil rights and liberties; and gave couples the right to marry across racial lines—societal shifts that helped move America toward a more perfect union.

I started getting calls and letters from citizens about the nomination, a good deal of them supporting my perspective. One man from Belleville, which is downstate, wrote to me saying, "I've followed your career. I think you should run for the Senate."

Running for Congress? A goal, someday, perhaps. I tucked it away in a corner of my mind.

That is, until a surprise visitor stopped by to see me. I'm not sure if Senator Alan Dixon just happened to be in the City Hall-County Building that day, or if he made a special trip to see me.

At any rate, the man known in Illinois as "Al the Pal" was in my office. As his nickname suggested, the gregarious Democrat relished old-school politics, from glad-handing and kissing babies to cutting deals.

He also had a reputation for civility, and a willingness to build consensus across the aisle. And, after four decades in politics, Senator Dixon had never lost an election.

I had no inkling that one of our sitting senators even knew my name but was honored by his presence. Yet, it was curious that a man of his stature was paying a call upon me.

There was a reason for the impromptu visit: Dixon wanted to discuss the confirmation hearings that had riveted our nation.

The country was waiting with bated breath to see how the Senate's one hundred lawmakers would vote on Thomas's nomination.

Senator Dixon asked my thoughts. I pulled no punches as we discussed the nominee, the tone of the hearings, and the long-term implications for women's and civil rights. I expected that Dixon, a moderate Democrat, would reject the nomination.

But he seemed to be leaning in the opposite direction, and sure enough later voted "aye." Paul Simon, then our junior senator, voted "nay."

When all was said and done, Thomas—who denied Hill's allegations and termed the proceedings a "high-tech lynching"—was narrowly confirmed. The vote was fifty-two to forty-eight, mostly along partisan lines. He joined the court that fall.

The process had been polarizing. In my conversations with women, the frustration was palpable. One sensed a groundswell building to push back against politicians—namely, men—who seemed out of touch. Women across the country were talking about running for office to shake up the status quo.

In my home state, Dixon's vote had infuriated many women, so much so that names were being floated as possible Senate candidates to challenge him. Mine was among them.

My friend Kay, the activist who first induced me to run for public office, was ready to go another round, along with a coalition of women activists to back me. "You must run, Carol!" she said.

I was pondering and praying about what to do, when Senator Dixon popped up again for another unplanned chat. This time, I imagine he'd heard the rumors that my name was on the list of possible challengers in the next election.

We exchanged pleasantries, before rehashing the explosive hearings. "Many women don't feel they are being adequately heard in Washington," I recall saying.

Dixon listened patiently, politely nodding his head. But he just didn't seem to get it.

After he left, I thought about the conversation. It sealed the deal for me: I was going to run for the US Senate.

Deciding to enter the US Senate race was just the first step. The next was trying to win the Illinois Democratic primary.

While the Republican candidate was running unopposed, the contest to get to the general election was a three-way race between me and two men.

There was Senator Dixon, of course, and Albert Hofeld, a multimillionaire and political novice. Incidentally, all three of us were lawyers.

Despite my credentials and electoral experience, I was considered the underdog.

Yes, I had some name recognition from holding office, but I was not a local legend like Al the Pal. Moreover, I did not have his hefty war chest, nor the deep pockets of Hofeld, a successful trial lawyer who pumped millions of his own fortune into the race.

By contrast, mine was a grassroots campaign that started out with a prop plane flight through a thunderstorm to announce my candidacy in Downstate Illinois.

At my campaign headquarters on Lake Street, I had a small team in place, led by Chris Long. But while everyone did their best, we struggled to find our footing.

I was missing key deadlines and events. We were not really canvassing. Campaign contributions were sparse.

I remember when my college friend Tony Podesta invited me to Washington to help drum up support for my campaign. He took me around to meet elected officials and power brokers on Capitol Hill. Some people were polite, others less so, but most were simply uninterested in a county official.

But campaign or not, I still had to perform my day job for the good people of Cook County. And, I remained diligent.

One weekday, I had a series of back-to-back meetings that had me literally running back and forth. After sitting down with a group of officials in my office, I ran across the street to a gathering of medical professionals. I then hustled to a third event, a press conference.

My car, a Lincoln Continental about the size of a small boat, was parked. I was on foot.

I was toting a purse on one shoulder, a briefcase bulging with assorted papers under my other arm, all the while teetering on high heels. I was huffing and puffing harder than a Chicago freight train.

My day did not end there: after clocking off work, I had campaign commitments and mommy duties.

I was frazzled and overwhelmed. At this rate, I would not win a seat for dogcatcher, let alone the US Senate.

I desperately needed help. That's when a knight in shining armor entered the picture.

By this time, I was divorced. My ex-husband had remarried and had a new family. I was focused on co-parenting our son, and my career. Still, I did socialize occasionally.

One weekend, I dolled up and went to a nightclub with a

few girlfriends. It was one of those ChiTown hot spots that attracted an upscale crowd. Well, that night none other than Michael Jordan was in the house.

Yes, the legendary NBA player and Chicago Bulls champion. The epitome of tall, dark, and handsome.

To my delight, we caught each other's eye across the dance floor. Some lighthearted flirting ensued. Michael was winking and blinking. I was winking and blinking. I flashed him a dazzling smile, and he beamed right back at me.

I was far too nervous to approach the hoop star, and he had fans swirling all around him. Our little moment ended as quickly as it began. It was all in good fun. The attention did make me feel special.

I dated a few other men in the early years of my singlehood, but nothing too serious.

Years later, I was at a birthday party for the Rev. Jesse Jackson in Washington, DC.

I have known the Rainbow/PUSH founder since we were both in our twenties. His celebration was packed with politicos, movers and shakers, and all manner of admirers.

I worked my way through the throng, hoping to get an audience with my old pal, but never got so much as a glimpse of his curly 'fro in the well-heeled crowd.

That's how I made the acquaintance of Kgosie Matthews. He introduced himself, and I tried to place his charming accent: he was South African with British citizenship. He had met Rev. Jackson at an anti-apartheid rally, and later joined his 1988 presidential campaign. Apparently, Kgosie's job was a cross between a special assistant and what politicians call a "body man."

We had a brief, cordial conversation, and exchanged business cards. Kgosie mentioned an upcoming trip to Chicago and said he would look me up.

As luck would have it, his visit coincided with my campaign meltdown. Kgosie called me up that same week and indicated he was in town. Since he'd worked on a presidential campaign, I figured it would be smart to pick his brain.

We arranged to meet at the Walnut Room, a popular restaurant known for its elegant decor and menu favorites like chicken pot pie.

As we broke bread, Kgosie shared more about his background. He had come to the States to study at Harvard's Kennedy School of Government. He split his time between London, New York City, and Cape Town.

Kgosie told me about his distinguished family. His grandfather was a co-founder of the African National Congress, the political party of Nelson Mandela and fellow freedom fighters who helped crush apartheid. His father formerly served as a deputy minister in South Africa. His sister was a high-ranking foreign minister.

I enjoyed our conversation, which at first was one-sided. But Kgosie was easy to talk to, and I found myself opening up. I poured out my woes about the campaign.

"Things are a mess," I said, shaking my head. "I can't keep up this pace." Kgosie looked me in the eye. He then wordlessly reached into his leather attaché case, and pulled out one of those clunky, early model cellular phones.

"I will not be flying back home," he told a relative on the other line. "I'm staying on for a while in Chicago to help a friend."

That simple, generous gesture was his way of offering to manage my campaign. I felt as if a weight had been lifted off my shoulders, and my gratitude was profuse. "Thank you," I said.

Kgosie wasted no time in getting to work. He had a Rolodex filled with contacts, fresh ideas, and a knack for organization.

In no time at all, my campaign was running with the efficiency of the Chicago "L" transit system.

We began to stump in Chicago and crisscross the state. I knocked on thousands of doors, meeting voters of every race, color, and creed.

I shared my inclusive platform of good government that lifted all, how I would tackle bread and butter issues, and the need to diversify the Senate. Reception was positive.

I once joked that my campaign was cobbled together with chewing gum, sealing wax, and rubber bands. Kgosie's strategy and execution, my drive and determination, and the efforts of hardworking staff and volunteers made an impact. We were making headway.

Early on, my poll numbers lagged behind the incumbent, Senator Dixon. Moving into the final stretch of the campaign, we began to close the gap.

I'd pushed for a televised debate with my opponents, and it took place nine days before the March primary. The forum, sponsored by the League of Women Voters of Illinois, aired on TV and radio stations across the state.

"The two Als are not qualified," I told viewers in my opening statement, as the camera zoomed in on my cherry-red suit and chunky gold jewelry. "I think we can do better and I'm prepared to make a difference."

For the next hour, the three of us sparred over substantive issues, tackling questions from viewers about the economy to jobs, health care, and taxes. I'm not sure if there was a definitive winner, but my poll numbers climbed dramatically afterward.

The debate followed weeks of slick attack ads from Hofeld's camp that hammered Dixon, painting him as a DC insider, beholden to special interests. The senator responded with his own negative ad blitz. One of them lambasted Hofeld for not bothering to vote in several prior elections. At some point, the men even had dueling press conferences.

I tried to stay (mostly) above the fray. My campaign was finally able to afford two radio spots, which hit the airwaves shortly before Election Day. In one of them, I emphasized the history-making nature of my campaign.

In the meantime, my campaign got a monumental boost from the world's most famous feminist: Gloria Steinem.

I'd first met the activist and journalist earlier in the primary.

She was in Chicago to promote her bestselling book, *Revolution from Within: A Book of Self-Esteem*. She found time during her book signing schedule to stop by our headquarters.

I was gobsmacked. During college and law school, I'd participated in women's rights rallies. Now, here in the flesh, was the woman who had co-founded the National Women's Political Caucus and *Ms. Magazine*.

At that point, the campaign was barely holding on. I think we had less than five hundred dollars in the bank. I felt defeated and was about to throw in the towel. Her appearance felt like a miracle.

Gloria insisted that I not give up. "Let's get out and meet some voters," she said. It was a frigid Windy City day, with snow and ice on the ground.

We bundled up and walked together over to a public space to pass out pamphlets. People were excited to see Gloria.

That day represented a turning point in the campaign. We picked up volunteers, and the contributions started to roll in.

The money came from small donors, although not exclusively. Groups like Emily's List—the powerful PAC that raises funds for Democratic women candidates—toward the end of our primary campaign and later did fundraising mailings to its base.

Fast-forward a few months. Momentum continued to build. There'd been a walk-a-thon organized—coinciding with International Women's Day—complete with my T-shirts for sale. They read "Make History. Carol Moseley Braun." Proceeds went to the campaign.

Now Gloria was back for an official, "meet-the-candidate" hybrid "get-out-the vote" rally. She was our special guest.

It was another cold day, with snow flurries swirling outside. Inside the campaign headquarters, with my signs decorated in patriotic red, white, and blue, the room was crammed to capacity, mostly with women.

Sisters of all races, ages, and backgrounds were milling about, excitedly. Some wore campaign buttons with my slogan, "A Real Democrat for Change."

"What do we want?" the call and response began.

"A woman in the Senate!"

"When do we want her?"

"Now!"

I had been out pounding the pavement. When I walked in, clad in a black dress and pearls, applause erupted. "Carol! Carol! Carol!" the ladies cheered. It was such a joyous, spontaneous expression of womanpower. I beamed in response, looking around the room with gratitude. I was grateful for their support and enthusiasm.

As we waited, members of the press positioned their cameras and microphones.

Soon, Gloria arrived to loud cheering. She looked fantastic, casually chic in a black blouse, a silver jeweled belt slung low on her waist, and a flowing print skirt. Her blond hair was pulled back in an easy ponytail.

We embraced happily. I offered a brief welcome about having a "role model" such as Steinem supporting our "historic campaign" and her leadership being "embodied in the spirit of this effort." I talked about the need for more women's voices in the Senate, so as to better articulate the concerns of women, minorities, and working people.

Gloria's remarks began, "I can tell that the trend line in this election is going the right way," she said, noting her previous visit and my rising poll numbers since that time. "This is the woman about whom they said it wouldn't be done but we're gonna do it, right?" she continued, to cries of "yeah!" and "woo!"

Gloria stunned me by presenting a campaign check for one thousand dollars. Cheers erupted. "I just talked to Marlo Thomas on the phone—" she smiled, referring to the actress and advocate "—and she is sending you her check for a thousand dollars." The crowd went wild. "And, as soon as I get home, I'm making a lot more phone calls!"

I thanked Gloria for her long-standing efforts and sacrifices on behalf of women, and for taking time from her busy schedule to "help us make history."

"We can make a difference," I said to those assembled. "With all of you. We're gonna do this. We're going to win this election!" There were more chants of "Carol! Carol! Carol!"

One week later, my words proved prophetic. God blessed me. I became the first Black woman in history to win a Democratic Senate primary.

The good people of Illinois had given me their votes. My support was a diverse coalition of women, Black and white liberal voters—as well as men, suburbanites, rural voters, and so on. The Thomas confirmation hearings were a factor, as was a general anti-incumbent fervor that swept other elected officials out of office.

On election night, my family and supporters gathered at the McCormick Place Hotel.

As the early precincts poured in, Dixon was leading. At one point, the race was too close to call. By midnight, I had pulled ahead.

Ultimately, I received 38 percent of the votes cast in the primary. Dixon came in second, garnering 35 percent. Hofeld was at 28 percent. His media adviser, David Axelrod, would join my camp for the general election; years later, he would help Barack Obama make presidential history.

Suffice to say, my victory was a shocking upset. Both of my opponents called me. The senator gave a wonderfully gracious concession speech.

"My dear friends, I have just called my friend Carol Moseley Braun to give her my heartiest congratulations on a great victory," said Dixon. "Now let me tell you something: I spent a lifetime in Democratic politics. And I spent that lifetime in Democratic politics playing by the rules. And I said in this primary campaign that I would support the winner, I would endorse the winner, and I would vote for the winner. And now... I will vote for Carol Moseley Braun, and I ask my friends and my supporters...to do the same thing that I will do."

The election ended Dixon's lengthy career in politics, as the longtime official made clear he would never seek office again.

"I have tasted the full glass, it was wonderful. And now I pass that glass along to a fine woman, and I say 'Carol, I'm for you.'"

Looking back all these years later, I truly appreciate this gentleman and statesman who was a true "pal" to the good people of Illinois.

Inside my victory party, on a stage decked out with an arch of red, white, and blue balloons, I was jubilant.

"You are historymakers!" I told the crowd. "This is what America is about... When they told us that a woman couldn't serve in the United States Senate, we told them, 'Wrong-o!'"

There were hundreds of people in the room that night. My son, Matthew. Mother. My siblings, Marsha and Joe. Extended family and friends. My campaign team. The Hyde Park "kitchen cabinet." College and law school chums. Activists like Timuel Black and Rev. Willie Barrow as well as Chicago officials and Springfield lawmakers. So many good folks celebrating democracy, celebrating progress.

People danced, toasted, and hugged. They cheered my name over and over.

"This democracy is alive and well and ordinary people can have a voice," I said.

"Our work has just started," I said of the next hurdle, the general election.

"We are going to make history in November."

HISTORYMAKER
PART TWO

My victory stunned the political establishment. We negated the negative polls, and disproved the pundits who said I didn't have a snowball's chance in hell of winning.

Cresting on a wave of womanpower, anti-incumbent zeal, and a message of inclusive government that benefits all its citizenry, I had come from behind to lead the pack. About 1.4 million voters cast their ballots in the Illinois Democratic Primary, and nearly 600,000 of those votes were for me. I was ever grateful to the good people of Illinois.

Now the general election in November loomed. Registered Democrats outnumbered Republican voters statewide, which, ostensibly, increased my electoral odds.

However, one can never, ever take anything for granted in an election. I expected the GOP to mount an aggressive campaign in what had become a high-profile race.

The race in Illinois was being closely watched by prognosticators nationwide. Not only was my Senate contest among the more highly contested matchups around the country, it coincided with a presidential election cycle. The stakes were high up and down the ballot.

Until my run for the Senate in the early nineties, only three Black Americans had served in the upper chamber. All were men. Two of them—Hiram Revels and Blanche K. Bruce—represented Mississippi in the 1870s during the era of Reconstruction that followed the Civil War. It would be nearly a century before Edward Brooke of Massachusetts won a Senate seat in 1967.

A quarter century later, I was one step closer to further diversifying the chamber. If elected, I would become not only the first Black woman senator, but the first woman senator from Illinois.

Beyond the gender implications, all of the previous Black lawmakers in the Senate were Republicans. Post-Emancipation, the "party of Lincoln" had the allegiance of Black voters (that is, if they were actually allowed to vote) until the twentieth century. If elected, I would be the chamber's first Black Democrat.

My worthy opponent was Richard S. Williamson, a conservative who had never held elective office, but was by no means a political neophyte. An attorney with degrees from Princeton and UVA, he was a senior policy advisor in the White House under presidents Ronald Reagan and George H.W. Bush. He was dispatched to Vienna, Austria, as the US ambassador to the United Nations International Organizations, among other key roles.

I was facing a formidable contender. Williamson had the support of the Republican National Committee, party stalwarts, and moneyed donors.

That said, I've been underestimated, outspent, and outorganized throughout my political career. I was determined that no one would outwork me.

I decided to take my campaign to the people, once again, this time on a wider scale. We made plans to embark on a statewide

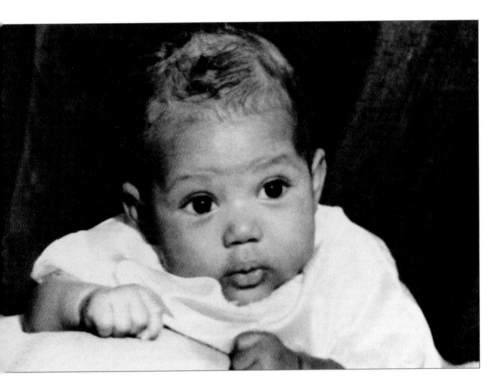

A wide-eyed baby photo of me.
Photo Credit: Author's personal collection

A childhood portrait of me, my brother John, and our parents seated near the family piano.
Photo Credit: Author's personal collection

My father, Joseph Moseley, was a musical prodigy who played multiple instruments, including the saxophone. Here he is performing with the Sol Hicks band. My glamorous Auntie Darrel is on stage with them preparing to sing.

Photo Credit: Author's personal collection

My maternal Southern relatives on the Alabama farm. Those pictured include: my great-great-grandmother Isabelle McNair, born in 1856; my great-grandmother Ollie Henry (touching the shoulder of her husband Pierce Braswell), and my grandmother, Edna Bryant, the little girl with a bow in her hair. In the rear (wearing overalls) is George aka "Chicken," whom my kinfolk took in. Photo Credit: Author's personal collection

My maternal grandmother, Edna Davie,
was born in Alabama and migrated to Chicago.

Photo Credit: Author's personal collection

This distinguished, dapper gentleman is my paternal grandfather, Wilson Moseley. "Papa Wilson" was a pianist who hailed from New Orleans before arriving in ChiTown.

My maternal grandfather, Thomas Davie, served during WWI as a member of the U.S. Army. This sketch was done while he was deployed in France. Decades later, I visited the country's Western Front and retraced the steps of our brave troops. Photo Credit: Author's personal collection

My maternal ancestor, George Davie, seated on the porch of his wood planked house. Born circa 1837 in Alabama, he survived the era of slavery and lived to be 108 years old.

Photo Credit: Author's personal collection

My paternal grandmother, Elizabeth, dressed in a gown while standing in her parlor. "Mama Liz," as we called her, was a trained opera singer.

Photo Credit: Author's personal collection

My maternal great-grandmother, Ollie, in her younger years. She is wearing a long black dress from that time period.
Photo Credit: Author's personal collection

My maternal great-grandmother, Ollie, wearing a wide hat
and standing near the headstone of her late father, Charlie Henry.

Photo Credit: Author's personal collection

My grandmother, Elizabeth, owned a grocery store in Chicago before later moving to Indiana. She sold everything from fresh produce to pickles. My first unofficial job was helping her serve customers.

My son Matthew, who is my pride and joy.

Attending my brother Joe's graduation from the police academy.

Photo Credit: Author's personal collection

Me and my family, including my parents, paternal grandmother, niece, and three siblings at my wedding.

Photo Credit: Author's personal collection

Thanksgiving 2024 with family.

Photo Credit: Ally Almore

Me and my fellow "sister" Senators.

Photo Credit: CQ Archive / Getty Images

My Senate swearing-in ceremony with Vice President Dan Quayle.
Photo Credit: Ron Edmonds / AP Images

With my son and family as Vice President Al Gore swears me in as Ambassador to New Zealand and Samoa. Photo Credit: Chris Kleponis / Getty Images

I enjoyed the company of Supreme Court Justice Ruth Bader Ginsburg.

Photo Credit: Jennifer Law / Getty Images

At a televised debate alongside my fellow Democratic candidates for president.

Photo Credit: Jim Cole / AP Images

My fellow Chicagoan, Hillary Clinton, has been supportive throughout my career.

Photo Credit: Chicago History Museum / Getty Images

With my friend and former Senator, President Joe Biden.

Photo Credit: Maureen Keating / Getty Images

With fellow Congressional Black Caucus members, Delegate Eleanor Holmes Norton and Representative Eva Clayton on the Hill. Photo Credit: Chris Martin / Library of Congress Prints and Photographs Division

Meeting civil rights icon, Rosa Parks. Photo Credit: Photo by Philip McCollum / Library of Congress, Prints and Photographs Division, Visual Materials from the Rosa Parks Papers

Me and Supreme Court Justice Ketanji Brown Jackson at the University Club of Chicago in February 2025. Photo Credit: David T. Kindler, University Club of Chicago

tour. Illinois has 102 counties. My goal was to visit each and every one, with stops in major cities, small towns, and everywhere in between.

Peoria. Joliet. Waukegan. Oak Lawn. Des Plaines. Calumet City. Libertyville and East Saint Louis. Evanston, Wilmette, and Niles, to name a few. I am reminded of a catchy marketing campaign the state did to promote tourism: "Just outside Chicago, there's a place called Illinois."

Back then, most candidates did not have fancy campaign buses with all the bells and whistles. I was traveling by car. Kgosie drove, with me riding shotgun. Colorful paper maps were our trusty navigation tools long before GPS and mobile phones.

We stopped by diners and pizza parlors. Barbershops and beauty salons. Volunteer firehouses. Sports stadiums. Bars and taverns.

I joined farmers in their fields. I knelt at worship services. I sat down with small business owners and addressed chambers of commerce. I passed out campaign fliers at the supermarket and the county fair.

I was typically logging eighteen-hour days, and as the saying goes, there was no rest for the weary. My mindset was that every voter I met, every hand that I shook, allowed me to learn more about the people of my state, and what they wanted and needed from their senators.

I found most folks to be receptive, open to dialogue and willing to listen. Many of them were generous, be it offering a cup of coffee, or inviting me to join them at suppertime.

One evening when it was getting late, a rural family insisted that I stay the night in their home. I have never forgotten their hospitality, nor the kindness of countless strangers with whom I became fast friends in every corner of the state.

Back in Chicago, our little campaign that could was chugging right along. The headquarters was bustling with staff and volunteers from myriad walks of life. College students. Suburban soccer moms. Retirees. The Moseley family was enthusiastically participating, eagerly sharing their time and talents.

Matt came in after school to stuff envelopes and man the phones. In between homework and extracurricular activities, he sometimes accompanied me on the campaign trail. My son was practically born into politics, and nothing made me happier than having him by my side.

My brother Joseph, with his law enforcement background, provided my security detail. Thinking back to my very first campaign when a rock smashed through our window, I knew there were crackpots and furtive forces out there. I trusted Joe implicitly, and he quietly worked behind the scenes to help keep me and my team safe.

My sister Marsha was working at the time as an advertising account executive for a cable company. In her spare time, she was one of the campaign's volunteers.

My younger sister approaches every task with excellence, and her understanding of both advertising and the early cable industry was extremely beneficial to the campaign. She used her know-how to get my campaign ads placed on channels across western Illinois.

Besides my relatives, a host of friends, allies, and fellow elected officials let me know they were in my corner.

One of them was Jerry Butler, the '50s soul crooner known to fans as "The Iceman." Like my family, his people had migrated from the Deep South to Chicago. In Jerry's case, from Mississippi.

A gifted singer, songwriter, and producer, he gained fame with The Impressions, whose talented members also included Curtis Mayfield.

The group had hit records such as "For Your Precious Love," which went gold, and Jerry climbed the charts as a solo artist with tunes like "Let It Be Me."

In the eighties, he launched a second career in politics, and was elected a Cook County commissioner. When Jerry visited my campaign headquarters one snowy day, he was one of the only men in the room.

He expressed his solidarity and offered encouragement. "Only the strong survive," he quipped, citing the lyrics from one of his hit records. His words would later echo in my head as I navigated Capitol Hill. Jerry is now singing in the Lord's heavenly choir, and I will never forget his support.

Campaigns can be chaotic. Turnover is not unusual. Egos may clash. My operation was no different. But we had an internal problem brewing that foreshadowed dark times ahead.

Several of my staffers abruptly quit during the primary. A few others threatened to jump ship before the general election, at a time when we needed them most.

At issue was Kgosie's management style, which various team members seemed to feel was autocratic. Complaints were flying left and right. "He's abrasive," some told me. "He won't listen to anyone's opinion," others suggested. Certain colleagues used less than polite language to convey to me what they thought of him.

It was distressing to receive such feedback, because I did not view my campaign manager this way. In my mind, he was doing an excellent job. Initially, I chalked up the criticisms to cultural differences. Kgosie was not American, and while that certainly made no difference to me, some considered him an outsider.

Midwesterners are known to be down-to-earth, friendly, and modest. Kgosie wore Armani suits. He spoke with a distinct upper-crust lilt. And he comported himself with the Brits' stiff upper lip—not to mention the demeanor of an African prince.

There was a reason that he carried himself with pride. In South Africa, Kgosie's grandfather was one of the authors of the country's Freedom Charter. The document he helped pen was akin to our nation's Declaration of Independence.

Just as Nelson Mandela was arrested for being a freedom fighter,

so were Kgosie's grandfather and father. They too were impris-
oned, but later released. When the government came after them,
both of the men went into exile.

His grandfather fled to Botswana, and eventually became its
ambassador to the US. He died in Washington, DC, and President Lyndon B. Johnson ensured his body was flown back to
the continent. At home and abroad, Kgosie's family continued
their fight in the anti-apartheid movement.

My point is, this man was part of a long legacy of political
struggle and sacrifice. I believe it was why he immediately grasped
the historic nature of my campaign and was determined to help
me win. The fact that he did not kowtow to anyone in the process made a lot of folks mad. It was like, "Who is this mysterious
African running around in designer suits telling us what to do?"

I will admit that his demeanor was not always warm and
fuzzy. However, anyone who has ever worked on a campaign
knows that tensions and disagreements are not unusual in the
pressure cooker of politics.

But the bottom line was that he was getting things done. I
relied upon his judgment, because his direction had breathed
new life into a once-dormant campaign.

The two of us were spending a great deal of time together.
We drew closer. The cordial relationship that I had kept strictly
professional during the primary blossomed into a romance.

We enjoyed each other's company. We bantered about ideas,
politics, and global affairs. I found him erudite and cosmopolitan.
He was handsome, and his touch made me feel alive. In short,
I fell head over heels in love. We discussed marriage.

People "tsk-tsked" about our coupling from day one. Many
in my circle viewed Kgosie with suspicion. My mentors—Kay,
Billie, and Ethel—considered him a wannabe political Svengali
who was using me. Sadly, I lost some dear friends and hardworking staffers due to the relationship.

The consensus was that I was a fool in love, who would wind

up hurt. "Carol!" I remember someone asking, "Have you lost your mind!?"

Maybe I had. I was in my forties, divorced, with a teenage son. At the time, Kgosie was nearly a decade younger, in his thirties, had never been married, and didn't have children.

But for all the brouhaha about our so-called May–December liaison (actually, our ten-year age gap was not all that considerable) we were two single consenting adults.

As the campaign progressed, the gossip intensified. The scuttlebutt was that Kgosie was in my ear, controlling me. I suppose people thought that as a couple, there was pillow talk about politics. Worse yet were the whispers that Kgosie treated me harshly. This was not true. I know something about tyrannical men, having been raised in a household where my father too often resorted to brute force. I take domestic violence seriously, and as a lawmaker have sponsored legislation aimed at helping women and their children survive.

Kgosie never laid a hand on me. Had he dared, the man would have regretted it. I would have kicked his butt! Seriously. I am a woman who will fight back. Even as a little girl, I tried to stand up for myself. That meant challenging my father and schoolyard bullies. Once I entered politics, I found myself battling naysayers and opponents alike.

Nor was Kgosie verbally abusive. Whatever my insecurities, I have never allowed a man—or anyone—to demean me or call me names. It's simply not in my makeup.

I only recall one occasion when Kgosie snapped at me, about of all things, my chipped nail polish. This occurred minutes before I was taking the stage for a televised campaign event. As my campaign manager, he was concerned that viewers would somehow equate my personal grooming with my politics. I was annoyed with him for bringing up something that seemed trivial and told him so at the time. That said, he may have had a point about a candidate putting their best foot forward during a public forum.

For a time, our love affair was euphoric. But mixing politics and passion became messy. We had opened up Pandora's box, and out flew all kinds of complications that began to strangle my career. And I could not help but wonder if, ultimately, my heart would be broken.

During the primary, I'd raised around $500,000. Even back in the nineties, it was considered a paltry sum in fundraising terms, especially compared to the millions my previous competitors had in their respective war chests.

What a difference a day—and a plucky primary upset—makes. Small and large contributions began to pour in as we marched toward election day.

Early on, we raised more than two million dollars. And the numbers kept rising to four, five, then six million.

I had a broad base of local and national support. The Democratic Senatorial Campaign Committee (DSCC), whose mission involves fundraising and related activities aimed at sending Democratic senators to Washington, pledged to back me.

I was championed by a network of powerful women. Besides the Hollywood set, groups such as the Women's Campaign Fund in Washington, DC, held a major fundraiser that benefitted me and other candidates. I also addressed the annual meeting of the National Organization for Women (NOW). NOW had launched its "Elect Women For A Change" campaign the same year that I ran for the Senate. The organization's PAC was tremendously helpful in providing resources to me and other candidates with feminist values at the local, state, and congressional level.

I was zipping to fundraising events all over the state and country. At one point, I flew to Atlanta for a reception where the civil rights heroine, Rosa Parks, was a special guest. I had studied her arrest, how it spurred the Montgomery, Alabama, bus boycott and the larger Civil Rights Movement. I can scarcely articulate what an honor it was to be in the presence of such an icon. Meeting her nearly brought me to tears.

Mrs. Parks was serene and soft-spoken, a woman whose strength and the courage of her convictions seemed to enrobe her like a glowing halo. We took a photo together, and I shyly asked for an autograph. Mrs. Parks signed her name, adding a sweet personal message on a scrap of paper. To this day, it remains one of my most cherished mementos.

I tried to keep my wits about me when engaging with VIPs. I've never been the groupie type, gushing and such. That is, until I came face-to-face with "the Greatest."

Muhammad Ali was born in Louisville, Kentucky, but spent many years in Chicago. He trained in local gyms, fought in tournaments, and had personal ties. Notably, he joined the Nation of Islam.

I was very familiar with the Black Muslim community in Chicago because my paternal grandmother, Mama Liz, was an adherent of the faith. She prayed at the mosque, and knew many of the early leaders, including the Honorable Elijah Muhammad.

Ali had a residence on Woodlawn Avenue on the city's South Side. The champ opened his beautiful home—a historic brick mansion with dozens of rooms overlooking an impeccably manicured lawn—for a private fundraiser.

By that time, Ali was battling Parkinson's disease, but in my eyes, he still seemed to "float like a butterfly, and sting like a bee." He was delightful, and the time spent with him was memorable. Ali even presented me with a pair of personally autographed boxing gloves.

Thinking back, I should have taken them with me to the Senate.

In the summer of 1992, the Democrats were throwing a big party in New York City.

Thousands of delegates, elected officials, and people from all walks of life converged on the Big Apple that July for the Democratic National Convention.

Bill Clinton, who'd twice served as governor of Arkansas, and Senator Al Gore of Tennessee became the youthful, telegenic stars of the Democrats' presidential ticket. On the Republican side was the patrician sitting president, George H.W. Bush, and vice president, Dan Quayle, a fresh-faced former senator from Indiana. Ross Perot, a colorful Texas billionaire, was running as an Independent.

The massive event was masterfully helmed by then-Democratic National Committee (DNC) chair, the incomparable Ron Brown, and his phenomenal team.

I was thrilled when the organizers offered me an opportunity to speak alongside other senatorial candidates. We would join a list of speakers who ranged from Barbara Jordan, the legendary Texas congresswoman, to Bill Bradley, the NBA basketball star turned senator.

The invitation to address the nation was the stuff of dreams, but it also filled me with trepidation.

I decided to write my own speech, something I'd done plenty of times before. This go-round, however, my thoughts were jumbled and I hit a brick wall. Ahead of the big event, I was sitting in the lobby of my hotel, feeling rather anxious. In what can only be described as God throwing me a lifeline, a young woman sat down near me. As luck would have it, she was a writer. She noticed my angst. When I explained my predicament, she offered to help. Her skills and calm reassurance helped me organize my thoughts and finish the final draft.

When I told Kgosie about the encounter, he raised an eyebrow. My campaign manager thought it was unwise to have shared such important remarks with a stranger. But the proof was in the pudding. My speech was finished.

Soon, it was showtime at Madison Square Garden. I stepped

onto one of the most famous stages in the world, and heard the roar of the crowd.

I was dressed all in white, complete with a long strand of pearls. Someone later commented that I looked almost angelic. I just prayed that my guardian angel would guide me on one of the biggest nights of my life.

Senator Barbara Mikulski, the dynamic lawmaker from Baltimore, Maryland, introduced me and other women candidates from across America.

"I will be joined by a team of spectacular women and I am proud to present some of them to you tonight," she said. "These are Democratic women who have already been nominated for the Senate."

I moved to the podium and spoke into the microphone. "Thank you! Thank you all! Thank you, Senator Mikulski!" I said.

"I have come a long way in my life from the South Side of Chicago," I said in my opening. "I stand here this evening overwhelmed by the magnitude of the opportunity God has given me. My mother worked in hospitals and my dad in law enforcement. Both had to struggle to give our family a chance to succeed," I explained.

"Tonight, I stand here as a living testament to the hope and faith of my parents who believed, as I believe, that America is the only country in the world where I would have this chance— the chance to speak freely as a woman of color; the chance to be heard in the forging of a new American agenda; the chance to make history."

I heard the applause building, which gave me confidence to keep going.

"I am here as proof that my parents' struggles and their faith in America were not in vain. I believe that the dream of America lives when every girl or boy, no matter what race, or color, or condition, has the opportunity and the freedom... This country is challenged to recognize that, in our diversity, is our strength. Quality and excellence have many faces, many voices. We grow stronger as a nation when we see those faces and when we hear those voices."

The audience began clapping. I went on to state my belief that our nation could "find a better tomorrow" by getting back to the basics. "Our cities can be rebuilt, our economy reconstructed, our environment saved, and health care provided for every American when we remember that the people who serve in high public office are the servants and not the masters of the people who elect them."

I looked out into the crowd. The delegates were cheering, clapping, and waving signs. I exited the stage to deafening applause. It was all very heady and exhilarating.

Of course, we were just a warm-up for the main event. Clinton and Gore represented a new generation of Democrats. The presidential candidates ignited a spark that night. As they took the stage alongside their smart, accomplished wives—Hillary Rodham Clinton and Tipper Gore—the convention ended in a shower of balloons and confetti. We all had incredibly high hopes for the future.

I was elated to be a part of the DNC's successful convention. The promise and possibility inherent in America's sacred democratic process is that with each election, history can be made.

Something else happened at the gathering, which took me by surprise. Practically overnight, thanks to the magic of television, people knew my name.

The next day, pedestrians were stopping me on the streets of Manhattan to say hello.

Cab drivers honked, and bystanders smiled. When I got back to Chicago, my phone was ringing off the hook.

I had become a political darling. Something of a sensation. A flood of headlines, articles, and broadcast reports highlighted my "charisma" and "megawatt" smile.

In the whirlwind weeks and months that followed, editors called from *Vogue* and *Harper's Bazaar* about features.

I graced the cover of national magazines: *Essence*, *Ebony*, and *Jet*, the latter two published in my hometown by the illustrious Johnson Publishing Company. *Chicago Magazine* and *N'DIGO* also featured me. There were local and national talk show appearances, invitations to address groups, and so on.

Initially, I basked in the positive attention, as any candidate or campaign would. Still, it was quite overwhelming. It was very odd, this phenomenon called celebrity. Back then, before reality TV and social media, I certainly had no idea of how to handle fans and media. This new element of our campaign felt like hopping aboard a runaway train.

Posing for magazines was exciting and glamorous, but it also posed a conundrum for me as a woman.

I had arrived at this stage of my career as an attorney, former federal prosecutor, and state legislator who'd risen through the ranks of leadership. I'd gone on to become the highest-ranking Black elected official in the largest county in Illinois, one who managed hundreds of employees and a seven-figure budget.

Any man with my credentials would have been taken at face value. No one would have focused on his "cheerleader" smile. I'd long held up the torch for women's rights and the rejection of stereotypical or sexist gender norms. But I was being treated like someone running for a high school popularity contest.

I did not want the overemphasis on my personality to usurp the substance of my campaign. I was eager to discuss the critical issues impacting our state and the nation.

Moreover, I had a platform. It centered around job creation, a vital economy, a national health care plan, and championing women and families. I believed in policies that would give the poor a safety net, and empower the middle class and all Americans to thrive.

HISTORYMAKER
PART THREE

Almost immediately, my GOP opponent came out swinging. Rich Williamson made it clear that this Senate race was going to be a slugfest.

The negativity commenced with a thirty-second spot that hit the airwaves about two months after the primary.

"Carol Moseley Braun," an announcer intoned. "Just another liberal machine politician."

I shook my head and clicked off the radio. When it comes to political ads, specious claims are to be expected. But this one, which labeled me "part of the Chicago Democratic Machine," conveniently ignored the facts.

I'd entered politics as a reform candidate, buoyed by community activism and grassroots support. Later, I sued my own party over redistricting. I was hardly controlled by the Machine or anyone else.

The commercial went on to distort my voting record in the

state legislature. The language was intentionally inflammatory. I cringed hearing the term "welfare cheats" to refer to struggling families whom I sought to uplift. The ad went on to say "she even opposes the death penalty." It was meant as criticism, yet I made no apologies for fighting as a lawmaker to end a barbaric practice of legal and moral dubiety.

Moreover, the ad had problematic undertones. It noted my support for Rev. Jesse Jackson as a delegate to the DNC convention when he ran for president in 1988. True. I was proud to back his groundbreaking campaign. I was also described as a "voice" for Chicago mayor Harold Washington in Springfield. Also, true. The late trailblazing mayor was a friend and mentor. The inclusion of these leaders seemed designed to remind voters that I was Black. It was not-so-subtle race baiting.

The commercial ran for weeks on stations across the state. In response, I released a radio ad of my own. I spoke directly to voters, letting them know of my commitment to focus strictly on the issues.

We continued to stump across the state throughout the summer. I maintained a healthy lead in the polls heading into the early fall. I was feeling pretty good about our chances. That is, until an "October surprise" rocked me personally and turned my campaign on its head.

Back in 1989, my mother received a windfall. The check for $28,750 was an inheritance royalty from the sale of timber rights on the family farm in Alabama.

At the time, Mother was in her golden years. She had survived a heart attack and two strokes. Her leg had been amputated. She was having trouble living independently. The siblings discussed her moving in with one of us, but our mother was proud. She did not want to be a burden to her adult children.

We moved Mother to a nursing facility, where she seemed content. On a typical day, she might be found navigating the hallway in her wheelchair to visit fellow residents, or cheerfully participating in daily activities.

Upon receiving the lump sum, more money than she'd ever seen in her life, my mother's inclination was to share it. She had no bank account, and asked me to deposit the check and distribute the funds between us siblings.

I'd paid for my brother John's funeral, and my share of the gift recouped those costs. My younger brother and sister each received a portion. We thanked Mother for her generosity, and that was the end of it—or so we thought.

Years later, our private family business became a public campaign controversy, after a local TV station broke the story of possible Medicaid fraud. I was in the eye of the storm.

Because my mother's nursing home care was underwritten by a government funded program, a slew of questions arose: whether the money she received was properly disclosed, if taxes were owed, and if a crime possibly had been committed. Worse yet, was the suggestion that my relatives and I had somehow colluded to hide assets.

I was aghast. The Moseleys are lawyers and police officers. Dedicated public servants. The last thing any of us would ever do is knowingly break the law, or even skirt the rules. Our entire family was extremely distraught.

I assembled my campaign team. We later held a press conference. I was trying to be fully transparent. Yet it stung that after decades in public office without blemishes on my record, my ethics and character were being called into question.

I tried to make clear that no one tried to game the system. The truth is, this was an unintentional error, one due to ignorance of the regulations versus someone scheming to do something underhanded.

Technically, I had no responsibility for reporting my mother's money. Despite her physical infirmities, Mother was of sound mind. That said, I should have had the foresight to ask questions, and guide her through whatever process was required in terms of the monetary surplus. Apparently, there was some question as to whether an official form to report this type of thing even existed at the time.

My attorneys and I met with the Illinois Department of Public Aid. We hoped to resolve the matter expeditiously, but the bureaucratic process took time. It was horrific to be under the microscope. At one point, there were several concurrent inquiries, including one that could have potentially jeopardized my law license.

As the matter dragged on, our family name was dragged through the mud. It was one thing for whoever leaked this information to cast aspersions on my character, but my loved ones did not deserve to be sacrificed on the altar of political gamesmanship.

At one point, members of the press were camped out near the nursing home. One guy even showed up with a bouquet of flowers for my mother, tricking the front desk into letting him go back to her room. She yelled for an aide, and the intruder ran off. It was frightening.

I tried to shield Mother from the maelstrom as best I could. I did not want to see her harmed, but she was devastated. Imagine winning the lottery and sharing the jackpot with your loved ones? And, then seeing your benevolence turned into half-truths that not only harmed you, but your flesh and blood.

The scrutiny was stressful on all of us but had a particularly deleterious effect on my mother's physical health and emotional well-being. Normally outgoing, she became sullen and withdrawn. When this story broke, with seemingly endless television reports and newspaper headlines, it often usurped important local and national news in Chicago. In many ways, this singular event defined my campaign. It devastated me both politically and personally, because it involved the people closest to me.

When all was said and done, my legal team worked closely with officials to help me right what was an inadvertent wrong.

I apologized. Once it was determined what we owed the state, I personally made restitution of more than $15,000. That payment settled the matter. Thank God, no charges were pursued against me, nor any member of my family or team.

Still, this was no contretemps, there was fallout. My legal fees were exorbitant, inching toward seven figures. The situation gave rise to massive campaign debt, as well. From the time the story broke, we poured money into ads to combat the misinformation that some outlets were reporting. We hired PR specialists to help calm the ruckus with positive publicity. The campaign hadn't anticipated any of this in our budget, and we wound up spending upward of half a million dollars.

The episode poisoned the well with voters. My poll numbers began to slip. We were dropping two points a day. For the first time, I began to worry if the good people of Illinois were still with me.

My first debate with Rich Williamson was scheduled for the twelfth of October. We traveled to Peoria, which is the oldest community in the state, and situated along the Illinois River.

The live televised event at historic Bradley University was being hosted by the Illinois League of Women Voters and WTTW-TV. The auditorium was packed, and the air seemed to crackle with anticipation.

The stage was bare, save for two wooden podiums, where we candidates stood just paces apart. Our speaking order was determined by a flip of the coin. My opponent gave his opening remarks first.

"Hopefully tonight you'll learn why someone said this Senate race in Illinois is the clearest ideological choice in America. And so it is," Williamson began. "The economy is hurting. People are suffering. We're in the longest recession since World War

II. Everybody's either facing unemployment or knows someone unemployed," he said, referencing members of his own family. "We have to do better, we have to change. Tonight, I hope to outline specific proposals for reform on the economy. To get quality education. To help get our neighborhoods safer for you and your children."

So far, so good. No attacks, I thought to myself. But my competitor was not done yet.

"And I think there should be one standard of ethics for everybody. No special privileges. I know that because of Carol Braun's Medicaid scandal, many of you are rethinking this election. I hope you'll give me a hard look. I hope I'll earn your support. Thank you. I want to be your United States senator."

I'd hoped this debate would not be filled with mudslinging, but five minutes in, it already was. I took a deep breath and tried to calmly address the spectators in front of me and viewers at home.

"I'm Carol Moseley Braun and I'm running for the United States Senate because it really is time for a change," I said. "The recession that we're in is the longest since the Great Depression. And in Illinois alone we've lost some three hundred thousand manufacturing jobs and over eight billion dollars in federal funds. Those losses were caused by the policies of the administration known as 'trickle-down economics.' And its handmaiden, the 'New Federalism,'" I said, referring to Williamson's writings as a policy wonk.

"Our people are hurting and worried. I agree with my opponent this is a choice—this election is about choice. But I submit to you that it's a choice between the failed policies of the past and a constructive concrete program for change. I want to get back to basics. I want our country, our state, to be a state of builders and producers with the best-educated workforce in the world."

Calling Williamson "the handpicked candidate of President Bush," I posited that his run for the Senate "translates into basically more of the same. But my candidacy came about because you chose me to be a fighter for working people, to propose an opportunity for hope, and to help lead our country in the way. That's why there's so much excitement about this race."

For the next hour or so, we sparred about everything from job creation to tax codes to education funding. I had hoped our exchange would be issue oriented, but Williamson took every opportunity to lob verbal grenades my way.

Besides the Medicaid flap, he brought up my tenure as recorder of deeds, accusing me of "patronage, cronyism, and corruption." He played the race card. He had a way of cherry-picking selective facts and spinning them into something misleading. It was maddening.

I tried to remain senatorial and gracious. But my opponent was hammering me. At a certain point, I had to push back.

I retorted by talking about how Williamson had flip-flopped on the issue of women's reproductive freedoms. And, I pointed out his hypocrisy about the money involving my mother.

"But he doesn't tell you that he was a lobbyist who made money on his White House connections," I said, noting his lucrative clients, among them foreign companies that paid him millions. "He basically went back to Washington and made a fortune.

"I have been a fighter for working people all my days in public life," I said.

Round and round we went. The debate finally ended. As I was removing the lavalier mic from my lapel, Mr. Williamson approached me with a smile. I, too, was determined to be a good sport. We shook hands and he hurried offstage.

Afterward, both of our camps claimed victory. Yet I did not feel triumphant about our discourse. All I felt was weary.

My opponent had gotten some backlash for his negative ads. In response, he softened the tone with less personal attacks, yet still ran commercials with pointed messages.

In one of them, Williamson told listeners the election was "not about color, not about gender, and it should not be about personality."

I took umbrage at the thinly veiled references to yours truly, in what was just a softer way to pan me, not to mention the historic nature of this race.

For months, I'd let this man engage in character assassination. He pummeled me, and I had not responded in kind. As the time drew near for our second debate, we decided to punch back.

My next commercial zinged him.

"Rich Williamson's been running a nasty campaign, but who is he?" a narrator said.

"As a Reagan aide, Williamson wrote economic policies that punished Illinois families and rewarded the wealthy. His next stop was Beatrice Foods, where Williamson bagged over a million dollars when a junk bond deal destroyed the company. Rich Williamson got a one-million-dollar golden parachute, while thousands of workers got their pink slips. That's Reagan, Bush, Williamson economics in action."

Campaigning is grueling. I was traversing neighborhoods in Chicago and crisscrossing the state. I typically had no less than ten engagements on my daily schedule, on top of my duties as a countywide elected official. The fatigue began to wear on me.

Meanwhile, as a loving mother, I felt guilty about leaving my son. I tried to have Matt accompany me to different cities and towns—both as an educational lesson in civics, geography, and history—and so that we would not be separated as much.

But then came press that I was constantly running late, a racist trope, or occasionally skipping events.

No one seemed to take into account that I was a working mom and a candidate. One cannot be in two places at once. If the PTA meeting runs long, you cannot tell your child's teacher, "Oh, I am running for office." If someone at the coffee shop wanted to talk to me about an issue in their community, I did not rush them. If the officer of a local club who invited me to speak to their members made a long-winded introduction, I was obliged to be polite. If I was at the beauty salon—where women know it can literally take hours—I could not tell the stylist to take me first. To the extent that they could, my campaign manager and staff made sure that I stayed the course. The encouragement kept me going. As did daily prayer and attending church on Sundays.

While the bruising tone of the race had taken its toll, at each stage, there were bright spots.

Maya Angelou flew into Chicago to support my campaign. Meeting the famous poet was a revelation. I'd watched her on Oprah Winfrey's celebrated talk show, which not only inspired people and changed lives, but created jobs and economic benefits for our city. But her powerful presence radiated even more brightly in person.

Not only was Dr. Angelou physically striking—statuesque and regal—but she was also warm, funny, and insightful. During our time together, we discussed politics, while also connecting as mothers, and as she put it in her mellifluous voice, "sista friends."

Dr. Angelou supported me in 1992, and then again in 1998 when I was up for reelection. I remember us entering my condo building and the doorman greeting me with "Hi, Carol." I was fine with it, but Dr. Angelou found his informality inappropriate and nicely told him so. "This is Miss Moseley Braun," she said with polite authority. "Our senator." The writer who penned the poem "Phenomenal Woman" and bestselling books such as *I Know Why the Caged Bird Sings*, gave respect, and demanded it in return. It was a valuable lesson. I only wish that I'd taken Sister Maya up on her offer to reach out anytime. Her sage wisdom might have aided me in some trying circumstances.

In late October, less than two weeks before the November 3

election, I took part in a second debate with Mr. Williamson. Once again the League of Women Voters hosted the forum, which aired on WLS-TV. This time there was a live studio audience, and two satellite locations—including a local library— where voters could ask questions.

The debate was equal parts substance and spectacle. We clashed again and again on the issues—from the economy and crime to health care and drug legalization. And my opponent persisted with the ad hominem attacks on me.

In his opening statement, Mr. Williamson acknowledged: "I know I'm the underdog. I'm behind in the polls but the gap is closing," he said. "When Carol Braun became the Democratic nominee, many jumped on the bandwagon, many wanted to believe, but now they are having second thoughts. They're disappointed, and even disillusioned by her inability to fully respond. And be consistent." He mentioned the Medicaid situation, yet again, and other alleged offenses.

I sighed inwardly before the moderator came to me. I said in part: "The people of Illinois chose me in the primary because they knew I would be a fighter for working people. They wanted a senator who listens. Who cares. And who can make Washington respect us again," I said. I referenced one of the national presidential debates and noted that the citizens wanted the candidates to focus on the issues, instead of attacking one another. "I agree with that view," I said. "I look forward to discussing with you the issues…and sharing my plan for Illinois."

Election Day dawned. After casting my vote with Matt at our neighborhood precinct and doing several interviews, I visited polling places around the city. At every turn, I was greeted with cheers, hugs, and smiles. I thanked the good people of Illinois endlessly.

Turnout was heavy, which made me feel cautiously optimistic. Besides my own Senate bid, I hoped voters would help Democrats clinch Illinois for Bill Clinton and Al Gore. The ticket would go on to reclaim the White House, after twelve years of the Reagan-Bush era.

That evening, once the polls closed, I snuck away to a quiet place. Then, I got down on my knees and prayed.

I would go on to defeat Richard Williamson with 53 percent of the vote vs. his 43 percent. We'd battled politically, but in the end, he proved to be a gracious gentleman. I actually received 2.6 million votes in my home state, which floored me.

I didn't spend a lot of time in reflection on election night, but I knew how far we'd come. My longshot Senate primary campaign had succeeded, and the final results were beyond my wildest dreams. It was a jubilant, unbelievably exciting time for me, my family, campaign team, and supporters.

I vowed to the cheering, ebullient crowd: "I'm going to work hard to be the very best senator Illinois has ever had."

OLD BULLS AND
SISTER SENATORS

My victory came during the "Year of the Woman," a slogan that began appearing in the press following record electoral wins by women nationwide. Indeed, our class of women lawmakers proceeded to shake up the status quo in Congress.

Back in 1993, women's representation in the Senate increased from two members to six. Meanwhile, twenty-four new women were elected in the House of Representatives, doubling its numbers to a total of forty-eight. And besides me in the Senate, the House had more women of color than ever before.

I remember the jubilation and sense of purpose as we proudly took our places on Capitol Hill.

While women have held Senate seats since the roaring twenties, only two were in the chamber when I arrived. Senator Barbara Mikulski was a Democrat from Maryland, and Nancy Kassebaum, a Republican who represented Kansas.

Dianne Feinstein, who'd won a special election, blazed trails alongside Barbara Boxer as California's first women senators. Patty Murray, who'd been derided early in her political journey as "just a mom in tennis shoes," turned it into a campaign slogan and made history representing Washington state. Later that same year, Senator Kay Bailey Hutchinson, a Republican from Texas, was elected.

The women senators of that era formed a sisterhood. Mikulski, a four-foot-eleven dynamo from Baltimore who became the first woman to chair the Appropriations Committee, gets the credit for bringing us together.

She would organize gatherings that took place on The Hill, and occasionally at her home. Over coffee and donuts, or sandwiches, we got to know each other. I learned that my peers had impressive credentials in law, education, and social work, among other fields.

Our bipartisan meetups were exclusively for us: no men, aides, nor press were allowed. In this sanctum, we could speak freely about current events and legislation.

We came together in a collegial way to create our own networks vis-à-vis issues affecting our constituents and the nation. Information sharing was very important.

That's not to suggest we were always in lockstep. Women are not a monolith, and there was an ideological spread among us. There were colleagues whose ideologies differed from my own. No matter what, we tried to respect each other. We did not get hung up on partisanship. We truly desired to work together for the good of our country.

At other times, the conversation was far more mundane.

We figured out a carpool schedule so that everyone had a ride to the Capitol. My road buddy was usually Dianne.

We celebrated birthdays and special occasions. I will never forget Dianne hosting a wonderful engagement party for me. I still have the gift she presented me that day, an ornate clock. It ticked longer than the relationship.

I had such respect and affection for these smart, strong, and highly capable women. There were days in which we shared what was happening in our personal lives and families. Over time, we bonded and supported each other. We laughed, hugged, and sometimes cried together.

Decades ago, my fellow trailblazers and I were not only focusing on legislative issues impacting all Americans, we were pushing for our own equal treatment in Congress.

Gender equality issues were front and center for me and my peers. We were navigating an institution that historically was the ultimate boys' club. We had to fight to keep from being marginalized or treated as novelties, and to ensure we were shown the same respect as our male counterparts. One scenario when I first arrived on The Hill stands out.

Men in the Senate have long had a private restroom, complete with an attendant, conveniently located near the chamber floor.

Yet when we newbies burst on the scene, there was only a tiny lavatory designated for women senators. And it was a decent distance from the chamber.

No senator wants to miss a vote, so if nature called, you either sat there squirming or made a mad dash. After one too many times racing down the hallway in heels, tapping on the door, only to find it occupied, many of us had truly had enough.

The women in the Senate began agitating for new restrooms. We pressed the leadership, all of whom were men during that period. Plans from the architect of the Capitol were finally approved, and a new ladies' loo was unveiled in 1993. Everyone was, shall we say, flush with excitement. Best of all, the washroom was paces from the Senate floor, just like the men's room. Alas, it would take nearly two more decades for women in the House to get their own restroom near the Speaker's lobby. Prior to that, the congresswomen had to use one of the building's public facilities.

The women of the Senate also demanded parity when it came to strictures around dress codes.

One day, I came to work in a pantsuit. I was all decked out and thought my designer outfit looked chic. As I made my way to the floor, suddenly, there was all this whispering. A few colleagues actually looked shocked. I was puzzled.

I am fairly meticulous about my appearance. It stems from my childhood.

I have always been a little on the chubby side. And in my youth, I went through phases of feeling like an ugly duckling in a family of swans. I recall back in grade school when my mother came to a parent-teacher conference. My teacher casually remarked, "Oh, your mother is so beautiful. What happened to you?" It was such a blow to my self-esteem.

Another time, my Auntie Darrel took me shopping for my grade-school graduation. We went to one of the upscale department stores that had begun to open their doors to Black customers post segregation.

Auntie Darrel—who was this glamorous model type—told me she would purchase any outfit that I wanted. Together, we pulled several beautiful dresses off the rack for me to try on.

When we went to the fitting room, the saleswoman was sort of eyeing us as I tried everything on.

These days, there's a movement centered around body positivity. It's fantastic to see. But back then, I did not embrace my curves. I tried on frock after frock and none of them fit. By the time we got to the last one, the saleswoman was snarky. "Well, you should be thin like your mama."

We stormed out of the store. In the end, my mother wound up sewing my graduation dress, and it was perfect. For a while, I refused to go shopping. It was too demoralizing.

Decades later, my appearance as America's first Black woman in the Senate was closely scrutinized. There was media commentary on my hair, which in my younger days I wore in an Afro.

Later, I relaxed my hair and would spend hours in the beauty salon, emerging with fluffy curls. Apparently, some in Chicago were asking stylists for similar hairdos. On hectic mornings, to save time, I'd pull my tresses back in a ponytail or chignon. I sported braids, too. Certainly, that natural style had never been worn on the Senate floor.

My fashion choices also elicited attention. A Chanel suit drew disapproving commentary. I think the ultimate insult was a photograph that zeroed in on my derrière as I walked up the Capitol steps. I had on a sweater set that was clinging to my backside. It was cited as an example of what not to wear.

But unbeknownst to me, I'd breached protocol by wearing slacks. The Senate has numerous rules, some of them unwritten. No one had told me that women lawmakers were expected to wear skirts and dresses on the floor. I recall that the only guidelines in place for us were fairly ambiguous, along the lines of "appropriate attire."

No one asked me to leave or change clothes, not that I would have anyway. If a woman in the Senate wanted to wear pants, and she was neat and pulled together, what of it? Besides, all of the men in the room had on pants!

To be clear, I was not the first woman in Congress to don a pantsuit. Congresswomen in the House of Representatives, which tends to be slightly less formal than the Senate, had worn pantsuits since the '60s.

Meanwhile, I wasn't the only woman in the Senate who bristled at the antiquated limitations on how women lawmakers and aides could dress. Senators Mikulski and Kassebaum decided to stage a protest. They wore trousers and encouraged women staffers to wear slacks to work, too. When Mikulski came onto the Senate floor, her attire ruffled some feathers. Yet what became known as "The Pantsuit Rebellion" did lead to changes.

At that time, the sergeant-at-arms (who enforces the Senate's rules) was Martha Pope, who'd made history as the first woman chosen for that important position. She updated the dress code. It seemed altogether fitting that a woman would help usher in a new sartorial era. I am proud that my colleagues and I took a stand. Decades later, whenever I turn on the news and glimpse one of the younger congresswomen or senators at a hearing or press conference, clad in a fashionable suit with slacks, the march of progress is apparent.

Meanwhile, the Senate lived up to its reputation as the ultimate boys' club. When I first arrived, there were ninety-four men. These gents read like a "who's who" of politics, public, and military service, as well as high society. Here are just a few of the senators who served alongside me: Joe Biden. Ted Kennedy, brother of John F. Kennedy and Robert F. Kennedy. Former astronaut, John Glenn. John "Jay" Rockefeller IV—the great-grandson of the wealthy Rockefeller family.

War hero, John McCain. Harry Reid. Bob Dole. Daniel "Pat" Moynihan, author of the Moynihan Report. Orrin Hatch. John Kerry. Phil Gramm. Mitch McConnell. Tom Daschle. Daniel Inouye of Hawaii, the state's first congressman turned senator.

Claiborne Pell, sponsor of the financial aid legislation that became the Pell Grant. Former NBA star, Bill Bradley. John Warner, onetime secretary of the navy, not to mention Elizabeth Taylor's sixth husband.

Patrick Leahy. Chris Dodd. Chuck Grassley. Arlen Specter. Trent Lott. Joe Lieberman.

Chuck Robb, former governor of Virginia. Russ Feingold, who co-sponsored a major campaign finance reform bill.

Bob Kerry, former governor of Alaska. Ernest "Fritz" Hollings. And, my senior Illinois senator and friend, Paul Simon. Upon his retirement, Dick Durbin was elected in 1996. Both men were fine colleagues, and we made a great team. I used to joke that Paul was comparable to an uncle, while Dick was closer to a cousin.

On The Hill, the male senators who possessed seniority, prominence, and power were known as the "Old Bulls." If the Senate was akin to Valhalla—the mythical place of the gods— then these were its warriors. They waxed eloquent on the Senate floor. They dressed the part in suits and ties, strutting and preening like peacocks. They happily held court before the media. The thing is, they were extremely effective in working across the aisle and delivering legislation for the American people.

Some of these senators had been elected decades prior when the times were very different. Strom Thurmond of South Carolina was in his nineties when I joined the chamber. Once an ardent segregationist, he would moderate his stances. Upon his death at age one hundred, his legacy was further complicated by the revelation that he'd fathered a biracial daughter. That said, Thurmond was among the first senators to welcome me, making a point to stop by one of my receptions and offer a few congratulatory words at the podium.

Senator Robert Byrd of West Virginia was elected back in 1959. He was a former Klansman who later apologized for his actions and denounced hate. Rising to speak on the occasion of his ten thousandth vote, Senator Byrd said, "Of the ten thousand votes, there are only two that I regret; one was the vote against the Civil Rights Act of 1964, and the second was the vote for airline deregulation."

Senator Byrd was in the chamber for more than a half century, which intersected with my tenure. He was very kind to me. As a honcho on the Appropriations Committee, his influence directly assisted my efforts to bring home "pork" to the state of Illinois. I recall his fervent support to help me secure $14 million in funding to convert an old armory into the Bronzeville Military Academy, a public school in the heart of Chicago's South

Side. Senator Byrd served until his death at age ninety-two, and he was always respectful to me.

But not everyone went out of their way to be cordial.

I recall walking to my seat one day and smiling at one particular senator. He just stared at me, a hostile expression on his face. And there were other slights.

Sometimes, when attending hearings, committee meetings, and events, the reception I received was cold as ice. I did not expect a parade upon entering a room, but common courtesy would have been nice.

I remember walking into a committee meeting where I was the lone woman and person of color. The senators were all older and they looked at me oddly. One even asked, "What are you doing here?" I replied, "What are you talking about? I am a US senator." After a while, as I joined in the dialogue and shared my expertise, they recognized that I had something to contribute. I had to claim my seat at the table.

Ted Kennedy was one of the nice guys. The senator sensed that I might need a sounding board. I'd served for a decade in the Illinois General Assembly, but this august body was a different animal. The place had a culture all its own.

Senator Kennedy invited me to lunch. I have never been (and pardon the term) a starfucker, but when a member of one of America's foremost political dynasties wants to break bread, you go.

Instead of the Senate cafeteria, we met at La Colline, a popular DC restaurant. The French brasserie had stunning views of the Capitol and a famous clientele of politicos, star reporters, and Washington socialites.

I'd dressed in all black for our meeting. I felt like someone in mourning. "How are you doing, Carol?" Senator Kennedy asked in his distinct accent. I couldn't pretend and didn't lie.

"Not so good," I replied.

I explained that there were days when I felt ostracized on The

Hill. At other times, I was treated like a political rock star, which caused resentment and was a hindrance to the allyship necessary to perform the work I'd been sent to do. Being "the first" Black woman senator and the isolation that accompanied it, sometimes got so bad that I occasionally escaped to my "hideaway"—the private spaces that senators have around the Capitol—to clear my head and pray.

"I am proud to be a symbol of women's rights, and civil rights," I said. "But for me, my role in the Senate is about more than symbolism. I am here to advance a true agenda of progress."

The senator was a good listener. He was filled with wisdom and friendly advice.

We discussed prioritizing family amid the hectic schedules that senators kept. Aware that certain media were on my tail, he advised me to exercise discretion, and not let my private life spill over to the Senate. We spoke a bit about our faith. The Kennedys, of course, are famously Catholic, as were my relatives. Mostly, he was compassionate and encouraging.

We parted that day as friends. "Let me know if you need anything, Carol," he said. My spirits were lifted enough to smile.

"Thank you," I replied.

I was just a few weeks into my role as a new US senator. We wasted no time in delving into issues that impacted the American people.

On January 26, 1993, senators addressed a range of topics during our legislative session. Jobs and the economy. The Clinton administration's major policy shift regarding gays in the military. The consideration of Madeleine Albright, to be US ambassador to the United Nations, to name a few.

Amid all of this, I delivered my maiden speech on the Senate floor. Delivering one's first speech is a long-standing tradition, one that usually receives a little fanfare in the chamber from leadership and colleagues, sometimes with invited guests watching from the gallery.

I stood up. Mindful of parliamentary procedure, I sought consent from the Senate's president pro tempore to be recognized for ten minutes.

I began speaking about one of my heroes, Thurgood Marshall, who'd died two days prior at age eighty-four. It is "hard to conceive that a heart as mighty and as courageous as his is no longer beating," I said of the nation's first Black Supreme Court justice.

I spoke of Marshall's youth in Baltimore, his educational development, and prowess as a civil rights lawyer. I praised him for the legal battles he fought and won to end segregation, and how he made a difference. "His work helped make my election to the US Senate possible. He opened closed doors and created new opportunities for me and for many, many others.

"I hope we will all remember Marshall by dedicating ourselves to the principles and goals he dedicated himself to—making American opportunity available to every American," I continued. "I am proud to have the opportunity, in some small way, to continue his work, and to try to build on his legacy."

When I finished you could hear a pin drop. Business proceeded as usual until Paul Simon, my senior colleague from Illinois, rushed in and asked to speak.

"I was not here, unfortunately, when my colleague, Senator Carol Moseley Braun, made her first comments on the floor of the Senate," he said. "I do not know that anyone was aware. I think it is appropriate that Senator Carol Moseley Braun, who is herself a pioneer, should in her first remarks pay tribute to someone who was a pioneer."

As my fellow Illinois senator continued, his kind words touched my heart. "We will be hearing much more of my colleague on a great variety of issues where her abilities and her strength and her compassion will become very evident to those of us in the Senate as well as to the American people."

After getting past the gatekeeper incident on the first day, I went about setting up my office in the Hart building.

I was in the process of trying to get situated, when a matter arose that would have never occurred to me. It had to do with the volume of mail coming my way. As the first Black woman in the Senate, it became immediately clear that my constituency went beyond Illinois. I had so much mail that it required a special room in the basement of the Capitol to store these huge fifty-pound postal sacks; they were as tall as I am. They were filled with cards, letters, photos, artwork from schoolchildren, postcards, and invitations.

The unfortunate thing is, I didn't have adequate staff to help me go through it all and answer everyone. I started to miss correspondence from the good people of Illinois, and from people beyond my home state. Some were VIPs. For instance, Harry Belafonte, the Hollywood actor, singer, and activist, wanted to sit down with me. Apparently, he'd sent a message that never reached me. I was mortified to think that a great entertainer and humanitarian of his stature was left wondering why I did not respond.

Another time, a prominent African American pastor invited me to attend Sunday worship services at his church. The church elders and congregation were expecting me to speak as a pioneering senator.

I was truly honored, but the wires had gotten crossed. If you know anything at all about Black churches, there was surely a gospel choir and a delicious feast. Not showing up was a major breach of decorum. I apologized profusely and truly hoped they would charge it to my head, as they say, and not my heart.

I went to the Senate leadership and asked for some additional staff to help me get through the mail. I did not get much sympathy. One of the leaders, who shall remain nameless, said to me, "Ted Kennedy and John Glenn were celebrities when they got here and they handled it." The basic attitude was, "Get over yourself and figure out a way to work through this." Well, what was I supposed to do? There was no equivalency between me and a famous astronaut, or a Kennedy for heaven's sake. I was a Black girl from the South Side of Chicago who had been thrust into the spotlight.

I was getting mail from Illinois, across America, and even from around the world. While the correspondence came from people of all stripes, Black Americans took special pride in me. In the minds of many, I was their senator. To this day, I get requests from Black folks who not only don't reside in Illinois, but who seem to forget that I haven't been in the Senate for decades. I certainly do not mind. I consider it a compliment and try my best to be of assistance, if and when possible.

But back then, dealing with fan mail was easier said than done. I was still finalizing my staffing and trying to find the right people. And frankly, I got some criticism because I was holding on to some former employees of my Senate predecessor, Alan Dixon.

I wasn't going to do a complete staff reset coming in. So, I kept some of the Dixon team. I felt retention of former staff made sense in terms of continuity, and it saved their jobs. But I got raked over the coals for that, too. The feedback was "Oh, she's too lazy to find her own people or train new staffers." Ironically, I'd been criticized during my Senate campaign for having a revolving door of staff. Go figure!

Meanwhile, I was feeling all kinds of additional pressures back home. The press was still hounding me about controversies that predated my Senate arrival.

Questions were still flying about my campaign and fiancé. During our relationship, we'd made a pact that Kgosie would not be involved in any way with my Senate duties. In fact, he never once stepped foot in my office on The Hill. Nonetheless, the endless curiosity about us continued. Amid all of this, I was a working mother whose teenage son was in a different time zone. After fourteen-hour days in the Senate, I put on another hat as Mom. I was devoted to my only child.

I would rise very early, and call Matthew before school. Just hearing his voice delighted me.

In the evening, once I got home from the Senate, we talked for hours. In those days before email was commonplace, he would fax his homework to me and I'd review it. On weekends, I often flew home to Chicago to see him, before catching a red-eye back to Washington, DC.

Long-distance parenting had its challenges.

When I first came to Congress, I rented an apartment large enough for us both, because I expected Matt to relocate and attend school in the District.

Somewhere along the way, he reversed course and opted to remain in Chicago. Now, this was a youngster who frequently complained about how much he hated his prep school. There'd been one gripe after another until it came time to leave. I thought Matt didn't want to stay in Chicago. I was taken aback when he told me, "Mom, I don't want to go anywhere. All of my friends are here."

I was sad but we decided that Matt would remain in town with his father. My ex-husband has always been a wonderful dad. Michael had a new family, so we agreed that Matt would stay with them during the week.

Then I'd fly back home on weekends, and we'd kind of trade off, with our son moving between our two respective homes. That was the deal.

In the aftermath of the election, my address was in flux as I house hunted in Chicago. I finally found a place, but between my Senate duties in DC and Illinois, had yet to officially move in.

Unbeknownst to me, my highly intelligent and very independent son had somehow established residence first. One day, I called my ex from Washington, expecting our son to be home with his father. Instead, Michael told me that Matthew was at my place. I was puzzled. "My place? I haven't moved in to my place."

"Well, he said he was going to go back to Hyde Park to spend the night with his friend Andy, but he could be reached at your place," Michael told me.

"What?!" I hung up and dialed Andy's mother. She said the boys were at Sean's house.

Sean's mother said they were at Andy's.

At this point, I was worried sick, and needed to ensure that Matt was safe. I immediately booked a flight from DC and flew back to Chicago. After we landed, I hurriedly made my way to our new home. Sure enough, a bunch of teenage boys were sprawled out with their sleeping bags, eating pizza and having a ball without any adult supervision.

While I was none-too-pleased that my son had played me and his father for fools, I was relieved. The episode hastened my plans to retrieve my furniture and household items from storage and establish stability for us.

Matt, always a good boy who had navigated divorce and my public life with aplomb, had made his feelings clear. He stayed in Chicago and lived with me and his dad part-time. It was an unorthodox arrangement for sure.

Being a US senator was one thing, and I took that role seriously. However, my most important job was to be a good mother. Some days, I wondered if I was getting either one right.

A senator's typical day is lengthy and jam-packed with activity. My schedule was an intense whirligig. Committee meetings. Town halls and community meetings back home. Voting on bills. Ribbon cuttings and ceremonial events. Making speeches. The list was endless.

Top of mind for me was constituent service and introducing legislation that would benefit Illinois residents and all Americans.

Alongside Senator Paul Simon, with whom I worked extremely well, our staffs set up regular meet and greets and welcomed people from our home state. We set aside certain days and anyone who wanted to come to Capitol Hill and talk with us could do so. I loved it. We met folks from every walk of life. Our trusty aides would be there with pen and paper, taking notes and following up on whatever the needs were.

My mornings and afternoons were largely dedicated to committee meetings and office hours, with votes often taking place in the evening. I sometimes joked that senators kept vampire hours.

Early on, I served on the Judiciary Committee, and was one of its first women members.

After I got elected, Joe Biden came to Chicago to congratulate me and talk about committee assignments.

He actually called me unexpectedly from O'Hare airport and said, "Can I stop by and see you?" Now, in my mind I was thinking the timing was not ideal because I had just moved in to a new place. I was unpacking boxes. I had on blue jeans. And I said, "Well, you know, I'm not really in any shape to receive visitors." He replied, "Oh, no need for you to go to any trouble. I'll just come on by and I won't take more than ten minutes of your time."

He was very nice, so I finally said okay. When the senator arrived, I warmly welcomed him. I had dashed downstairs to the grocery store in my condo building and bought a frozen cherry pie. I threw that in the oven and made a pot of coffee. So we sat there on the boxes eating cherry pie and talking at length. A friendship was born.

Joe explained that the reason for his visit was that he wanted me to be on the powerful Senate Judiciary Committee. At the time he was the chairman. I had zero interest. A bunch of lawyers debating how many angels could dance on the head of a pin? No thanks.

So my response to him, kinda tongue in cheek, was, "You just want Anita Hill on the other side of the table." And while I thought my joke was hilarious, I could tell he didn't think it was funny at all. He politely persisted, saying my perspective was needed. And while I didn't decide right on the spot, I later accepted the offer. It was the right decision.

Dianne was another trailblazer on Judiciary. Thus, the Senate went from a situation of having no women at all on the committee during the Thomas hearings, to having us, and the numbers would continue to rise.

I also served on the Small Business Committee and the Bipartisan Commission on Entitlements and Tax Reform. Later, I became the first and only woman at the time to serve on the powerful Senate Finance Committee. The backstory is that Senator Tom Daschle of South Dakota was vying to become Senate Minority Leader. I'd backed him over another senator, and he gave me his coveted seat on the panel. I was also a member of the Banking, Housing and Urban Affairs Committee, and the Special Committee on Aging.

I worked diligently to establish myself as an effective legislator right out of the gate. During my tenure, I introduced nearly one hundred fifty individual bills, resolutions, and amendments. I also co-sponsored hundreds of bills in tandem with Senate colleagues and the administration. The list of bills I sponsored and passed is long and extensive, and it is matched by a comparable list of the actual funding of Illinois projects I fought for and delivered.

As a member of the Senate Finance Committee, I participated in crafting tax policy that restored the interest deduction on college loans, and that gave ethanol (corn-based alcohol fuel), which is an Illinois agricultural and energy product, a market boost.

As a longtime champion for women, I helped widows receive

pension benefits via legislation that made those laws simpler and more equitable for women. I said at the time, "Unmarried, widowed, and divorced women are particularly apt to be living in poverty," during their retirement years, during their retirement years data showed. The legislation, which had the support of labor secretary Robert Reich, was designed to simplify consent forms, help women access spousal pension benefits, and ensure broad financial protections.

I also advocated for federal procurement contracts to benefit small, women-owned businesses.

Another women-centric bill of mine involved lupus, an autoimmune disease that disproportionately affects women of color. In 1995, I introduced legislation on behalf of myself and Senators Simon and Inouye, later co-sponsored by Senator Mikulski. It sought to amend the Public Health Service Act to increase research and funding at the National Institutes of Health around lupus. Three years later, Utah senator Bob Bennett (one of my favorites on the Republican side of the aisle) and Senator Richard Shelby of Alabama joined me in successfully passing the legislation. I will never forget seeing a young woman wearing a T-shirt about the fight to cure lupus. I believe we raised awareness and helped to save lives.

I worked on measures that encouraged retirement saving, and that expanded opportunity for the poorest citizens to receive the Earned Income Tax Credit.

I was the sponsor of the important brownfields tax law, which assists environmental remediation and cleanup and encourages economic development via additional empowerment zones in Illinois and communities nationwide.

I played a role in passage of the Child Support Orders Act, legislation to require noncustodial parents to continue paying child support when they move out of state.

I pushed for the military to enact procedures for handling racial and sexual harassment cases. I introduced a measure to protect the retirement plans of local and state firefighters and law enforcement officers.

I sponsored a bill to provide health care to low income individuals, and pushed for measures to protect children from abuse.

As a member of the Banking Committee, I sponsored the creation of the dollar coin, which honored Native American explorer Sacagawea. I co-sponsored a bill from New York senator Alfonse D'Amato called the Jackie Robinson Commemorative Coin Act, which honored the legendary player who broke the color barrier in Major League Baseball.

I worked to fix what are known as unfunded mandates. When the federal government enacts sweeping, often game-changing measures (e.g., the Clean Air Act), local, state, and tribal governments must adhere to these standards. But officials in various jurisdictions, including my state, were saying they often lacked the funds in their coffers to fully enact the provisions. My bill called for cost-benefit analyses and more. It took a while, but my legislation became the basis of a larger unfunded mandates bill that became law in 1995.

Via a series of different resolutions, I officially addressed the rise of church burnings happening at that time in the South. I formally congratulated the Chicago Bulls on championships. I put on the record the need to restore democracy in Haiti.

I am proud to say that as a senator, I provided national leadership in education, and started an important debate about repairing and renovating our nation's elementary and secondary schools. My team believes we coined the term "crumbling schools" to illustrate the urgency for upgrades, especially in underprivileged communities. My Senate office also coordinated what was known as Project Synergy, a public/private partnership that gave Chicago students an opportunity to access computers and software donated by local companies.

I pushed for the promotion of men and women's athletic programs at institutions of higher learning. I pushed for more funding to preserve buildings and structures at our nation's Historically Black Colleges and Universities (HBCUs).

As a member of the Judiciary Committee, I brought about authorization for the National Park Service to preserve historic Underground Railroad sites around the country. There's a photo of me and colleagues in President Clinton's office when he signed the measure into law.

I was attuned to the issues of the day, as was my staff. One moment, we might be working on nuts-and-bolts stuff such as securing money for roads and reauthorization of transportation funding. The next day, we might be tackling the Disadvantaged Business Enterprise (DBE) rules to help women, African American, Hispanic, and Asian American business owners in Illinois and around the country.

I fought hard for every piece of legislation that my staff and I introduced. The stratagems of the Senate involved going around and talking to people. You try to convince them of the soundness of your position, you listen to their perspective. You communicate why it would be a good thing for them and no downside for them signing on.

I tried to work not only with Democrats, but across the aisle. And in those days, bipartisanship was more common.

I was grateful anytime we scored a legislative victory. There is tremendous satisfaction in walking into the White House, being ushered into the Oval Office, and witnessing the president of the United States sign one of your bills into law. On days like that, it felt as if I was making a difference.

There were also disappointments. Times when my staff and I sponsored bills that I thought would benefit our state and country, only to receive little or absolutely no support.

I recall introducing a measure that would temporarily suspend the tariff (a tax levied on goods, etc.) on HIV antiviral drugs. I had zero co-sponsors. During one legislative session, I introduced two economic bills related to agricultural products, which would have benefitted my state and farmers nationwide. I had one co-sponsor for each.

Or, we'd toil away on a legislative initiative only to see someone else take the credit for it.

Meanwhile, the unwritten rules of the Senate still tripped me up from time to time.

There's a gym which the women in Congress integrated in the '80s. I had messed up my knee working out, which to be honest, is not really my thing. Every time I get the urge to exercise, I lie down until the feeling passes.

I went to the hospital, and the doctors wrapped my knee up, and gave me a cane to temporarily get around. I came onto the Senate floor for a vote.

And when I did so, a senator who was usually very nice to me stood up and objected to my being on the floor.

I didn't know what was going on. I'm standing there like, "What?" So then another senator asked that the rule be waived. I'm standing there. The two men are having this conversation. I had no idea, no clue what was happening. Then, one of my colleagues comes up and he's laughing, and says, "Oh, you just violated a rule that comes from the Civil War era."

And it turned out that circa 1856, a House member had come over to the Senate and beat a senator half to death with a cane. Subsequently, canes were banned on the Senate floor.

Thus, when I came on the Senate floor with this cane, even though I needed it to walk, I had violated an unwritten rule. The epilogue to that story is that one of the senators who was involved stopped me later.

He offered me, shall we say, a natural remedy for my knee. And he says, "I'm the local bootlegger for this. It may help you." I laughed. And I have to tell you, it actually did.

CAROL VS. THE CONFEDERACY

"Oh, I wish I was in the land of cotton…"

I had just stepped onto the private elevator in the Capitol building, a perk available only to senators. Suddenly, I heard someone singing the unmistakable verse from "Dixie"—the unofficial anthem of the Confederacy during the Civil War. The sound was not very loud, yet it pierced my ears with the intensity of a dog whistle. Indeed, that is what it was in a sense. I stood there, in stunned disbelief, my emotions bubbling up slowly, rising from my core.

Now, some might think that hearing someone hum a tune is no reason to get upset. But "Dixie" is no ordinary song. And hearing it in the building where we US senators perform our jobs for the American people who elected us, jolted me. Written in 1859, the minstrel tune romanticizes the antebellum South and mocks the horrific realities of the institution of slavery. While there are multiple versions of the song, including reworked verses that some historians say actually championed the Union, the most popular versions were decidedly pro-Confederacy.

I wish I was in Dixie
Hooray, hooray!
In Dixie's land, I'll take my stand to live and die in Dixie!
Away, away, away down South in Dixie!
Away, away, away down South in Dixie!

It was a relatively tight space, so I could see clearly that the
crooning was coming straight from the mouth of Jesse Helms,
a Republican and one of the most powerful men in the Senate
at the time. The gentleman from North Carolina was looking
over his spectacles straight at me, the only Black member of the
Senate. He grinned and continued singing in a loud, clear voice.
"Oh, I wish I was in the land of cotton…"
Senator Helms glanced at one of his friends, a fellow senator,
and boasted, "I'm going to make her cry. I'm going to sing 'Dixie'
until she cries." I could not believe my ears. I couldn't believe
a member of the Senate was singing such a blatantly offensive
song in my presence, and bragging that he'd sing until I cried.
But clearly, the good senator had never tangled with a Black
woman raised on the South Side of Chicago. I was accustomed
to bullies, racism, and men trying to wield their power over me.
"Senator Helms," I said calmly, "your singing would make
me cry even if you sang 'Rock of Ages.'" The elevator went silent, but someone snickered at my witty comeback.
Meanwhile, Helms glared at me and said nothing. I reached
my floor and exited the elevator, fuming. Later, he would dispute this, and offer his own version of the way things transpired
that day.
His off-key crooning of "Dixie" was not accidental or happenstance. A few weeks earlier, I had crossed swords with Senator Helms about his legislative attempt to renew a long-standing
patent related to the Confederate flag insignia.
The morning in question had started ordinarily enough. My
legislative duties began with a committee meeting in the Can-
non building. I was listening to Utah senator Orrin Hatch, one

of the "Old Bulls" who had been courtly and considerate to me as a colleague.

He was talking about a bill that involved reproductive freedoms for women and the controversial issue of "choice." Senator Hatch, a staunch conservative, had compared abortion to slavery, a talking point frequently used by the right wing at the time. I was horrified and outraged by such a comparison—both as a woman and a Black person descended from enslaved ancestors. I told him so, in no uncertain terms.

We were debating back and forth, when suddenly my chief counsel, Geoff Gibbs, hurried into the room and motioned that he needed to speak with me. I was reluctant to step away. I was three rounds in with Senator Hatch and not eager to give up, but my trusted aide—one of the few Black male staffers in Congress in those days—looked concerned. He whispered that something major was going on over on the Senate floor. "You need to get over to the Capitol ASAP!" he said.

I gathered my things and hurried toward the Capitol building, using the underground tunnel system that feeds directly to the intricate maze of offices on The Hill. Even with miniature trams zipping riders around, it is not a short walk to get from building to building, especially in high heels. When I arrived, slightly out of breath, I beelined for the chamber. I pushed the doors open and rushed to my desk. I heard my colleagues debating an omnibus bill called the National and Community Service Act. The measure itself was not controversial, per se, because it mostly dealt with national service and educational awards. Yet lawmakers routinely slip all sorts of amendments and changes into bills of this kind. It may be "pork" or funds to help their district, or something more controversial that they hope to sneak in under the wire. And what my staffer had warned me about was one such addition: an amendment having to do with the Confederate flag was being tucked into this seemingly routine measure.

Specifically, the amendment sought to renew a patent, sought by the United Daughters of the Confederacy (UDC), established in 1894 by wives, widows, and daughters of the soldiers who fought against the Union for the South during the Civil War. Their insignia featured the first national flag of the Confederacy.

The first congressional patent for this specific insignia was granted way back in 1898. These sorts of patents, which are not uncommon and have previously been granted to patriotic institutions such as the Ladies of the Grand Army of the Republic, expire after fourteen years, and must be renewed. Throughout the twentieth century, the UDC never had any trouble obtaining approval for their insignia's renewal. Apparently, no one questioned renewing an insignia that proudly bore the Confederate flag, despite the fact that the Civil War was long over, and the South had lost.

In 1992, the year I was elected, a renewal effort had been considered in the Judiciary Committee and passed by the Senate. However, Congress adjourned before it could be officially voted on. In 1993, when I was sworn into office, the issue remained unresolved. The matter reared its ugly head again when South Carolina's legendary senator Strom Thurmond resurrected the patent issue in the Judiciary Committee. I suppose he expected it to pass easily.

Why should he think otherwise? The UDC patent renewal had been approved routinely by a chamber of mostly white men. Yet the composition of Congress was no longer the same and there was new blood, namely, more women in the mix. I was a freshman senator, but I sat on the powerful Judiciary Committee, having been asked by then–Committee chairman, Joe Biden.

As the first Black woman in the Senate, and the first Black woman seated on Judiciary, I wasn't about to let this measure pass again. At least not without a fight. If the UDC wanted to use its symbols to celebrate their "heritage" as was often claimed, that was their business.

However, an official nod from the United States Congress, allowing the use of a Confederate flag symbol in public, was a step too far for me.

"I'm not voting for that," I made clear to my colleagues when the Senate Judiciary Committee met on May 6, 1993, to discuss the measure. Our meetings were held behind closed doors, where senators could, ostensibly, speak freely about the issues.

"Those of us whose ancestors fought on a different side of the conflict or were held as human chattel under the flag of the Confederacy have no choice but to honor our ancestors by asking whether such action is appropriate," I said. Indeed, this issue went way beyond the Confederate flag itself. It touched the meaning of the flag, and how for millions of Americans whose ancestors were enslaved, it represented hatred not heritage.

After raising my concerns, the Judiciary Committee voted twelve to three against renewal. I was proud of my colleagues, and thought the matter was settled. I was proven wrong.

A few months later, on July 22, Senator Helms appeared on the floor of the Senate, seeking approval of an amendment that would renew the UDC patent. He'd taken up the fight where Strom Thurmond had left off in the Judiciary Committee. I was livid not only that the senators supporting this measure had revived this matter, but that they had slyly waited to do so until the chamber was mostly empty. But I was here now, and ready once again to go to the mat to explain why the Confederate flag was problematic and offensive. It launched the fight anew, and just as during the Civil War, battle lines were drawn.

"Mr. President," Helms said, addressing the Senate president pro tempore, "the pending amendment, co-sponsored by Senators Lott, Faircloth, Coverdell, and Cochran has to do with an action taken by the Senate Judiciary Committee...that the distinguished senators on that committee did not intend.

"The action was, I am sure, an unintended rebuke unfairly aimed at about 24,000 ladies who belong to the United Daughters of the Confederacy, most of them elderly, all of them gentle souls." He went on to espouse the "many, many" charitable actions of the UDC—from aiding veterans to feeding the homeless and awarding youth scholarships.

For almost a century, he continued, "Congress has granted patent protection for the identifying insignia and badges of various patriotic organizations," including the UDC. Renewing the patent was not an effort "to refight battles long since lost, but to preserve the memory of courageous men who fought and died for the cause they believed in.

"...I emphasize that most of the ladies now live in a few remaining rest homes established decades ago. Scores of these homes once dotted the landscape of the South, which I love," said Helms. "But as the numbers of the children of the Confederacy have dwindled with each passing year, the homes and the memories have all but disappeared. The last living Confederate veteran died in 1959," he noted. "In a short time, he will be joined by the last true daughters of the Confederacy and we will be left with nothing but fading recollections of these proud and gallant women."

Only a handful of senators were present. I believe it was no accident that yours truly was there in that moment. Listening to my colleague's revisionist history, I could not let his diatribe pass without a response.

I immediately sought recognition from the presiding officer to take the floor, as was protocol, and began addressing my colleagues. "I would like to respond to this amendment and to suggest that it is absolutely ill-founded and to oppose the amendment.

"I submit to you...as I did in the Judiciary Committee, that the United Daughters of the Confederacy have every right to honor their ancestors...however, those of us whose ancestors fought on a different side in the Civil War, or who were held, frankly, as human chattel under the Confederate flag, are duty bound to honor our ancestors as well as by asking whether such recognition by the United States Senate is appropriate.

"Whether we are black or white, Northerners or Southerners, all Americans share a common history and flag—the flag, the Stars and Stripes Forever is our flag—that is our flag."

I explained how giving the symbol of the Confederacy a patent sends a powerful message about history, and whose stories have value over others. "To give a design patent—" a rare honor "—that even our own flag does not enjoy, to a symbol of the

Confederacy seems to me just to create the kind of divisions in our society that are counterproductive."

I added that "symbols are important. They speak volumes. They speak volumes to the people in our country. They speak volumes to the people outside our country who follow and who care about what happens in this, the greatest nation in the world."

I further reminded my colleagues that given the debates and arguments that have raged since the Civil War, it was time for our country to get beyond the "separateness" and "divisions" and "fanning the flames of racial antagonism."

Following my speech, I introduced a motion to table the Helms amendment, which would have essentially blocked its passage.

The chamber was still mostly empty at this point, although as a vote was called on my motion, my colleagues began filtering in, largely unaware of what had just transpired. I sat anxiously, waiting for the votes to be called. Seeing as how we Democrats were in the majority, if everyone voted along party lines, it should have been successful. However, Southern loyalties run deep, and the majority of the Southern bloc of senators, both Republican and Democrat, supported Senator Helms. The final tally was forty-eight to fifty-two. My motion to table the amendment did not pass.

I was stunned. That said, I was not about to give up. I am the daughter of a World War II veteran. The granddaughter of a World War I veteran. Moreover, I am a descendant of a formerly enslaved Virginia man who fought for the Union as a member of the US Colored Troops during the Civil War. This issue was far bigger than the UDC. My issue was with an insignia related to the Confederate flag, a symbol of oppression.

To me, this was also about democracy. It was about shaking off the yoke of the Civil War and laying to rest arguments and debates that have been entertained ever since. It was about healing the divisions in our nation and showing empathy for all of America's people.

That's when I decided I was not going to give up the floor. This freshman senator was prepared to filibuster. Again, I sought recognition to speak. As I stood up a second time, my voice became louder and more urgent. "I have to tell you this is about race," I told my fellow senators. "It is about racial symbols...and the single most painful episode in American history."

I had not arrived for work that day anticipating that America's racial history would fall upon my shoulders. But this was an important battle, and one I was prepared to wage. History belongs to each of us, and while Senator Helms and Senator Thurmond saw their history as Southerners through a different lens, I have to believe they understood that the Confederate flag represented an agonizing chapter in our country's journey.

I could not allow history's truth to be co-opted. For Black Americans whose ancestors, including my own, were removed from Africa against their will, ripped from family, transported across the ocean in chains, and once here, sold, whipped, raped, and dehumanized beyond comprehension—the Confederate flag is a reminder of the pain.

During my filibuster, I tried to block any forward movement until we addressed the issue.

Since most of my colleagues had been out of the chamber during my first oration, I realized that I had to explain the context of my protest, and why the vote was worth reconsideration. While some of them might not have considered this amendment worth me taking a stand, I made my intentions clear. "If I have to stand here until this room freezes over, I am not going to see this amendment put on this legislation."

As I continued, reiterating my arguments with renewed passion, I noticed a change in the chamber. Senators began to buzz and talk among themselves in hushed tones. Eventually, a few of my colleagues took to the floor, acknowledging their previous lack of understanding, and expressing regret for their earlier vote. I prayed that my words were getting through to my colleagues. The entire debate stretched to three hours, as several senators called for another vote. I looked out into their faces with cautious optimism, gaining more confidence as more voices rang out in support of my motion.

But I wasn't in the clear. Many Republicans were still against the motion, and the Southern Democrats weren't a lock either. I was anxious as Senator Howell Heflin of Alabama took the floor. A son of the Deep South, he was a prominent Democrat with conservative views who had previously voted for the patent renewal. When he spoke, I braced myself. Instead, I was surprised by his wisdom and sensitivity.

Senator Heflin acknowledged his family background, which was deeply embedded in the Confederacy, but he also recognized that this was, at its core, an issue of symbolism. The UDC had performed good works, he said, but times were changing. Said Senator Heflin, "We must get racism behind us, and we must move forward." To my shock, he supported a reconsideration of the motion.

While I might not have expected that response from Senator Heflin, his words touched me, and reminded me of the evolving nature of democracy toward a common good. With Heflin leading the way, other colleagues followed. Senator Robert Bennett of Utah introduced a motion to reconsider. I was on pins and needles the entire time, nervous energy coursing through my body as they read out the names. When the roll call ended, to my surprise and great relief, seventy-six senators supported me.

To say that I was elated is an understatement. I had managed to convince dozens of senators, including ten from onetime Confederate states, to change their respective votes. It was a triumph not only in the sense of blocking the patent renewal, but for the democratic process, and of the good that can come from honest, impassioned, and compassionate debate. It was one of those rare moments in the Senate when I actually felt that my peers were listening and respected me.

With the passage of that motion, my next move was to table the earlier amendment from Senator Helms. My amendment came before the body and passed by a vote of seventy-five to twenty-five. This was monumental. The US Senate would not be renewing the confederate insignia.

I thanked my colleagues, "for having the heart, having the

intellect, having the mind and the will to turn around what, in [my] mind, would have been a tragic mistake." That day, I spoke for my constituents in Illinois. I spoke for Black Americans. I spoke for my ancestors. I spoke for all Americans who dream of a more perfect union.

Today, decades after my fight on the Senate floor, I pray that symbols don't divide us. I pray for goodwill across this land. Let us remember that each and every day we have a choice: to reject hate and embrace peace. To lift each other up, no matter our differences. To celebrate all that is beautiful about our country. I pray that we find ways to come together, understanding how truly fortunate we are, and respecting our nation's official motto: "E pluribus unum," which means "out of many, one."

COURTING CONTROVERSY

"Mom, guess what I found? Take a look!"

My teenage son could barely contain his enthusiasm. "It's a ring!"

We were cruising at an altitude somewhere around thirty thousand feet. I was reclining in my seat but sat up and glanced down at Matt's hand. I gasped. He held in his outstretched palm an emerald sparkler. The gleaming green gem was huge; it looked to be at least five carats. "I wonder who it belongs to," he said breathlessly. "Whoever it is, they must be rich!"

Indeed. We were aboard the Concorde, the exclusive supersonic airliner renowned for flying faster than the speed of sound.

On any given day, its flight manifest might have CEOs to celebrities and even royals. Passengers could sip champagne, nibble on caviar, and arrive at their transcontinental destinations in record time. It gave new meaning to jet-setting.

I buzzed for a flight attendant, and one appeared almost instantaneously. "My son found a ring in the bathroom," I told her. "I'm not sure if you have a lost and found. But we're turning it in."

As Matt gently placed the ring in her hand, she thanked us and proceeded down the aisle. I was proud of my son. I'd raised him to be honest, and always tried to model good behavior. Some kids might have slipped that ring into their pocket. But not my boy.

When we landed, word filtered back about the precious jewel. We heard the rock belonged to Liza Minnelli, the fabulous Broadway star and daughter of Hollywood legend Judy Garland and director Vincente Minnelli. We felt good knowing that the gorgeous ring was (hopefully) with its rightful owner.

My first time on the Concorde had been quite memorable. I was flying back home after a nearly month-long vacation in Africa, taken with my son and campaign manager turned fiancé, Kgosie. Yes, we'd quietly gotten engaged. I was wearing a ring myself, although perhaps not quite as impressive as the emerald Matt found on the plane.

That December, we journeyed to the African continent. Our itinerary included stops in several countries, including Kgosie's homeland, South Africa. His large tight-knit family wanted to meet me ahead of any future nuptials.

We also touched down in Nigeria, where Kgosie connected with an old friend. At the time, I had no knowledge of who he was beyond a simple introduction. They caught up over lunch and we were on our way. In Botswana, we embarked on a safari with the most stunning vistas, landscapes, and exotic animals. The entire odyssey was one filled with natural wonders. But that's not why the trip is etched in my mind. The fallout from our expedition practically derailed my Senate career before it got started.

Days after November's general election, Senate orientation was held for incoming freshmen on Capitol Hill.

I flew in from Chicago, along with senators-elect from states across the country. I was particularly excited to see my fellow trailblazers elected in "The Year of the Woman," namely, Dianne Feinstein and Barbara Boxer, both of California, and Patty Murray of Washington state. Another trailblazer in our class was the nation's first Native American senator, Ben Nighthorse Campbell of Colorado. We became fast friends.

Vice President–elect Al Gore, fresh off a massive electoral win, and congressional leadership welcomed us. Senate majority leader George Mitchell, was asked by reporters about the diversity of the incoming cohort.

"Well, first of course, it will make the Senate more representative of the nation as a whole," said Mitchell. "I believe that's a good and healthy thing."

Our two-day congressional introduction was a primer on everything from setting up one's office to filing a bill. We heard from caucus leaders, and attended breakout sessions. We also received a tour of the magnificent Capitol.

We took a trip seemingly through time in the Old Senate chamber, located in an older wing north of the Rotunda. Benjamin Henry Latrobe, a native of England who'd migrated to the new United States, became the country's first architect of the Capitol.

He modeled the semicircular chamber, complete with a covered half dome and marble columns, after structures he'd seen in Paris that were inspired by Roman amphitheaters.

Crimson and gold decor, a gilded eagle, and historic paintings filled the ornate space. Senator's desks and chairs were crafted of mahogany by a New York cabinetmaker.

We each took seats that once belonged to senators from our home states. Mine was that of Illinois senator Stephen A. Douglas, elected in 1847. A prominent yet controversial figure, he was perhaps known for a series of debates with then–Senate candidate Abraham Lincoln around the issue of slavery that captivated the nation. Douglas subsequently ran for president, losing to his longtime rival, but rallied behind Lincoln and supported the Union.

More than a century later, the nation's first Black woman

senator was sitting in Douglas's chair. Once again, I was struck by the gravity of my new role and the onward march of history.

After my trip to Washington, DC, I floated around in a deliriously happy haze. I spent several days making calls and saying "thank you" to staffers, volunteers, donors, and the good voters of Illinois. Most of all, I was thankful to the Good Lord for enabling victory.

Winning the race for Senate was one of the greatest days of my life. Other than giving birth to my precious son, nothing topped it.

Yet the topsy-turvy campaign season depleted me physically and emotionally. There'd been months of marathon campaigning and more melodrama than expected leading up to the general election.

A barrage of attack ads. The controversy around Mother's nursing home and Medicaid liability. Relentless media coverage that became increasingly mean-spirited. I recall one editorial cartoon that showed my opponent standing in the muck with the words, "Look at what I have on Carol Moseley Braun!" In another illustration was a caricature of me as a puppet with a man's hand up my dress, an apparent dig at my campaign manager turned beau. One blatantly racist sketch depicted me as a monkey in a tree.

Meanwhile, we discovered that people were even going through my trash.

Winning was one thing. Shaking off the residue of a dirty campaign season was another.

Thus, the vacation to Africa. It was my first time visiting the motherland, as well as Kgosie's homeland. The bonus was getting some much-needed R & R before fully diving into my Senate role.

Rather naively, I failed to realize that when we returned, I'd be subjected to a fresh round of questions about my campaign, personal, and professional life.

I'd sold my home and used the proceeds to move in to a new condo on Chicago's lakefront. It was a penthouse, with sweeping views. I selected the building because of its security features. The rent was a tad pricey but I'd budgeted accordingly. Unfortunately, even though I was a professional working woman earning a good salary, my move elicited all kinds of questions about how I could afford it.

Around that time, I'd also traded in my older model Lincoln and bought a Jeep, a vehicle that seemed more practical given the Windy City's winters. This too, became a big deal.

Eager to look my best in Congress, I'd gone shopping for a new wardrobe—including a few designer pieces and jewelry. The blowback was swift. But the truth is, it was my own hard-earned money!

I tried to make sense of why some people seemed fixated on my lifestyle. Yes, I was a public official, and certainly I should be held to a high standard. That said, not every single detail of my private life needed to be fodder. I was entitled to do normal things and periodically treat myself, without the suggestion hanging over my head that I was somehow doing something untoward, or even illegal, while simply living my life.

But I learned, belatedly, that anyone in the public eye, especially, must think through decisions carefully. Rumors, innuendo, and allegations can destroy people's lives. There were reports about me in the media with sensitive information that clearly had been leaked. I have to wonder who exactly was gunning for me.

In terms of public perception, I realize now that many people simply did not have a reference point for someone like myself and even fewer for a man with my boyfriend's background. The criticisms struck me as "A Black woman comes into this position and she is not entitled to anything fancy. She ought to be more humble and not get too big for her britches."

The truth is, I really hadn't changed my lifestyle all that much. I had a middle-class upbringing. My parents owned our house, we had cars, and food on the table. We had nice clothing and went on vacations every summer. We had parties that drew musicians, artists, and intellectuals of all races and backgrounds.

My father's issues and the divorce my mother wisely sought to escape domestic violence sent us into a downward economic spiral. Yet, that does not negate my upbringing, and what my parents were able to attain in better times. And, what I have been blessed to accomplish through education and hard work.

My travel, housing, and fashion choices would lead to false allegations of campaign finance irregularities. The claim was that I'd diverted several hundred thousand dollars in campaign funds and used these donations for personal use. The Federal Election Commission launched an audit. Later, the Internal Revenue Service sought to impanel a grand jury about the possibility of tax crimes. This request was denied (more than once) by the Justice Department. And, for good reason: I'm no tax cheat.

The whole notion that I would plunder my own campaign was extremely upsetting to me. It is anathema to my upbringing and moral values.

Dipping into the till? No. I'm a former federal prosecutor whose caseload encompassed white-collar crime. I know better than to try some shenanigans. I've had multiple campaigns and have never misappropriated the monies for personal use. The very thought is insulting, actually, because it suggests that merely having access to that much money makes one dishonest.

And in spite of all the noise around these matters, after an audit by the FEC, no noncompliance was found, nor was any enforcement action taken. Bottom line: the money was accounted for. There may have been less-than-perfect record-keeping, but the issues raised were resolved. The money was not misused.

I think that's why they did not level a fine after combing through reams of documents. It took them about four years to find nothing damning.

I was never fined, sanctioned, or censured in any way by the FEC, IRS, DOJ, or any other government agency. Ever.

That was the good news. But my love affair was causing me grief. Mixing romance and professional endeavors had become a hornet's nest.

When we visited Nigeria, I'd unwittingly been brought into the orbit of General Sani Abacha. He's now deceased but was leading the country at the time and had been accused of human rights abuses. My first visit caused an uproar. I would later return to the country twice more, including for the funeral of Abacha's son, Kgosie's friend, who had been killed. It spiraled into another morass of regrettable decisions that haunted me.

In retrospect, I should not have accompanied my beau on these visits, especially as a senator. My intentions, which are always centered around promoting the best of our country and its democratic principles, were misconstrued. The State Department did not ever reach out to me to protest any of this. But I realize it sent the wrong message.

That was not the only problem. Kgosie was accused of sexual harassment by two women working on the campaign, accusations which he vehemently denied. I'd been mailed an anonymous letter, and although the individuals never came forth publicly, the story was widely covered.

I had run for the Senate, in part, because of a core belief that women's voices should be heard—be it Anita Hill's, or in the halls of Congress. I was troubled that any woman, particularly on my team, would feel unsafe or had allegedly experienced treatment that was harmful, or, worse, unlawful.

When I confronted Kgosie, he insisted nothing inappropriate had occurred. He was furious about the media coverage and threatened to file a lawsuit. I hired an independent investigator to look into the accusations; they could not be substantiated. Nor did they ever lead to any charges or claims.

The damage, however, had been done—to him, to me, to both of us. Kgosie was someone whom I cared for deeply. I do not believe he deserved all the harsh criticisms that came his way while involved with me. That said, looking back on this period, was it prudent for me to begin dating my campaign manager? No. He was an employee on my payroll, and technically I was his boss. Legally and ethically, it was a minefield. I must confess that my heart overruled my head.

Being in politics opens one up to inspection of every single area of your life. It was not a piece of cake, that's for sure.

Someone once said to me, "Well, you had to expect that you'd be held up to a special kind of examination in your career."

I never objected to scrutiny. What I did object to was having to accede to the notion that it was okay to be held up to a different set of standards, seemingly in many cases because of my race and/or my gender. A lot of people suggested that I should have just kowtowed, tucked tail, and conceded that's just the way it is, and not get personally upset about it. That wasn't me.

Alternatively, the other option was fight back which (for better or worse), I have done for decades. In which case you often find that your resistance is further pissing your enemies off, and giving you more problems.

There are no perfect people. There are no perfect public servants. But as the Bible says in James 5:16, "Confess your faults one to another, and pray one for another, that ye may be healed."

REELECTION

At times during my Senate tenure, I felt a bit like Icarus, the figure in Greek mythology who flew too close to the sun and then plunged from the sky.

Winning a Senate seat and having the opportunity to serve the people of Illinois and America was a monumental high. Conversely, that period of my life brought earth-shattering lows.

My beautiful mother passed away during my first year in the Senate. She died of cancer at the age of seventy-one. Before her death, Mother's health had been in decline, so much so that she had been unable to travel to DC for my swearing in with the rest of the family. We missed her that day, but every lesson my mother had taught me up until that point helped to propel her firstborn into the pages of history books.

Mother was a hardworking, tenacious, and resilient woman. Her life had its share of hard knocks, but she sparkled and smiled and never complained.

However, I could tell the whole Medicaid flap during my Senate primary campaign weighed heavily upon her emotionally and physically. I believe it killed her. A friend said, "Oh, Carol, your mother was very sick."

Certainly, that's true. But at the same time, in my mind the episode hastened her demise.

What was essentially a personal family matter, morphed into a local and then national news story. Every time there was coverage, I noticed Mother's condition would worsen. If she was doing better, a new story on TV or in the newspapers would cause a relapse.

Various media outlets were camped out near the nursing home as if some major catastrophe had taken place. Around the same time, the military conflict Operation Desert Storm was in the headlines. It baffled me that the Medicaid debacle received as much or more attention locally than major global news about our brave troops.

Mother got sicker and sicker. One magazine did a lengthy profile about me—something I considered a scathing, searing, hatchet job. Although it was a national article, it trickled into the local news cycle.

One day, the nursing home called to say that Mother had suffered another heart attack, and had been transported by ambulance to the hospital. I was giving a speech that day, and rushed to her bedside. The entire family was worried sick about her. It turned out to be an anxiety attack. Praise God, the medical team was able to help her.

As an elected official, I realized that my personal life in the public eye was fair game. But there is something sinister about hounding and targeting someone's family. Not to mention a defenseless elderly woman. My loved ones were being ripped to shreds for something that was not their fault. All because mysterious forces—and I never learned who was behind everything—were out to get me.

Back on The Hill, the Senate's chaplain acknowledged my

loss as he recited the daily scripture. "As we pray, let us remember in silence the mother of Senator Moseley Braun."

We buried Mother on a cold winter morning, and truly it felt like winter in my heart.

I was not only grieving, but racked with guilt. The only thing I could take solace in was that Edna Davie Moseley knew and loved the Lord. Until it became difficult for her to get around after the amputation, my mother was a daily communicant who attended Mass every single day, and received holy communion. A devout Catholic, she worshiped the Father, Son, and Holy Spirit. She believed in Mary, the blessed Mother of Jesus Christ; his earthly father, Joseph; and all the loving angels and saints. I prayed that finally, her precious soul would be at peace in heaven, among the divine ancestors.

That season of my life produced more loss. My relationship with Kgosie was faltering. The engagement that had led me halfway around the world, and practically caused an international incident in the process, ended without a wedding.

In hindsight, going on vacation when I did was a huge mistake. Not that there was anything substantively wrong. There wasn't. I was worn out. I needed to get away. I had marriage on my mind. I wanted to go and meet my fiancé's family. But I indulged myself, when I should have been more cognizant of the fact that this was a window of opportunity. I should have used it to get my Senate plans mapped out, put a press team in place, get advisory committees set up, begin fundraising to pay off the campaign debt and so on. If I had taken advantage of that time frame between November and January and done all those things, who's to say how it might have impacted my Senate tenure and my political future? At any rate, it's wishful thinking now.

In terms of Kgosie, there'd been so much animus directed toward us. It overshadowed the happy times we'd shared. He had so many good qualities, chivalry among them, and was often my escort at the banquets, galas, and soirees that I was invited to as a senator in Chicago and beyond.

Back in 1993, I was honored at the Essence Awards, a splashy celebration in New York City that aired as a televised special on CBS.

Founded in the '70s, *Essence Magazine* has long been considered the preeminent publication for Black women.

Then-editor-in-chief, Susan L. Taylor, and her talented team made me a cover girl in October 1992 during my Senate campaign. For the generations of Black women and girls who have come up reading *Essence*, this award was a special honor.

When I entered the Paramount Theatre that evening, the venue was filled with a galaxy of stars and icons. At every turn were stunning sistas of all ages with stellar achievements.

Lena Horne. Rosa Parks. Aretha Franklin. Tina Turner. Olympic gold medalist Gail Devers. Community advocates. These ladies were my fellow honorees.

The show's co-hosts were the fabulous Patti LaBelle and actor/ activist Danny Glover. Gorgeous Halle Berry and Ann-Margret were among the Hollywood celebrities who appeared as presenters, while songstress Anita Baker and a roster of talented performers brought the house down.

I was thrilled when Ron Brown, our nation's secretary of commerce, presented my award. Dolled up in a flowy red ensemble with dangly earrings, I made my way onstage.

My remarks were brief. I thanked everyone involved for allowing me to be in such "illustrious" company. I stated my sincere belief that the Lord "had brought me to the Senate for a purpose." I closed by promising to "do the best I can to be a great US senator," and to "make all of you very proud of me."

When I glided back to my seat, Kgosie—who cut a dashing figure in his tux—was beaming. It was a magical night.

About a year later, we were on the road to splitsville. I wished him well. I harbored no bitterness for someone who transformed my campaign, helped me pave a path to victory, and in the process, captured my heart. Our relationship was akin to a fever dream. Given all the trouble our coupling seemed to cause, my head told me that perhaps breaking up was for the best.

Still, sadness enveloped me. Anyone who has ever loved and lost the object of their affection understands the ache of a broken heart.

But there was no time for me to sulk. I was committed to my role as a senator and moving forward. I threw myself into delivering for the good people of Illinois.

One of a senator's most solemn responsibilities is the duty to offer advice and consent on the nomination of a justice to the US Supreme Court. I was privileged in my freshman year to participate in that process.

In June of 1993, Ruth Bader Ginsburg was nominated by President Clinton to sit on the Supreme Court, replacing retiring justice Byron White.

After trailblazer Sandra Day O'Connor, this was only the second time in American history that a woman had appeared before the Senate Judiciary Committee as a Supreme Court nominee.

I was part of that momentous day. That July, I joined my fellow committee members for confirmation hearings. Dianne and I were the only women, and this was our first proceeding related to the High Court.

Two years ago, I'd watched the Senate confirmation hearings for Clarence Thomas on television from back home in Illinois with a sense of helplessness and exclusion. Now I was here representing the people of Illinois and part of American history.

I began my remarks paraphrasing a quote from India's first woman prime minister, Indira Gandhi. She once said that if you study history, you will find that where women have risen, that country attained a high position, and whenever they remained dormant, that country slipped back.

"Regrettably," I said, "history teaches us that many obstacles have been placed in the way of progress for women in this
country. Judge Ginsburg's own personal history, including being
rejected for employment by leading law firms and by the very
court to which she is nominated today, demonstrated vividly
the nature of gender discrimination..."

I looked at Ruth, and around the room, before continuing.

"This is the greatest country in the world, and I believe the
US Constitution to be the finest exposition of democratic principles ever written.

"I make these statements, Mr. Chairman, fully aware of the
fact that, in its original form, the Constitution included neither
this senator as an American of African descent, nor our distinguished nominee as a woman in its vision of a democratic society.

"But the greatness of the Constitution lies in the fact that it is
a living document. Or, as Dr. Martin Luther King Jr. once said,
a declaration of intent regarding America's unlimited potential,
a document that, through an often painful process of amendment and interpretation, has broadened its reach to extend to
the previously excluded its promise of equality and justice for all.

"Over the years, the Supreme Court played a glorious role in
that process. It was the justices of our Supreme Court in their
bold, independent, and faithful interpretations of our living Constitution, who outlawed racial segregation in our schools, guaranteed indigent criminal defendants the right to counsel, brought
wiretapping within the restrictions of the Fourth Amendment,
demanded freedom of speech, and recognized a woman's fundamental right to control her reproductive destiny.

"In some of the most difficult areas of our history, the Supreme Court has shown the courage to give life to the promise
of the Constitution. It seems to me that a central issue of our
time is whether that courage has been lost to timidity and partisan politics.

"It is troubling to me, Mr. Chairman, that the Court's general approach to constitutional interpretation—the willingness of some recent nominees to embrace the jurisprudence of so-called strict construction and original intent—all too often has resulted in a narrow reading of the Constitution that has curtailed, rather than expanded, individual rights and has left those who are not rich or powerful or privileged with fewer and fewer rights and less and less liberty. Regular working men and women, ordinary people, can no longer be sure that the Supreme Court will be their champion of last resort.

"All of the conversations that we have heard today about judicial philosophy boil down to this: Can the people be secure that this nominee will be a champion of their liberties, a jurist committed to the rule of law in the service of society, someone willing to see our living Constitution as a declaration of intent?"

I went on to say that our committee would be exploring some of the most complicated doctrines of constitutional law with the nominee, "a brilliant jurist and legal scholar."

"Let us never forget that the Supreme Court does not belong to the Senate Judiciary Committee, nor to this country's eight hundred thousand lawyers, nor even to the nine distinguished justices themselves.

"Mr. Chairman, the Court belongs to the American people, and the Court belongs to the American people for one very simple, yet profound reason, because the Constitution belongs to the American people."

Justice Ginsburg was confirmed. We would become friends.

I also participated in the confirmation hearings that year for our nation's next surgeon general.

At the time, the administration was intensely engaged in the issue of health care reform, and pushing to create a universal health care package for the American people. I was passionate about the issue, one that I'd advocated for since my days as an Illinois state legislator. I participated in discussions with First Lady Hillary Clinton and key officials.

President Clinton nominated Dr. Joycelyn Elders for the top post. Hers is a fascinating American journey. The daughter of an Arkansas sharecropper, she won a scholarship to college, then served in the US Army, later utilizing the G.I. Bill to attend medical school before becoming a board certified pediatric endocrinologist.

Later, Dr. Elders was appointed head of the Arkansas Department of Health, and had a record of success in everything from immunizations to terminal care.

During a July hearing, I offered a full-throated endorsement. "Dr. Elders represents the kind of positive change that we need to have—that we need to recognize, we need to support, we need to celebrate in our country," I said. "I am very honored to speak in behalf of her nomination and to encourage the members of the committee to recognize the high quality and caliber of this nomination and of this nominee, the importance and significance of the confirmation vote that you are about to undertake, and encourage you to proceed with great dispatch to confirm Joycelyn Elders as the next surgeon general of the United States."

Dr. Elders was confirmed that fall, becoming the country's first Black surgeon general and only the second woman to hold the post. I was elated. Unfortunately, her tenure was brief, about a year and a half. Her progressive views and outspokenness on topics such as sexuality led to criticisms that hastened her ouster. It was disappointing to witness. The good news is that Dr. Elders continued her groundbreaking work in medicine, albeit on a different stage.

I was serving on the Judiciary Committee when Lani Guinier, the first woman of color to become a tenured Harvard law professor, was tapped by the president to lead the Office of Civil Rights within the Department of Justice. At the time, Janet Reno, was our nation's first woman attorney general.

Professor Guinier had been hailed for her brilliance and talent. Yet the nomination process became rocky as conservatives pounced on some of her academic writings.

The Congressional Black Caucus—launched in 1970 by thirteen pioneering lawmakers in the House of Representatives—came out in favor of Professor Guinier. So did civil rights leaders.

I was a proud CBC member, and its only Black senator.

However, I felt strongly as a Judiciary Committee member that my weighing in prematurely might potentially impact the process. This led to me taking heat publicly for not going to bat for a fellow Black woman.

As the media onslaught continued, Professor Guinier called my office and reached one of my aides. I told my staff to patch her through right away. We had a cordial conversation and agreed to meet that following week. I was looking forward to dialogue. Unfortunately, it never happened.

I was not privy to decisions of the executive branch, but before I could sit down with the esteemed legal scholar, the White House withdrew the nomination.

Professor Guinier remained in academia. When she passed in 2022, her formidable legacy was widely hailed.

I voted on other nominees during my Senate tenure. The president appointed a record number of African Americans to his cabinet, including women such as Hazel O'Leary who was confirmed as secretary of energy, and Alexis Herman who became secretary of labor in his second term. As the full Senate deliberated, it was gratifying to cast a "yea" vote for these accomplished, dedicated public servants.

One of my Senate duties, from time to time, was serving as the chamber's presiding officer.

The Constitution allows for two officers to preside: the vice president (who can break tie votes) and the president pro tempore, a senator with seniority elected by the majority party.

When neither one of these leaders can be present, fellow senators are assigned to handle proceedings, and execute their attendant rules and procedures.

I first presided as a freshman senator.

Here I was, a girl from the South Side of Chicago, occupying the famous chair with a gavel in hand.

The notion of how far our country had come in my lifetime filled me with emotion. I thought about the countless warriors of all races, colors, and creeds who'd fought for civil and women's rights.

I thought about legal eagles Thurgood Marshall and Constance Baker Motley and what they did to make quality public education available to all children regardless of race.

I thought of the good teachers who taught me, as one of my grandmothers would say, to "read, write, and cipher." I thought of the public and private resources—from college scholarships to affirmative action—that opened up when I came along, making it possible for me to obtain a degree, attend law school, and later ascend to the Senate.

Each time I presided, the experience was moving.

There were times, of course, when being a senator meant wading into controversy.

I was serving when Congress passed the 1994 crime bill, a Clinton administration initiative. While campaigning two years prior, the future president had shed light on his views: "We cannot take our country back until we take our neighborhoods back... I want to use it to unite America. I want to be tough on crime and good on civil rights. You can't have civil justice without order and safety."

As the country grappled in the '90s with brazen gun violence, and the scourge of illicit drugs, people were hurting and desperate for solutions. Lawmakers in Congress were hearing from besieged communities nationwide, and big-city mayors where a crack epidemic had taken hold in urban centers, demanding the government do something. There were public polls and calls for elected officials to get tough on crime. The bill put more cops on the streets, expanded prisons, and had a "three strikes" provision, along with significant crime prevention, addiction treatment, and other resources. Given my background as a federal prosecutor, and coming from a law enforcement family, I agreed action was necessary. I was a proponent of certain elements of the sweeping legislation, less bullish on others such as capital punishment.

I strongly supported the Violence Against Women Act, which made gender violence such as sexual assault and domestic abuse a federal crime. It increased penalties for perpetrators and provided a range of services for victims, as well as civil remedies. There was also an important assault weapons ban, and the crime bill helped fund the Brady Law, which imposed a waiting period for handgun purchases and background checks.

I put forth a measure to establish midnight basketball leagues as a preventative crime diversion effort for youth, which wound up grandfathered into a larger education bill. More punitive was another amendment in the crime bill I sponsored which allowed teens to be charged as adults for certain violent crimes. Today, society has more knowledge and understanding about everything from adolescent brain development to the perils of mass incarceration. My perspective has evolved with the times. What I can say, unequivocally, is that my intention has always been to ensure that the American people have every opportunity to live in communities that are safe and secure in every way.

As the nation was grappling with rising crime, members of Congress convened a series of hearings on rap music to see if there was any link or possible causation.

To be clear, I do not loathe rap or hip-hop.

In fact, as someone raised in a family of musicians, I listen to all kinds of music: gospel and blues, country and classical, R & B and rock 'n' roll. And so on.

Not that I inherited any musical talent myself. In my youth, I briefly played the clarinet. One day, Uncle Tommy, my mother's brother and a professional jazz cat, heard me practicing. "Sweet-heart," he said, his expression deadpan. "I think you better try something else."

Years later, hip-hop had taken America by storm, and teens like my son were partying to the beats. While some lyrics were affirming and uplifting, or shone a light on adverse social con-ditions, others threatened women with misogynistic choruses or promoted violence. I was horrified when Matt mentioned one song titled, "Beat that B—with a Bat."

Both the House and Senate held hearings that served as a fact-finding mission to hear concerns, and suss out possible solutions. Among the witnesses who testified was C. DeLores Tucker, an NAACP activist who had marched with Dr. King in Selma and later broke ground as Pennsylvania's first Black secretary of state.

Tucker, who chaired the National Political Congress of Black Women, a group she co-founded with Shirley Chisholm, had been on a crusade against rap, questioning its broader societal implications. "It is an unavoidable conclusion that gangsta rap is negatively influencing our youth," she said at the time.

Rev. Calvin Butts, pastor of Harlem's famed Abyssinian Bap-tist Church, was among those who came to The Hill. He'd gone on record as saying not all rap lyrics were offensive, but he de-cried those that glorified sex, guns, and violence.

He and supporters would eventually lead a dramatic protest in New York City, crushing a pile of records with a steamroller and delivering the contents to a major record label.

Meanwhile, some scholars such as Dr. Michael Eric Dyson and members of Congress, such as Congresswoman Maxine Waters of California had an alternative view. Both touted hip-hop as an art form. Representative Waters said the artists had their fin-gers on the pulse of what was happening, and it made no sense to scapegoat the messengers for societal issues.

As a stalwart defender of First Amendment rights, I knew that whatever one thought of the music, censorship was out of the

question. Decades later, hip-hop has become a global phenomenon. We did our best to discuss the issues that were confront-
ing the nation at the time.

There was one event on The Hill that drove home for me
how interconnected America is with the rest of the world.

It happened in September 1998 when Nelson Mandela visited the US to receive the Congressional Gold Medal. What a
marvelous day that was on Capitol Hill.

As I listened to President Clinton's presentation, it occurred to
me that only the hero who helped break apartheid could bring
together everyone from California congressman Ron Dellums
to conservative Republicans.

Mandela, ever eloquent, thanked our country.

"In all these ways, the United States and its people have played
a significant role in the birth of our new nation," he said. "Since
the achievement of democracy, the relations between our countries have been steadily growing. We appreciate the commitment
to our future..." he said, adding that the people of the United
States occupy a "special place" in the hearts of South Africans.

"The breadth of our relationship makes the United States an
indispensable partner in bringing material improvement in the
lives of our people, especially the poor, without which our democracy would remain a hollow shell and our stability fragile."

On that glorious occasion, I had the opportunity to meet
Mandela and take a photo with one of my heroes. That event
ranks up there as one of the best days of my professional life.

Back in the Senate, however, I was still running into the brick
walls of sexism and racism. It did not happen all the time, but
each episode left an indelible imprint.

I recall being in a committee meeting involving the Com-
modity Futures Trading Commission. Its commissioners were
appointed for terms by the administration, but they had to undergo Senate approval.

I'd gotten some critical feedback about a professional who was either already on the commission or being considered. I thought it merited further examination, and put a hold on the person's nomination. Upon doing so, a senator from another state whom I gathered supported this individual became quite upset. He sort of bum-rushed me after the meeting and said, "We need to talk about this! Can you come to my office later?"

"Yes," I told him. One of the things I prided myself on as a lawmaker was being open-minded, and trying to discuss matters and, where possible, try to reach consensus.

I stopped by my colleague's office. When we sat down, he apologized for his earlier outburst. "There's a reason I reacted that way," he said.

I was perplexed. If a senator has concerns or questions about a nomination, it's standard procedure to place a hold on it. "What I did is not unusual," I told him.

My colleague then confessed that he was uncomfortable with a woman senator questioning his decisions. He used a horse racing analogy. "Once a stallion is bested by a filly on the racetrack, he's never the same."

I could hardly believe my ears. I've certainly heard lawmakers make off-color comments, but this analogy was ridiculous.

And so I said, "Well, Senator, we don't want you to be embarrassed. I'm not looking to do any harm to you."

I continued, "So is there some way we can come up with a compromise about this?" He was noncommittal, which was my cue to end the meeting.

This "filly" needed to get back to her own stable. I politely bid him goodbye and left.

Later, we wound up—rather, he wound up—withdrawing the guy's name. However, he did so in such a way that it did not appear that he was responding to my hold. A win-win.

Still, I was not there to appease my fellow senators. I answered to the people of Illinois. Interestingly, even that became a hurdle for me. I got some criticism that I was never around, or my constituents had not seen me. It simply wasn't true.

Particularly with the kinds of schedule demands that I had, I was dashing here and there. However, it was never enough. I had folks on the South Side saying that I wasn't spending enough time in the Black community. I had people downstate in the rural communities saying I was not in their neck of the woods enough. And yet I was regularly commuting back and forth between DC and Illinois, not only for all sorts of events but to see my son whom I sometimes brought along.

One afternoon I was down in Springfield, in the center of the state. There was a function taking place, and a preacher I knew stopped me in the lobby.

"Oh, Senator Braun, it's great to see you. How ya been?" he said.

"I'm doing fine, Reverend, how are you doing? It's good to see you."

He remarked, "Well, we don't see you around these parts much."

I was very sensitive to this, so I nicely replied, "Now, Reverend, I was just here two weeks ago for a community meeting. I was here a week or so before that, attending a big convention. I was here before that for a speech at the university," I said.

After I ticked off my recent stops, he looked at me. "Well, that may be so, and I'm sorry that I missed you those times. But, Senator, you haven't visited my church."

I tell this story because it really illustrates the conundrum one faces in public service. It didn't matter one whit to the pastor that I'd been to all those other places. Constituents want you to be wherever they are. Being an elected official means that you must be all things for a wide swath of people all of the time.

I was busting my butt, but no one seemed to care. There were times when my staff would answer the phone, and some mean-spirited person would be on the line, calling me names. At times, I even received hateful and dangerous threats, which had to be reported to the proper authorities. I felt so beleaguered.

Some days I asked myself, "Why am I here?" And on a couple of occasions, my roller coaster of emotions took me low. I was depressed and came close to throwing in the towel. I thought, "I'm gonna go back to Chicago, practice law, and just have a nice quiet life."

But it's funny, every time my mind veered in that direction, the Man Upstairs played a joke on me. I'd go home and pick up my Bible and start to read, or I'd turn on the television. Invariably, there'd be something like the miniseries *Roots*, or a documentary about women's suffrage. I took it as a spiritual nudge for me to keep going.

I realized the blood, sweat, and tears that had been sacrificed for me in the name of freedom, justice, and equality to even have this Senate seat. I truly cared about people, and utilizing the power of good government to uplift all Americans. I knew that the first Black woman in the Senate could not quit.

That settled it. I was staying put. At least, that was my plan.

While I was contemplating my future on Capitol Hill, somebody else was eyeing my seat.

Peter Fitzgerald was a young Republican from suburban Illinois and the heir to a family banking fortune. A lawyer by profession, he first ran for the state legislature in 1988 and lost, but four years later won a seat in the state senate.

Mr. Fitzgerald was an arch conservative on such issues as a woman's right to choose. While in the legislature, he introduced tough-on-crime legislation and was an independent voice on protecting the environment and fighting against higher taxes.

During his term as a state lawmaker, Mr. Fitzgerald had run unsuccessfully for Congress. A few years later, he set his sights on the Senate. The seat I held, to be exact.

Back in March 1998, Illinois held its election primary. No other Democrat had tossed their hat in the ring, so this go-round I was running unopposed. Thank goodness.

On the GOP side, Mr. Fitzgerald was matched up against Loleta Didrickson, a longtime public official who at the time was state comptroller. Senator Bob Dole and other top Republicans were backing her campaign, which was a pretty big deal.

Yet Mr. Fitzgerald beat her. That was my first sign to take this guy seriously. To ignore him would be folly, especially with my reelection on the line.

I was perceived as vulnerable. There'd been a steady drumbeat of ethics controversies, some due to my own poor decision-making and others the provenance of my known and unknown enemies.

Early on, the pundits and prognosticators were saying that my chances looked good.

Months later, however, there was a definite shift.

It was around this time that Mr. Fitzgerald, who reportedly spent upward of twelve million dollars to self-finance his campaign, began to run attack ads. The word in political circles was that an infamous GOP operative was one of his campaign consultants.

Whoever was behind the ads, they were nasty and hammered me. On television and radio, they rehashed every single controversy I'd ever had, over and over again throughout the campaign.

I wound up being on the defensive all the time.

Finally, my advisers convinced me to do what became known as a "mistake ad." It said in part: "I know I've made some mistakes and disappointed some people, but I want you to know that I've always tried to do what's best for Illinois... I'm aware that it has not all been hunky-dory and it's not all been perfect, and I'm sorry to the extent that I failed to communicate or failed to meet expectations."

I didn't like having to do that, personally. But I finally reached the conclusion that my team was correct in saying that I was better off doing a mea culpa with the public around errors, both real and perceived, leaving it general in hopes that would stop the conversation about what the specific errors might have been.

Did it make a difference? It's hard to know what kind of impact the "apology ad" had. But we thought it was important to do.

People were beginning to say this election was far from a fait accompli for this sitting senator. Yet, I hoped the tide would turn.

Looking back, the so-called experts had written off my campaigns from the beginning. Frankly, I never worried about what doomsayers put out there because we'd done the seemingly impossible to get me to the Senate.

However, perception can quickly become reality in politics. My poll numbers began to slip. In one survey, when voters were asked who was the more trustworthy candidate, they chose my opponent. Anytime your polling is down—and mine was by percentages that concerned my advisers—fundraising is even more difficult. We needed everyone from individual donors to the Democratic Senatorial Campaign Committee to remain confident and invest in our campaign until the end.

Fortunately, my fellow Democrats around the state and in the administration had rallied for me, including visits by the president and First Lady Hillary Clinton, a fellow Chicago native. We got on very well, and she was helpful and encouraging throughout my political career.

I still had celebrity supporters, among them Jackie Kennedy Onassis whom I'd met through a mutual friend. The former First Lady, as chic and lovely as her photos, indulged me with her time over lunch. I blabbered on and on, and she could barely get a word in edgewise. But when she spoke, in the softest, silky voice, I understood why men were so enchanted with this icon.

I pressed forward at work, continuing the job I'd been doing as a senator for Illinois.

I had achieved a legislative record second to none in my class, but some voters seemed surprised to learn that despite the legitimate discussion about me being a "symbol" that I was actually getting things done.

I thought that was funny—not funny "ha-ha" but ironic, because while I really did appreciate the "symbolism" of it all, I felt compelled to focus on the substance.

Indeed, the symbol of a Black woman senator without substance made no sense to me.

So, I worked hard to develop a strong legislative record and to be seen as a senator for all of Illinois—from the agricultural community which dubbed me the Ethanol Queen (a label which I wore proudly) to developing welfare-to-work programs.

I focused on delivering as a senator, not just on the big picture issues, but also the personal needs that my constituents might have.

During the campaign, I was stumping in Champaign-Urbana. I'd gone back to my hotel and was winding down for the night.

Among my habits before bedtime is sipping water. I often keep a glass of water on my nightstand. If I'm traveling, I will drink bottled water. It doesn't have to be mineral water or anything fancy. But there wasn't any in the room.

I called downstairs to the front desk. A very nice clerk answered. I asked her if they had any bottled water.

"The kitchen is shut down but I'll see what I can do," she said. In the meantime, I started taking a hot shower. I was rinsing off when I heard a knock at the door.

I grabbed a towel and hurried to the door, still dripping wet. I cracked the door open a little bit. A young woman in a housekeeping uniform was standing there with the water.

She handed the bottle to me through the door, and I thanked her. My purse was not handy, but I made a mental note to leave her an extra tip later.

Before I could close the door, she shyly asked, "Are you really Senator Moseley Braun?"

"Yes," I said.

"I just wanted to have an opportunity to meet you so I could thank you in person."

She paused, seemingly to work up her courage. "Senator Moseley Braun, I just want to thank you from the bottom of my heart. Because when I lost my daughter you were the only person who listened to me."

At this point, I opened the door a little bit wider and stuck my head out. I wanted to give her my full attention.

What I heard left me reeling. A young mother trapped in a bad marriage. A violent husband. An innocent baby caught in the crossfire. She told me that her spouse had crossed state lines and disappeared.

The young lady called my district office seeking assistance. I had not heard of her situation, personally. But she shared that someone on my staff answered her call, connected her with the proper law enforcement agencies, and provided resources to address her trauma. "I'm so glad they treated you with respect," I said.

"Yes, Senator Braun, they did," she replied.

She stood there with tears streaming down her face. I was shivering, clutching onto my towel, with tears in my eyes. I empathized with her more than she would ever know. Every single one of my constituents, had their own stories. Maybe not as dramatic as this one. But they all mattered to me.

The month before the general election, I met my opponent for a live televised debate at the University of Illinois.

The forum, which was sponsored by the Illinois Press Association, had a panel of reporters from outlets across the state asking questions.

After a coin toss, Mr. Fitzgerald spoke first. "Thanks for this opportunity. Because I'm the challenger in this race," he said, "many of you don't know as much about me as my opponent."

He proceeded to speak of his upbringing, education, and family. "I was blessed with love," he explained, before sharing that he was a husband and proud father to a six-year-old.

I began my intro by invoking Illinois's own Abraham Lincoln and his message of America being a beacon. "He was referring not only to the land of opportunity, but to the triumph of our ideals and shared values over limitations and our divisions," I said. "This United States Senate election is a test of those ideals and sacred values."

I then referenced my opponent's deep pockets. "The real reason people are willing to spend millions in pursuit of this office is not personal. It is nothing less than a contest over who will dictate the direction of our government."

For the next hour, we fielded tough questions on topics such as how we would protect Social Security, education reform, and a national health insurance plan. There were queries about how much scrutiny there should be into the private lives of politicians, a topic I knew all too well.

I did not hold back on criticism and neither did he. Our exchange was mostly civil, although we had a few verbal skirmishes. I accused my opponent of flip-flopping on his views, painting himself as more moderate than he really was.

He called on me to explain my overseas trips, questioning both my commitment to human rights and judgment.

In turn, I asked whether his judgment in voting to support a concealed weapons bill was wise given the bloodshed in our society.

Along the way, we delved into things such as internet safety for children and reproductive freedoms for women.

At the end of the hour, we each had time for a closing statement.

"If I'm your senator in Washington, I will fight vigorously to protect the interests of families and taxpayers in this state," Mr. Fitzgerald said. He spoke of "wasteful government spending" and a "higher tax burden." But also, "we want to create a climate which is better for our children and their futures. I've talked to parents all across the state of Illinois who recognize that the single greatest reform that we could have for our kids are their futures…"

When it was my turn, I said, "I'm so pleased to have the rare opportunity to actually debate my opponent. Unless he agrees to another televised debate this may be the last time you will see him discuss the people's business. He's able to afford a lot more commercials than I can, but he has avoided frankly talking about his record in Springfield. And talking about his real views on the issues."

I continued by noting that my opponent had reinvented himself and his positions. "There are fundamental differences between his view of Illinois and mine," I said, adding "the Bible says we are known by our stripes. I have given my all to the people of this great state. Even in the face of controversy. Because I have the courage of my convictions. And an abiding belief in the good of America. I fight for Illinois because I care about its people and its future."

The weeks before Election Day flew by.

I had barely slept. My feet were sore. I had met, engaged with, and hugged thousands of voters across Illinois. In the end, 1.6 million of them—47 percent—cast ballots for me. But they cast 50 percent of their votes for Mr. Fitzgerald.

I had hoped that my service in the Senate would have been a point of pride for Illinois, and all the American people. I'd hoped that people would say, "We've finally integrated the United States Senate, again, in this century. That's a good thing for America, and something that we can be proud of."

I had run for office in multiple elections up to that point and never lost one. But, I lost my Senate reelection race narrowly. I came close, but as the old saying goes, close only matters in horseshoes.

I gave it my all, but it wasn't my seat to begin with. It belonged to the voters, the good people of Illinois.

AMBASSADOR TO PARADISE

I was down in the dumps following my crushing Senate reelection loss, not to mention facing unemployment.

Senators with my qualifications typically receive a flood of offers from prestigious law and lobbying firms, as well as invitations to join corporate boards.

However, given the ethical cloud that hung over my head, there was barely a trickle of interest. From Chicago to Washington, DC, it seemed that no one wanted to hire me. I'd gone from being a political rock star to persona non grata.

It was a very low period in my life. Some days, I blamed myself for a series of self-inflicted mistakes. At other times, I was bereft and bitter about what felt like a prolonged smear campaign against me.

I felt so forlorn. When one is in the public eye, people seem to forget that you are a human being and feel pain. Were it not for my faith, I might have gone over the edge of the precipice. Looking to Jesus Christ, my Savior, gave me some solace. I was searching for peace and purpose.

First, I needed a new job. Thanks to allies within the Clinton administration, I was fortunate to land a role with the US Department of Education as a consultant.

Education is one of my core values. It has been the foundation and gateway for every single one of my accomplishments. I have long championed educational initiatives as a pillar for societal progress.

In Congress, I sponsored a bill to repair crumbling schools, and I've pushed or supported numerous educational measures throughout my legislative career. During my post-Senate transitional period, it was gratifying to focus on policies meant to empower students, teachers, and our communities.

I'd been out of office for maybe ten months or so, when a call came out of the blue. To my astonishment, it was the White House. President Clinton, who had won reelection to a second term, wanted to appoint me as the US ambassador to New Zealand. I nearly dropped the phone. This was phenomenal news, and right on time.

The very idea of an ambassadorship was like a dream. I first began traveling the globe as a young woman and had amassed numerous stamps on my passport.

My father had always pushed us to expand our horizons. And I credit a well-known Chicagoan with helping me spread my wings and see the world.

Leon Despres was an alderman, lawyer, and activist. He was known as a fiercely independent advocate for the people, who frequently did battle with The Machine. Leon lived to be a centenarian, and during his long, fascinating life and career, he exemplified the meaning of public service.

Like me, Leon lived in the city's Hyde Park neighborhood. One day, long ago, we got to talking. He asked how I was doing. Nothing was wrong, per se, but I confessed to feeling restless. He listened, then asked if I had ever traveled abroad. I had not, but the thought of spreading my wings was instantly appealing.

Leon subsequently put me in touch with a lovely woman at the British Consulate in Chicago. She told me about the European Union Visitors Programme. It was established in the 1970s to strengthen Europe's ties with people around the world.

The program was geared toward individuals with an interest in government, public service, journalism, and related fields. Participants were offered the chance to tour various countries in Europe, all expenses paid.

I applied and crossed my fingers. When word came back that I'd been selected, I was elated. Faster than you can say O'Hare airport, this Chicago girl was on a transcontinental flight.

I spent the next few weeks backpacking across Europe and beyond. My stops included England, France, Turkey, Israel, and Jordan. Each destination was sui generis.

As a youngster, I used to take my books and read on the Chicago waterfront. It gave me the chance to escape to new worlds. What a thrill it was to be on a real-life excursion.

I was introduced to the culture, language, and history of countries on distant shores. I met interesting people of various nationalities and ethnicities. I made new friends of many races, ethnicities, and religions, and relished hearing their unique origin stories, while sharing my own.

I climbed mountains, strolled through ancient streets, and gazed up in wonder at frescoes adorning cathedrals erected centuries ago.

Little did I know back then that my wanderlust would help lay the groundwork for a position on the international stage. I thanked the Creator for opening the door to yet another unexpected adventure.

President Clinton formally nominated me to be ambassador to New Zealand and Samoa on October 8, 1999. It was one of the proudest moments of my career.

But almost immediately, the pushback came from detractors.

There were those who deemed me unfit to represent our great nation as a global ambassador.

At issue were the campaign finance allegations that had dogged me since my first Senate run. And, lingering questions about my unofficial visits to Nigeria while a brutal military regime was in control.

It was a dagger to my heart that these controversies, and the rumors and innuendo that surrounded them, kept arising over and over again. Then I learned that an old opponent was leading the brigade in resurrecting them.

As a freshman in the Senate, I'd tangled with Senator Jesse Helms over the Confederate flag. He once tried to rattle my cage while we shared an elevator ride. We butted heads again over a bill that I co-sponsored to federally fund the Martin Luther King Jr. Holiday Commission.

Now my former nemesis was chairman of the Senate Foreign Relations Committee, the powerful panel that would recommend whether or not to send my nomination to the full Senate.

Early on, the gentleman from North Carolina signaled that he would halt my confirmation process. Weeks passed with no hearing. If he was determined to exact political revenge, I could lose out on a potentially once-in-a-lifetime opportunity.

Fortunately, I had my defenders. The White House, civil rights organizations, and various members of Congress were in my corner.

Congressman Danny Davis, a representative from my home state of Illinois, stood on the House floor on November 4 and delivered an impassioned speech.

Extolling what he termed my "extraordinary life of breaking stereotypes, a life of shattering glass ceilings, a life of public service," he questioned why the confirmation process was taking so long.

It is "the long-standing tradition of the Senate to welcome former colleagues who have been nominated to high office by the president of the United States and to extend them the courtesy of prompt hearings, in accord with their constitutional responsibilities to advise and consent," Davis pointed out. "A senator has not been rejected for an ambassadorial appointment since 1835.

"Mr. Speaker, make no mistake, our democracy is being weighed in the balance in the coming days," the congressman continued. "If fairness does not prevail, if Senator Carol Moseley Braun is denied confirmation, then those responsible will have offered up proof, proof to the American people, proof to the world, that fairness and justice are still wanted in America five generations after the end of the Civil War. I find that possibility abhorrent, detestable, and obscene."

The next day, a confirmation hearing was hastily convened to consider my nomination. Dressed in a black suit, complemented by pearls and a jeweled American flag pin, I took my seat before the committee and a scrum of photographers and cameras. I was willing to answer any questions that came my way. I'd already submitted a boatload of documents requested by the committee, as had the White House.

The wood-paneled room in the Dirksen office building was packed. My family had flown in. The light of my life, Matthew, was there, as were my siblings, Marsha and Joseph, to offer love and moral support.

Quite a few congressional colleagues showed up for me. It made me feel good to see legislative warriors such as Representative Sheila Jackson Lee of Texas, Delegate Eleanor Holmes Norton of DC, and Representative Maxine Waters of California, as well as other members of the Congressional Black Caucus. Also in the audience was Senator Mary Landrieu of Louisiana, a friend whom I'd first met during my state political career.

Senator Helms was not present. He had allowed Senator Craig Thomas, chair of the Foreign Relations' East Asian and Pacific Affairs Subcommittee, to preside over the televised hearing.

The Wyoming lawmaker opened by speaking about the historic, close ties between the US and New Zealand. Then, he put me at ease about the elephant in the room.

"As we're all aware, a number of issues regarding your qualifications have been brought to the attention of the committee," Thomas said.

"Our failure to further investigate them would have been a dereliction of our duty. In my opinion, however, the allegations have been competently investigated and dealt with prior to this hearing by other government agencies."

Inwardly, I was relieved. "There are members of the committee who still have questions," he went on. "I'm sure they will ask them. However, I have none. I hope that we will follow soon with a hearing to complete this process."

Then-Senator Joe Biden of Delaware, who'd been pushing behind the scenes on my behalf, spoke after the chairman.

"I want to welcome our old friend, Senator Carol Moseley Braun back," he said. I smiled.

"There's been a good deal of hubbub surrounding this nomination," he said, noting the timeline.

He went on to express his full confidence in my qualifications. She has "the political experience, personal charm, and street smarts," he said, to handle the post. "I don't believe there's any evidence, any shred or scintilla of evidence that would disqualify Senator Moseley Braun."

He wrapped up by describing me as someone he considered, "a very close personal friend." I felt the same about the man who would one day become the leader of the free world.

I had so much gratitude to Joe and many of my former colleagues for going to bat for me.

Illinois senator, Dick Durbin, who formally introduced me to the committee, elicited laughter when he cited some lyrics from Stevie Wonder's hit song to describe our collegial bond in the Senate. We were like "ebony and ivory, in perfect harmony," he said. Senator Barbara Boxer of California, one of my sister lawmakers elected in "The Year of the Woman," spoke of her "love and support for this very qualified nominee."

When it was time for my opening statement, I thanked my loved ones, President Clinton and his staff, former colleagues, and supporters. "I feel very blessed to have this opportunity to appear before this committee today," I began.

I went on to share that "serving as a member of the United States Senate was a great honor and privilege for me. And I would be sincerely grateful to be afforded this opportunity to continue in public service."

I acknowledged that there had been "a number of issues raised in the media," and sought to debunk those that were not true or had been taken out of context.

During my 1992 campaign, I told the committee, our fundraising generated upward of eight million dollars. The Federal Election Commission, the independent agency charged with oversight and enforcement of campaign finance law, subsequently "conducted a hundred percent audit" of the campaign's credit card activity. Of that vast sum in my war chest, I explained, only $311.28 was unaccounted for, and we believed that negligible amount was an overpayment.

The campaign was not fined or sanctioned, I told the committee. "There was no corrective action. Nothing."

Concerning my trips to Nigeria, paid for using no taxpayer monies, I let the committee know that promoting democracy on the continent of Africa was important to me.

I also pointed out that other members of Congress had traveled to countries led by autocratic rulers and less than politically correct governance, a fact with which several committee members concurred.

"I meant no harm to anyone," I said. "I certainly meant no harm to our policies.

"I have always taken the public trust as a solemn responsibility and I will continue to do so."

A few days later, committee members determined that my nomination would be reported to the full Senate. There was only one dissent. I wasn't at all surprised to learn who it was.

Helms told colleagues that he'd watched the hearing on television and called it "a sight to behold."

"In fact, what it was was a political rally, lacking only a band and the distribution of free hot dogs, soda pop, and balloons," said the senator. He then launched into a litany of my alleged ethical lapses. Never mind that I had just spent hours before the committee discrediting them and had provided reams of documents as proof.

Following Helms's remarks, Senator Durbin stood up and rebutted the accusations, saying in part: "What Senator Moseley Braun was subjected to during the course of this process is a standard, which frankly may exceed a standard imposed on any other person who comes up for an ambassadorship," he said.

"In other words, she was subjected to more rigorous examination and questioning than virtually any person" nominated by the president.

He was right about that. I shared with the committee that years of being under the microscope had been "very difficult for me" and my family.

That said, I wanted to focus on the path forward. I prayed that this door to a new opportunity would be opened to me.

Leading up to the full Senate vote, Senator Biden was once again a vocal supporter, as were Senators Dianne Feinstein and Ted Kennedy. Each of these individuals had befriended me during my Senate tenure in kind, caring ways, and it was heartening to know they were still in my corner.

Helms made a half-hearted effort at being magnanimous. He expressed his "sincere" hope that I would "serve diligently, effectively and honestly," because I would be "representing the United States, the country of all Americans. For the sake of our country, I pray there will be no further reports of irregularity regarding her conduct. In short, I wish her well."

Senator Peter Fitzgerald, who won my former seat in Illinois, repeated the laundry list of unfounded charges against me. He closed by saying: "While I cannot in good conscience support her nomination, I wish her well in her new post."

On November 10, 1999, the Senate voted on my nomination. Two senators were "necessarily" absent.

I was on pins and needles, but word soon filtered to me that I'd been overwhelmingly confirmed. The vote was ninety-six to two. Hallelujah!

President Clinton—to whom I was grateful for the appointment—hailed the Senate's bipartisan vote as a "strong endorsement" of my "outstanding experience and credentials for the position."

"I expect her to do a superior job representing our country's very significant interests in New Zealand," he said.

In early December I was sworn in, as my loved ones looked on. Vice President Al Gore presided over the brief ceremony.

My official title was quite a mouthful. Ambassador Extraordinary and Plenipotentiary of the United States of America to New Zealand and Samoa. In addition, my portfolio included the Cook Islands and Antarctica.

I would soon be jetting off to the other side of the world to perform my duties. But first, I had to attend the Foreign Service Institute, also known as "ambassador school."

The training encompassed topics that envoys need to know: History and geography. Linguistics. Etiquette. And proper protocol and rules governing one's behavior while abroad.

By day, I listened intently to the experts. At night, I stayed up late, poring over briefing materials, books, and maps. There was so much information to absorb.

I was single-minded about representing the United States with distinction while abroad. My goal was for every official engagement, every interaction, to reflect positively upon me and upon America.

★ ★ ★

The day dawned for my journey to New Zealand. I was headed to an island nation nestled in the South Pacific Ocean.

It's believed ancestors of the Māori people navigated their canoes from Polynesia to these shores sometime around 1200 AD.

By the 1600s, European explorers had arrived. A Dutch name, "Nieuw Zeeland," would become New Zealand. In the Māori language, the country is called "Aotearoa," which translates to "Land of the Long White Cloud."

In the 1800s, both Great Britain and France were interested in colonizing New Zealand. In 1840, hundreds of Māori chiefs were invited to sign an accord—the Treaty of Waitangi—with the British crown. By the twentieth century, grievances over unjust land confiscation would lead to the New Zealand government settling with various tribes to the tune of billions of dollars.

New Zealand was part of the Commonwealth for well more than a century. The country gained full independence in 1947.

I was mulling over all this history and more, as we boarded our flight.

My son was accompanying me on my latest adventure. Matt had recently graduated from college, and as a young adult, was in that exploratory stage of life. We weren't sure exactly how long he would visit, but it was a pleasure to share this momentous experience with the person I cherished most in the world.

After twenty hours, the plane touched down. I'd had the longest nap of my life. I thanked God for our safe arrival, and prepared for bright, new beginnings.

Back in Chicago, we would have been preparing for a snowy Christmas, but it was actually summer in New Zealand.

I disembarked from the plane and stepped into the bright sunshine. The skies were impossibly blue, and a balmy breeze was blowing. The temperatures hovered around seventy degrees, so I needed no coat. For a Chicago girl accustomed to bundling up in December, the weather was blissful.

At the airport, we collected our luggage and waited for our transportation.

As is standard for ambassadors, I would have a full-time chauffeur to shuttle me back and forth to the embassy, as well as to official appearances and so on.

We were whisked away to the ambassador's official residence in Lower Hutt, a riverside city situated in the country's North Island.

We proceeded through a suburban-ish neighborhood down a short driveway, before stopping in front of a creamy white mansion with a manicured lawn, neatly trimmed hedges, and mature trees.

The house was named "Camperdown." Built in the 1920s, it had five bedrooms, three baths, and a fireplace. There was a garden bursting with colorful native flowers, plants, and shrubs. The entire property was lovely.

We were greeted warmly by members of the small household staff. A local couple, a husband and wife duo, lived onsite and had been employed for years. I was told their duties entailed housekeeping, meal preparation, and general upkeep. There was also a professional gardener, which was appealing to me as someone who'd spent summers on a farm, immersed in agriculture.

I was given a tour of the spacious house, which was decorated in a classic style with heavy mahogany furniture, handwoven rugs, antiques, and art. It was elegant and ideal for the entertaining that ambassadors are expected to do in their host countries.

While many diplomats bring their own stylistic touches to a home, that was not an immediate priority for me. It was more important to get settled in and prepare for all of my new responsibilities.

I did some unpacking, enjoyed a light dinner with Matt, and hit the sack.

I awakened to the sweet trilling of birdsong. I'd slept soundly. A good thing, too, because I learned later that the house was supposedly haunted. The story goes that the original homeowner, who built the structure, had a daughter who met a tragic end. There was a room between the first and second floors where her ghost reportedly appeared. Thank goodness, no one told me this creepy tale on my first night, or I might have hurried back to the States. Thereafter, whenever I passed that nook, there was an odd energy that made me shudder.

But real or imagined apparitions could not deter me from my mission. I was eagerly anticipating my first day of work at the US Embassy.

Bright and early, I made the short drive into Wellington, the capital of New Zealand. I gazed wide-eyed at the sights (and sites) along the way.

My first impressions of this port city included its expansive harbor and waterfront. Modern high-rises and neoclassical buildings existed in harmony, and bright red cable cars climbed its scenic hills. Wellington bustled with people (about 350,000 residents during my time there) and boasted cafes, museums, and public art. There were outdoor trails galore, and an observation deck at the top of Mt. Victoria, with panoramic views of the metropolis below.

When I arrived at the embassy, the entire team of about one hundred people were there to receive me.

Some of my colleagues were Americans, among them our brave military personnel, who provide vital embassy security across the globe. Still others were New Zealanders, part of the locally employed staff.

As I sought to connect names and faces, the reception was cordial and polite. I also sensed a bit of curiosity, which was not especially surprising. As a professional Black woman, I've often been in environments, the Senate being a prime example, where no one else looks like me. I've gotten stares upon entering certain rooms that would make you think someone spotted a duck-billed platypus. However, I have learned to put people at ease, simply by being my authentic self.

Early in my tenure, I had a major event on my official schedule. I would be officially presenting my credentials to Sir Michael Hardie Boys, New Zealand's seventeenth governor-general, who acted on behalf of the British monarchy.

At that time, Queen Elizabeth II reigned over the United Kingdom, and Sir Michael was Her Majesty's representative in New Zealand. He handled a wide range of constitutional duties from appointing judges to ceremonial duties such as welcoming foreign dignitaries.

We were invited to his official residence, Government House, where everything from state dinners to community functions are held. The main house is a heritage building that dates back to 1910. The grounds and gardens were impeccable. Inside, official portraits of the Crown and heads of state hung on the walls.

I wore a black suit, a peach blouse, and heels to present my credentials, namely a letter signed by our president with the seal of the United States. It officially enabled me to speak on behalf of our government as an ambassador.

"I hope to build on a relationship that is already as solid as they come," I said.

The presentation of credentials was one element of the welcoming ceremony. Another highlight of the day was a "taki" challenge, a time-honored custom of the Māori people.

We assembled outside Government House. A Māori warrior—bare-chested and clad in a "piupiu," a skirt made of palm leaves, and brandishing a spear—appeared in front of the stone columns.

He began rituals of the challenge, which is meant to test the intentions of a visitor. I was told that as a woman, I would not be put to the test (if only the rest of my life was that simple), so my son dutifully did the honors. The warrior placed a tree branch on the ground in front of Matt, and he picked it up. It was a sign that he'd come in peace. One is supposed to main-

tain intense eye contact throughout the challenge. My son later
told me he did not dare blink or look away.

It was my first peek into the rich culture of the country's Indigenous people, and an auspicious start to my new role.

Afterward, at a reception, I had the pleasure of mingling
with Sir Michael and fellow officials. Everyone was most gracious. After being kicked in the teeth during my Senate years,
the refined environs and genteel conversations were a welcome
change. It was as if God said, "Carol, you have suffered enough,"
and blessed me with the perfect job in a gorgeous setting. My
mind, body, and spirit were being healed.

Now that I'd been formally welcomed, it was time for me to
see New Zealand and Samoa up close and personal.

In the days, weeks, and months that followed my presentation
ceremony, I embarked on a series of whirlwind tours.

I'd heard these nations were among the most beautiful places
on the planet. They did not disappoint. And, at every stop, the
people whom I encountered were affable, generous, and well-
disposed to Americans.

New Zealand's manifold charms are diverse, encompassing
cosmopolitan cities to lush rainforests and abundant agriculture.
The joke there is that they have more sheep than people. The
people affectionately refer to themselves as "Kiwis"—a nod to
the long-beaked and whiskered flightless national bird.

During my expedition, I saw coastal, desert, and mountaintop vistas. Geothermal waters and spurting geysers. Whales and
sea lions. My guide pointed out the native kauri trees, and the
kakariki, a local parakeet with bright plumage.

Samoa was my next stop. The small island is situated between
New Zealand and Hawaii. It took us several hours to get there
by air.

It is well worth the trip. Samoa boasts cerulean-blue waters
and pristine, powdery beaches. Its hidden beauty includes coves

with natural swimming holes. I marveled at sparkling water-falls, and even fields of lava.

Later, my team and I met at the Samoa Consulate in Auckland, a major city on the country's North Island.

The US has had a presence, and specifically, a consul in the Samoan islands dating back to the 1850s. Samoa became independent of New Zealand in the '60s, and the US formed a diplomatic relationship in 1971.

I had the honor of meeting the chargé d'affaires and the vice consul for trade. We discussed US, Samoa, and New Zealand relations, Indo-Pacific security, and how to tackle the pressing issues of climate change in the Pacific. I reaffirmed America's commitment to a prosperous and resilient Pacific region and told them I looked forward to my next visit to Samoa.

The Cook Islands were also part of my portfolio. Its neon blue waters, pastel coral reefs, and tropical fish draw tourists from across the world.

Each place was breathtaking. Unofficially, I started referring to my position as "Ambassador to Paradise."

In 2000, one of my embassy assignments took me somewhere that never in my wildest dreams did I ever imagine visiting. I traveled to the continent of Antarctica. Yes, the coldest place on earth.

I flew to the South Pole in order to tour a scientific research facility associated with the US Antarctic Program.

New Zealand and the US are among the original signatories to the Antarctic Treaty of 1959, wherein twelve countries vowed international cooperation to help protect and preserve its natural environment and resources.

I met some of the hardy personnel who cycle in and out during certain times of the year.

You see, humans cannot stand the remote environment and harsh climate for too long. Antarctica is no joke. The average temperature is minus 57 degrees Celsius!

The advance team tried to prepare me. I stopped in Christ-church, the largest city in New Zealand's South Island, to be outfitted in warm clothing and protective gear.

Then, I took a military flight to the South Pole, which is about ten thousand feet in altitude. When I got off the plane, we had to hike a short distance and I could barely breathe. The pilot offered me some oxygen and said, "Are you okay? Is it too cold?"

I instinctively answered, "No, I'm from Chicago, and this is nothing. We Midwesterners are not weather wimps!"

I have never been so cold in my entire life, but it was a phe-nomenal experience.

During my trip, I also visited the historic huts of early ex-plorers. And during my flyover, I marveled at the sight of pen-guins, seals, and whales below. I felt a sense of awe at seeing God's handiwork.

There's a picture of me standing outside near the US facility, where an American flag is planted in the snow and ice. I liter-ally had icicles in my nose. But I was smiling.

That September, I attended a presentation by the Antarctic Heritage Trust, a New Zealand–based organization which had representatives from the United Kingdom and US. As ambas-sador, I was among the trustees back then, and the prime min-ister thanked me that evening.

These days, there are tourists going to Antarctica.

Of course, I was not merely sightseeing. As an ambassador, my role was to help maintain the strong bilateral relationship that the US and New Zealand have enjoyed for nearly two centuries.

Our ties date back to the 1830s, and a formal diplomatic re-lationship was established in 1942.

We've been allies in peace and war. During World War II, New Zealanders served and thousands of American service members were stationed in the country before their engage-ment in Pacific campaigns led by General Douglas MacArthur. Moreover, the Māori have served in both world wars.

For well more than a century, the US has made valuable economic, developmental, and security contributions which benefit
the region and beyond. These efforts are both large-scale and
lesser known: for example, the coast guard working to thwart
illegal fishing in Pacific waters. Or, the peace corps dispatch-
ing volunteers to remote communities in need.

Our mutual interests notwithstanding, the two countries have
weathered periodic frictions. They have ranged from nuclear policy disputes to questions involving trade and agricultural imports.

I ran into a sticky wicket soon after my arrival. It involved
F-16 fighter planes.

The US government had reportedly negotiated a lease-to-buy
deal of more than two dozen aircraft. The agreement was struck
under New Zealand's National Party.

But when the new Labour Alliance Government came to
power, the deal was suddenly at risk. At stake was $700 million
dollars, and long-standing goodwill.

Not long after, I scheduled a sit-down with the prime minister, Helen Clark, the country's second woman to be elected
its top leader. The timing of her election in 1999 synced with
my arrival.

The prime minister's office was in the city's parliament buildings, and the executive wing was situated in a conical-shaped
edifice nicknamed "the Beehive" because of its unique architecture. You might say Prime Minister Clark was the "queen
bee." Fortunately, she did not sting me. I liked her very much,
in fact. I conveyed the concerns of our government. She shared
her official perspective. We got the ball rolling so that a suit-
able solution could be reached. Two women using their smarts
and cooperative spirit to get the job done.

Not everyone was cooperative. One of my colleagues at the
embassy seemed to resent my very presence. A few weeks into
my arrival, it appeared this individual was trying to sabotage me.

I suspected the daily missives that were dispatched to all the embassies and ambassadors were being hid. At the time, email was just becoming widely used, and the rise of social media was years away. How was I to perform my job on behalf of the American people, if I had no idea of developments abroad and back home?

I also sensed what appeared to be attempts at sowing dissension, with what seemed to be gossiping about me. At some point, the tricks seemed to become more devious, with one stunt that could have cost me my post.

US ambassadors maintain a discretionary budget that can be used for everything from entertaining to decorating one's official residence.

Both are important because ambassadors regularly host events outside of the embassy in our homes. Of course, our official residences should reflect positively upon America.

The house was in good shape overall but needed a few minor updates. The wooden shutters on the windows had seen better days. I decided to have them removed, and have drapes installed. I was pleased with the results.

However, what happened next was unbelievable: I was accused of stealing the shutters. I was absolutely aghast.

Apparently, my colleague had contacted the brass at the state department, which took the claims seriously. Two investigators were dispatched halfway around the world to probe these ridiculous accusations.

I was incensed at how quickly the lies of a co-worker had escalated. And, having barely survived multiple professional storms, I immediately understood the detrimental impact false charges could have on my career, as well as that of others.

Black American women ambassadors are a bit like unicorns. Approximately fifty to sixty have served over the decades around the world. During my tenure, there were maybe five. One of them, Ambassador Diane E. Watson, who served in Micronesia, became a friend. We talked on the phone, holidayed together, and encouraged each other as proud representatives of our country.

I was performing my diplomatic role in New Zealand with integrity and skill. When the inspectors arrived from the States, I told them my side. Then, I politely walked them upstairs to the attic of the house and showed them the "evidence"—the shutters. I'd asked the groundskeeper to put them in storage. Case closed on the great shutter caper.

My plate was full. Each day was different. I might be meeting with a high-powered politico or providing guidance to the embassy team.

We assisted American citizens living in New Zealand with a multitude of requests, from replacing lost passports to birth certificates for newborns. We hosted cultural exchange programs. And the embassy staff interviewed those who desired to visit the US for educational, business, or other purposes.

We tried to solve problems. I recall one situation involving children of American servicemen, who sought dual citizenship. This seemed to me a reasonable request. I made numerous phone calls and inquiries, hopeful that we could help these individuals. Ultimately, I was told this matter was not within my purview.

I had better luck with influencing hiring decisions. Upon my arrival at the embassy, I noticed there were few, if any, Māori among the locally employed staff. That made no sense to me, especially from a diplomatic standpoint. I moved quickly to remedy the situation, which generated respect within their community. I was later made an honorary member of the Māori Te Ati Awa tribe.

I was able to witness the haka, a ceremonial dance. It is visually arresting, complete with swift and rhythmic movements, guttural yells, and foot stomping. In a word, it was magnificent.

Back at Camperdown, I was the official hostess for dinner

parties. These gatherings are about building the bonds of friendship. The guest list was eclectic: local officials, academics, and
artists, etc.

The menu planning was enjoyable, especially for an amateur
chef like me. I'm known for my home cooking; gumbo is among
my specialties. That said, I did not regularly prepare meals while
overseas. Usually, the cook would whip up a combination of
American fare and popular local dishes, such as fresh salmon.
We set a formal table with china and freshly cut flowers. There
was a piano and we always had music. I moved around, making sure everyone was comfortable, and tried to keep the conversation flowing.

I enjoyed many memorable occasions, but one in particular
stands out. We'd finished dining and retired to the living room
for dessert and coffee. I stood up, retrieved the water pitcher, and
began filling everyone's glasses. The room suddenly went quiet.
I was baffled until someone spoke up. Apparently, no one had
ever seen an ambassador serve guests in that manner. I smiled
and let them know that in the States we aren't quite so formal.
We all had a good laugh.

In addition to hosting locals, I also had the pleasure of welcoming American dignitaries.

One of them was Supreme Court Justice Ruth Bader Ginsburg, the second woman to serve on the nation's high court.
We'd first met at her Senate confirmation hearings and had
stayed in touch.

When Ruth and her husband, Martin, an attorney and law
professor, traveled to New Zealand, they stayed at the residence
for a couple of days.

I thoroughly enjoyed their visit. Despite there being a trio of
lawyers in the room, we did not really talk shop. This couple
was brilliant and had social standing, but neither of them put on
airs. Ruth related a funny story about the security dogs sniffing
their bags at the airport. She recalled telling her husband: "I told

you not to bring those little jars of jelly from the hotel!" When it was time for them to say goodbye, I felt a wee bit homesick.

By that time, my son had returned to the good ole US of A. Matt had a fantastic experience in New Zealand, making friends and, at one point, finding employment in his field as a tech geek. But he also wanted to live his own life. I completely understood.

Years later, after Matt got married and my twin grandbabies were born, Justice Bader Ginsburg autographed a onesie for the girl as a historic keepsake. It slipped out of my possession due to a delivery snafu, and somewhere, another baby may be sporting the visage of RBG.

When Ruth passed away in 2020, it hit me hard. I cherish the time spent with this American heroine, and her memory is a blessing.

I made memories to last a lifetime in New Zealand, Samoa, the Cook Islands, and Antarctica. But my time was up after the nail-biting election between Al Gore and George W. Bush, and the Supreme Court decision that returned the GOP to the White House.

I served until 2001. I fondly look back on that period as one of the happiest times of my life.

The ambassador's residence was graced with beautiful, mature trees. I'd look out and see assorted native birds nesting and fluttering butterflies. One tree was always covered with butterflies, and they were a shade of blue. The day of my departure, they all took off in a fluttering blue cloud.

TAKE THE "MEN ONLY" SIGN OFF THE WHITE HOUSE

"Auntie Carol! Auntie Carol!" The angelic voice of my nine-year-old niece, Claire, rang out, beckoning me to her bedroom.

The year was 2003. I was back in Chicago. My extraordinary ambassadorship had ended two years prior, and I'd taken some time off afterward to travel before returning to the States. I was happy that God had given me the opportunity to see more of His great, wide world.

My brother Joe had invited me over for dinner. I relished the chance to spend time with him, his wife, and children after my time abroad, and living down South.

Little Claire was studying in her bedroom, and had her social studies book open. I noticed she had a look of consternation on her face. "Auntie Carol," she began, her voice rising, "all the presidents are boys!" She pointed to the photos in her textbook as irrefutable proof.

I was slightly taken aback by her innocent, yet astute observation. I was not sure how to explain this to a little girl, in an age-appropriate manner.

"Sweetie, girls can be president, too," I said, hoping that my words sounded convincing.

Fortunately, my niece seemed satisfied with my answer. She hugged me and returned to doing her homework. Yet something about her words—out of the mouths of babes, as it were—rattled me.

When I walked back into the kitchen, my brother saw the distressed look on my face. "What's the matter?" Joe said.

"I just lied to Claire. I told her that girls can be president. We both know that hasn't happened yet." I sighed in resignation.

"Well, what are you going to do about it?" my brother said, a hint of challenge in his voice.

"What can I possibly do?" I retorted.

We stood there a few seconds in silence. Suddenly, it was as if a lightbulb went off in my head. I made a bold declaration that surprised us both. "I'm gonna run for president!"

The first American woman to seek the presidency was Victoria Woodhull, a suffragist and labor activist, back in the 1872 election. She did not secure a single electoral vote but is viewed as a pioneer who set the stage for a long line of women who aspired to the office.

Today, we can look to political heroines who have boldly sought the highest office in the land in the twentieth and twenty-first centuries. Kamala Harris. Hillary Clinton. Elizabeth Dole. And Shirley Chisholm, to name a few.

When I was in New Zealand in the late nineties and early aughts, its citizens had already elected women as heads of state. So had countries in Europe, Asia, South America, the Middle East, and elsewhere around the globe.

I believed we could shatter this glass ceiling in America, too. I began to see it as my patriotic duty to run. And, I was far from alone in feeling this way.

Donna Brazile, the famed political strategist whom I first met years ago through a mutual friend at a party in her native New Orleans, was among those who encouraged me. I also found a champion in Mosemarie Boyd, the visionary behind American Women Presidents. The national political action committee was founded with the mission of seeing women elected to the presidency and vice presidency.

Boyd is a Brown and Georgetown alumna who previously worked as a staff assistant to Senator Dianne Feinstein during the same period that I served on The Hill.

As fate would have it, our paths crossed again a decade later when I ran for president.

Her PAC had been sending out candidate recruitment packets to bipartisan women leaders nationwide—from members of Congress, to governors, cabinet secretaries, and corporate CEOs. The goal was to convince one (or more) female powerhouses to run for president.

Simultaneously, she was doing media and organizing forums in several states, designed to get women presidential candidates in front of voters.

But there was one problem: no women stepped forward and accepted the PAC's invitation to run. That is, until I entered the picture.

As word filtered out that I might be entering the race, my nascent ambitions garnered attention from the press. One C-Span interviewer asked me why I was running:

Me: Because I believe the country is on the wrong track and I believe I have something to offer in terms of putting it on the right one, and to talk about peace and prosperity, and progress for America. And I just think that the challenges of our time require every person to step up to the plate and that's what I'm doing.

Following the media coverage, the American Women Presidents' team reached out to me with an enthusiastic invitation. I would attend a series of voter events they were hosting in three states over the Presidents' Day weekend. The timing seemed fortuitous. Until the storm.

Snow was coming down in a crescendo of silvery flakes. Of course, as a Windy City native, I am accustomed to the cold and frigid weather. But the forecasts indicated this storm was going to be a doozy.

I was en route with a staffer to Iowa, New Hampshire, and South Carolina—three of the nation's early primary states.

American Women Presidents had taken care of the logistics and arranged for us to have Democratic party co-hosts and sponsors from local leadership in each locale. This was critically important for a national campaign.

I was eager to connect face-to-face with voters and share my views and vision for the country.

Mother Nature had other plans. A blizzard hit that holiday weekend. And the severe weather system was moving east.

State troopers and officials were urging everyone to stay home. That was certainly good advice given the conditions, yet quite a disappointment in terms of what we'd hoped would be a significant turnout at the events.

Iowa's famed political caucuses, where voters meet to select their party candidates, date back to the 1800s. The state has long had a reputation for predicting whether a candidate could go the distance.

Iowa is also the home of what's known as the Brown & Black Forum, one of the oldest minority-centered platforms for engaging presidential candidates in the nation. Over the course of the campaign, I attended their events. That summer, Iowa senator Tom Harkin invited me to participate in his popular "Hear It from the Heartland" candidate series in Waterloo. "She really has broken a lot of new ground," he told the capacity crowd in his introduction.

"I may not look like any president you have ever seen before," I said. "But I have a platform and a plan to rebuild America both physically and spiritually that I hope resonates with the American people." There was clapping as I shared my views on education, health care, the economy, jobs, tax fairness, and keeping the homeland secure, without sacrificing privacy.

Voters in the Hawkeye State take their civic duties very, very seriously. Thus, it did not surprise me that despite the inclement weather, one hardy soul showed up for the American Women Presidents gathering at a hotel ballroom in Des Moines.

Whether one voter or hundreds were in the house, I was going to give them my best. I debuted a speech called "Take the 'Men Only' Sign Off the White House Door." It aired live for voters at home on C-SPAN's program, *The Road to the White House.* Here is an excerpt:

"I have been fortunate to be the beneficiary of the efforts of a lot of everyday people, who moved our country in the direction of its highest ideals. Their contributions reached for the core values from which this country was created. They left a legacy of a more inclusive society that came closer than ever before in reaching the goal of equality and liberty, promised by the Constitution. We look back now and call them patriots for what they did to transform America. I believe we must also look forward toward the continuing transformation that will fulfill the promise of America.

"The people who worked to end Jim Crow, Black and white alike, made this nation begin to live up to its promise of freedom so that we could be here together today. Those who gave life to the intent of the Declaration of

Independence paid the price for the reality that we are experiencing right now. They transformed our society one person at a time, one opinion at a time, one conversation at a time. They shaped public opinion in ways that made civil society more of a reflection of what Abraham Lincoln once called the 'higher angels of our nature.' They created a climate of opinion that made our country begin to live up to its highest ideals.

"One of my heroes, the late congresswoman Barbara Jordan said, and I quote, 'What the American people want is simple. They want an America as good as its promise.' Well, women want an America as good as its promise and we are here to tell them to take the men-only sign off the White House door!"

As I spoke, the lone attendee paid rapt attention and was receptive. At the end of my speech, there was vigorous applause.

We packed up and prepared to travel to our next stop. The original plan was to fly out of Des Moines International Airport, and, after a layover in Chicago, take a connecting flight to New Hampshire. Unfortunately, when we called the airport, we discovered that ours was among dozens of flights that had been canceled in multiple states.

The public would be expecting me at the next forum, so I was determined to do everything possible to get there. We decided to drive through the night to O'Hare airport, aiming to pick up the connecting flight from there to New Hampshire.

Driving conditions were perilous. Countless vehicles and huge trucks had jackknifed and skidded off the highway. We proceeded with caution, inching along. I praise God for getting us there safely.

Very early the next morning, we flew from Chicago to New Hampshire for an event in the city of Manchester. The audience turnout was solid. I found the people of the Granite State very hospitable and receptive to my message. One little girl who was with her family ran up to me afterward, practically bouncing with glee. "When I grow up, I want to be president!" she said.

Our next stop was South Carolina. But as the blizzard continued to move across the country, our flights were canceled yet again.

We scrambled to find an alternative flight. Mosemarie raced from ticket counter to ticket counter. I tried my best to remain calm. The weather was out of my control. As we boarded and settled in our seats, I said my prayers. It was a bumpy ride. Our skillful pilot wound up rerouting around the worst of the storm and we landed at Raleigh-Durham airport in North Carolina.

By a stroke of luck, we were able to get the last available rental car. There were four of us. Mosemarie drove the first shift, until after midnight. Eddy Moore, her boyfriend at the time, picked up as temperatures dropped. They'd met on The Hill when he was an aide to Senator Ernest "Fritz" Hollings of South Carolina. She was in the front passenger seat. I was in the back seat along with my campaign consultant, Kitty.

We traveled along icy roads as snow fell through the night. Around 3:00 a.m., I was jolted awake. We were on a bridge that was covered by a sheet of ice. The vehicle began slipping and sliding. Everyone was terrified.

Mosemarie instinctively reached over and grabbed the steering wheel. Together, she and Eddy managed to keep the car from spinning out of control.

It all happened so fast. I made the sign of the cross and looked heavenward, praying silently.

After alternating behind the wheel through the night, our fearless co-navigators delivered everyone safely to the hotel. Mosemarie would later tell me that images of a dramatic crash plastered across the front page of every major newspaper in the country flashed through her head. All I could do was thank Jesus and our guardian angels.

My team and I had very early morning meetings at a local college, ahead of the AWP event later in the state capital, Columbia. We drew a phenomenal crowd. I added an impromptu line to my remarks, giving Eddy a shout-out in his home state for the heroic driving. I look back in gratitude to the Palmetto State that day, and all of the people we met that snowy weekend for embracing my message and truly seeing the possibilities for women to lead at the highest levels.

The next day, I flew back to Chicago for a press conference. There, surrounded by my family, friends, and supporters, I announced the formation of my presidential exploratory committee. The crowd held up "Ms. President" signs and cheered. Besides local coverage in the *Chicago Tribune* and *Chicago Defender*, the event yielded articles in the *New York Times* and *Ebony Magazine*, along with photos.

My latest political endeavor made me a lightning rod, as always. Some people cheered me on. Other folks believed that I'd lost my marbles.

Skeptics came out of the woodwork. My campaign was deemed a "long shot" and "silly." Comments and questions followed as to whether I was in the race merely as a spoiler, or if I was being paid to run. This was not only untrue but insulting on its face.

I had filed the paperwork for a presidential exploratory committee with the purest of intentions. Basically, it was a chance to test the waters of my candidacy before fully committing. The FEC rules allow one to fundraise for travel, polling, and the like. Candidates are not required to establish an exploratory committee, but it's commonplace in national politics. And for me, it was an essential step before deciding if I was officially leaping into the 2004 race.

My team and I spent time talking with people in different

parts of America, listening to them, registering voters, and engaging in passionate dialogue about our country's direction.

I was grateful to Americans who opened their homes and hearts, to those who shared their experiences with me, and who made it possible for me to explore the prospect of a presidential campaign.

That same month, the Democratic National Committee was holding its winter meeting where presidential hopefuls would be speaking. I made a note to call then-chairman Terry McAuliffe and tell him to hold a place for me.

The Democratic field was shaping up to be a large one, filled with prominent names. When all was said and done, ten hopefuls—all of them men except for me—were contenders.

Senator John Kerry of Massachusetts. Howard Dean, the governor of Vermont. Senator John Edwards of North Carolina. Civil rights activist, the Rev. Al Sharpton. Retired US Army general Wesley Clark. Representative Dennis Kucinich of Ohio. Senator Joe Lieberman of Connecticut. Representative Dick Gephardt, House minority leader from Missouri. Senator Bob Graham of Florida.

In September 2003, I kicked off my campaign at Howard University in Washington, DC. It was part one of a whirlwind launch that would take me to three states. As always, my beloved Matthew was by my side. So was my small but talented team.

I chose the storied HBCU for its tradition of educational excellence dating back centuries. The scenic hilltop campus was just a few miles from The Hill, where I'd served in the Senate. I invited the student body to attend the speech in the student center. I wanted young people with me, symbolizing generational progress, and reinforcing that democracy is a participatory process and not a spectator sport.

My son gave me a wonderful introduction in front of a crowd of students, professors, community members, and supporters. An audience member held up a sign that said "Elect Women Now."

I'd been endorsed by the National Organization for Women and the National Women's Political Caucus, among others. This type of sister support and advocacy gave me the hope I needed to engage in this monumental undertaking.

"Today, I am officially declaring my candidacy for the Democratic nomination for president of the United States," I said. "I am running for the Democratic nomination because I believe this party ought to stand for inclusion, hope, and new ways to resolve old problems.

"I am fighting for the nomination because I am determined to move our party in the direction of our nation's most noble ideals, and live up to our generation's duty to leave the next generation no less freedom, no less opportunity, no less optimism than we inherited from our ancestors," I told those assembled.

"I am dedicated to building partnerships for peace, prosperity, and progress based on new ideas that are as practical as they are innovative," the speech continued. "These partnerships will help us shape an American renaissance and renewal in the best traditions of our country.

"I have the experience, the ability, and the ideas to heal and renew America. In all of my public service, I have broken down barriers, built bridges, and brought people together to achieve solutions that put the public interest first!"

I shared my accomplishments and outlined a platform to "make our economy work for everyone, not just the already wealthy, and assure families that they will be able to provide decent housing, health care, education, retirement and safety to those they love the most."

I continued by speaking about global conflict in the aftermath of 9/11 and my approach to foreign policy.

"What makes this country great is not the size of its military or its budget or its wealth, but the spirit of her people."

I spoke further about ensuring "a real end to this Iraqi war," and "bringing our troops home with honor," as well as "partnerships for peace to give our international institutions new support for global collaborations to fight crime and terrorism, poverty and disease."

Of course, I outlined my domestic agenda, one focused on creating jobs and engaging the private sector in ways that would bolster their bottom line, while ending the exploitation of workers and the environment around the world. I spoke of restoring our nation's infrastructure; unleashing innovation and technology to create new jobs, industries, and wealth; and forging new policies to stop the slide toward embedded wealth, entrenched poverty, and a shrinking middle class.

I promised that as president I would center issues such as fiscal responsibility, fight for social justice, and help the needy. I talked of a single payer system of health insurance.

Additionally, I stressed education reform, positing that our "national interest is bound up in providing quality public education for every child."

"As president, I will give you an America as good as its promise. I will reach out to bring us together to create an American renaissance, revival, and renewal.

"We will lift up the hearts of the American people. We will inspire hope. We will renew the American Spirit. And we will win. Together, failure is impossible!"

After I finished, there was resounding applause. The reaction affirmed for me that I'd done the right thing by entering the race.

I immediately flew to Columbia, South Carolina, and re-announced my campaign at Benedict College. The HBCU was founded in 1870 by Bathsheba Benedict, an abolitionist with ties to the American Baptist Home Mission Society. Several students on campus came up to me, enthused about my candidacy.

From there, I hopped onto yet another plane bound for Chicago, to deliver a third announcement at my alma mater, the University of Illinois.

Three stops in twenty-four hours on the campaign trail fore-shadowed what would be an inordinate amount of work ahead. I was up for the task.

My campaign received coverage from major newspapers, lead-ing magazines, television and radio, including media in Chi-cago and across the country. To each of them, my message was the same: don't marginalize me or treat me merely as a vanity candidate. I'm in it to win it.

One day, I was being interviewed by CNN. The host de-scribed me as "the only woman and the second African Ameri-can" to enter the race for the Democratic presidential nomination.

The segment then cut to video of me saying: "We've never had a woman, or a Black, or a minority as president of the United States. And it's time."

Anchor: You said, in these difficult times, "I believe women have a contribution to make." Are you saying that men can't represent women, can't speak to women's needs?

Me: Oh, no, but that women's voices should not be ex-cluded from the leadership of this country. That women can come up with—can respond to the concerns of all Americans, that women can bring the point of view that has been excluded, frankly, from the highest level. I call it the last great glass ceiling in American politics.

Anchor: How is that different, though, from the view or the leadership role of men?

Me: It's because I think women bring different experiences. They bring the benefit of those experiences. It's not that they are dispositive of anything, but they do add. And our country needs everything that everybody can contribute now in these difficult times. And I think that people should be open to the prospect of having a woman in leadership.

Anchor: Obviously, there's another prominent African American already in this race, Al Sharpton.

Me: Well, all of the men who are running have something to say. And I will meet them on those points and make my point that I believe I have a plan for peace, for prosperity, for progress in this country. And so, I see all of the candidates as having their own platform, their own contributions to make. I'm prepared to make one that I think helps to bring to the fore contributions that women, particularly, can raise.

The anchor went on to mention there'd been a "fair amount of talk" that I was supposedly encouraged to enter the race by Democrats who wanted to see Rev. Sharpton's votes undercut, especially in the crucial primary state of South Carolina. I was asked point-blank if I'd had any conversations along those lines.

"No, of course not," I replied, explaining that my campaign would never be directed at one candidate versus the whole field. "I'm looking to hopefully encourage voters, Democratic voters from across the board—male, female, from the various communities, instead of dividing us as Americans. I think it's time for somebody to stand up and say, let's come together as Americans, because we're one country. We're one people, and we have to approach the rest of the world like that." The interview ended on a high note.

"I'm excited and the people who have come up to me have been excited, too."

In late 2003, Patricia Ireland, a former president of the National Organization for Women, joined our team as the campaign manager. Her intellect, feminist roots, and leadership were a gift. She believed in me and our larger cause, telling one national media outlet, "There's almost a mission feel to the whole thing that is building."

Indeed, I can think of no more extensive and intensive exposure to America than a presidential campaign. And my campaign schedule was grueling.

A candidate has to choose and balance between competing demands, between the many invitations one gets and those you would like to have.

You physically have to go both to those places where events are dictated by others, as well as to those locales your own campaign strategy and analysis suggest hold the most potential for you to personally influence and connect with voters. Thus, mine was a physical challenge of traversing the country by way of planes, helicopter, boats, trains, automobiles, and even mopeds.

One day, I might be on the West Coast, the next day back East. Or in the South.

I recall flying out West for the California Democratic Convention. During my convention speech, my team and supporters held up the "Ms. President" signs that had become a hallmark of my campaign.

While there in Sacramento, I made time to speak at a peace rally and march. I shared my views on the dangers of a preemptive strike against Iraq without the support of the UN.

"Duct tape is no substitute for diplomacy," I said. "We must end the saber rattling that has made us all hostages to fear. And we would do well to foster cooperation to freeze the very ground in which extremism can fester."

That summer, my audience consisted of thousands of Black clergy members at the annual Hampton University Ministers' Conference in Virginia. I was honored to be onstage with two icons: Coretta Scott King and Dr. Dorothy Height, president emerita of the National Council of Negro Women Inc., the storied organization founded by Dr. Mary McLeod Bethune in 1935. I'd been invited by Rev. Dr. Suzan Johnson-Cook, herself a trailblazing faith leader who was later appointed ambassador-at-large for International Religious Freedom. Because churches must be mindful of political activity that would violate what's known as the Johnson Amendment, I did not campaign. Rather, I took part in what was billed as a "First Ladies of the Civil Rights Movement" conversation. It was an extraordinary honor just to be onstage with these women of courage, conviction, and faith whose contributions to our nation not only changed the course of history but impacted lives in ways that still resonate today.

At every stop, I came away positively inspired by what I saw of the openness and the generosity of the American people.

I was somewhat pleasantly surprised by the receptivity to the idea of a woman president. And I was blessed to have the privilege of holding up the banner as the only woman candidate in that campaign cycle.

As can be expected, being the only lady in the field required some adjustments.

The guys likely did not spend as much time picking out their outfits and clothing accessories as I did. Most of them probably did not spend much time worrying about hairdos and manicures. And, they didn't have to concern themselves about the physical layout of the debates and climbing up on stools that showed off their legs. Moreover, when it came time on stage to raise our arms in a victory salute, the men could do so without their boobs becoming perpendicular!

Speaking of debates, there were a number of them around the country. I recall one in New York on the campus of Pace University in Manhattan.

All ten candidates were in attendance. As always, I was the lone woman. One of the reporters quipped that we were one player short of an official NFL roster.

Our speaking order was determined in advance by lottery.

This was a good thing because in the early debates, I had a hard time getting a word in edgewise. I'd be cut off or not called upon or given less microphone time than the male candidates. But many television stations began to get angry phone calls and letters from voters who complained bitterly about the unequal treatment, and it changed. By the time the network debates happened, the commentators were downright focused and even solicitous about the equality of exposure I was afforded down to the very second. At one debate, a cry from the audience, "Let her speak," was met by the commentator turning around during the commercial break to explain how many seconds each candidate had spoken, as if to prove he had been fair.

At this particular debate, the topics ranged from jobs and the economy to the billions it was costing for ongoing wars in Iraq and Afghanistan.

Later in the debate, when the discussion turned to tax cuts for the wealthy versus the middle class, it was my turn again.

Reporter: Ambassador Moseley Braun, who's rich and who's in the middle class?

Me: The economic policies, the trickle-down economics that this administration has given us has created a situation, probably in our recent memory, that we've never seen before in our memory, of embedded wealth, entrenched poverty, and a shrinking middle class. That, it seems to me, is the antithesis, the opposite, of what the American Dream is all about. ... We're not talking about class warfare, which I think is suggested by your question. This is not holding it against someone for doing well. But as people do well, I think they have a responsibility to build community. And that means getting away from an ethos of greed, that we have seen all too much of in recent times, and making certain that the economy works for every American and that opportunity is kept alive in this country.

The campaign was rigorous and demanding and required a degree of stamina and fitness.

Everything from round-the-clock candidate meetups with voters, to embedded reporters and daily press, all of that impacted the rhythm of my campaigning.

There was the campaign calendar to contend with. The states jockey—and it can become a battle royale—around the timing of their respective primaries or caucuses. Then there's the timing and scheduling of the state conventions, the public debates, and the unique rules that each state has to qualify for its ballots. I call it a campaign calculus. That calculus requires mastery of the mechanics of campaigns, from election law compliance, to pressing the flesh, meeting voters, and maximizing the impact of candidates' time and interactions with the voters.

Today, technology and social media have substantially changed the playing field, and campaigns are different now because of them.

And, of course, money plays a huge role. Political ads can create a candidacy overnight, even if it is often not enough to sustain it. I believe that the role of money in campaigns has been a challenge, precisely because historically certain candidates—be it women, people of color or those outside the political mainstream—have largely been at such a financing disadvantage, particularly for national campaigns. So much money is spent on campaigns and the process for raising that money is itself so difficult and expensive to access. Back when I ran, women were seen as nontraditional candidates, and often had a harder time raising money to be considered competitive.

Decades ago, I discovered during my campaigns that there was what people called the money primary. This was an almost-daily sampling by the media and your colleagues, your opposition, of how much money has been raised and from whom, as a test of the viability of a candidacy or a candidate.

Let me be candid: money, or the inability to raise it, can foil one's presidential aspirations. Our electoral process in this country is conditioned on access to money in ways that in my opinion are not healthy for our democracy, but that is the reality. Fundraising is necessary to open campaign offices, ensure there's a ground operation in place and more. Ultimately, that was a key factor in me exiting the race.

All that said, it was gratifying to me that people responded so well to my candor and straight talk about the questions that they asked about America and our future.

If I had a nickel for every man from the heartland, or a young person, or the countless women who came up after a speech or debate to tell me how much they liked my message, I would be rich. That was probably the most edifying part of the campaign experience for me.

Ordinary citizens seemed to be much more willing to give me a shot and to listen and consider me along with the men than many in the political class were prepared to concede. The voters, it seemed, were a lot less dismissive of a Black woman candidate for president than the professionals and the pundits.

My own shoestring effort went as far as we could. I withdrew in January 2004 because we couldn't afford to stay in long enough for the first voting in Iowa.

A few months later, the March for Women's Lives was held on the National Mall. I hosted an event at a venue near the US Senate offices.

For hours that day, Mosemarie, her mother, Dr. Vickie Boyd, and Eddy toted a huge "Ms. President" banner, moving through the crowd and up toward center stage. That sign was broadcast on screens around the world, and photos appeared in media outlets such as the *Washington Post*.

The sterling patriot, John Kerry, would go on to become

the Democratic standard bearer that cycle, winning the popular vote, but not the electoral college. The younger Bush went on to serve a second term. When it comes to politics, I try to weigh in on policies and not judge people personally regardless of party. The Bush family has a history of service to our nation.

I believe my campaign made a difference.

We qualified for more ballots than any other major party women's campaign at that time in American politics. I was the only woman to appear on the presidential primary debate stage throughout 2003 and 2004.

I believe my very presence helped redefine possibilities. I hope that my run helped pave the way for future generations.

I pray that it helped open the White House door a little wider for women, people of color, and all who wish to lift up our communities, country, and the American people.

What my experiences made clear to me was that the American people believed that women have a right to be treated as equals in the political arena. And that was a revelation and a transformation. An expectation of equality that revealed a profound shift in attitudes. It was evidence of a transformation in this country.

Besides Congresswoman Shirley Chisholm, at least a dozen Black women in our country have run for president over the decades, although most did not do so with major parties and thus their campaigns have oftentimes been more obscure.

I actually got to meet Rep. Chisholm during her 1972 campaign swing through Illinois. I was a law student at the time, and we spoke for a bit and took a photo together.

Her crusading campaign laid the groundwork for countless public servants, myself included, to Representative Barbara Lee, whom Chisholm mentored. It gave the American people a glimpse of what was possible.

By the time I embarked on my presidential journey, one of the best congresswomen and public servants our country has ever seen was retired and living in Florida. I reached out to Mrs.

Chisholm seeking guidance and any observations. She was kind and her advice was simple: just do the very best that I could, in service to our nation and all of its people.

LETTER TO MY GRANDCHILDREN

What shall I tell my dear grandchildren? What words of wisdom might I share with the offspring of my beloved son and daughter-in-law?

When I was a child, parental advice often seemed separated from any reality I understood. When adults spoke, often in rhymes or riddles, it was literally in one ear and then out the other. In hindsight, I wish I had listened more closely. I pray that you will give me the benefit of your sincere attention.

The first thing I want you to remember is that you are unique. No two human beings (even twins like yourselves) will live the exact same existence. And while every person on the planet has similarities, each individual is a reflection of the Divine.

I call that spiritual force the Holy Trinity: God, Jesus Christ, and the Holy Spirit. What you may call it depends upon your faith traditions or beliefs. But one does not have to be religious to appreciate and understand that you are you because the Creator of all life deemed it so. You came here for a reason. The good news is that you have free will to define that reason. This is where your uniqueness is so important. You get an opportunity to show the world who you are and what kind of influence you will exert on planet earth.

What you do with your life, while shaped by external forces, depends mostly on your choices. It will also be impacted by the role you decide to play in the life of the community as a whole.

Some people want to shut themselves away like a hermit, having no impact at all. Others opt to change the world, either by fixing something objectionable, or solving some problem. I hope in the time that has been allotted to each of us on earth, that you will be a positive force in our nation and/or world.

If you become a teacher, for example, every student with whom you interact will carry forth into the world with your influence. You might decide, as I did, to pursue the noble values of public service. You could be a world-class scientist. Whatever way you decide to contribute, know that it could have a ripple effect on not just you, but billions of people on the planet.

The next thing that I will encourage you to do is to stay curious. Curiosity is not just the spice of life; it speaks directly to its essence. Being inquisitive is a delicious addition to an otherwise routine and boring existence. It makes the journey worthwhile.

Life has its wonders, but I also want you to understand the dichotomy that it can be complicated, and sometimes difficult.

In my experience, life can also be confusing at times. For if everything one does is important, how do you discern what matters most? This is why your individual personhood is so important; every human being reaches their own conclusions about situations and questions based on their composition. Rarely do two people reach the same conclusions for the same reasons. Yet, how you meet, address, and resolve the complications of life defines you.

The tricky part is that life and the universe constantly changes.

Each generation inherits a world shaped by who and what has gone before. I was born in the twentieth century. The world that is so familiar to me will undergo countless changes by the time you inherit it. Every generation sets the table for the ones that follow, for good or for ill, and you will get the world as we have left it. For children like you who arrived in the twenty-first century and beyond, I hope you will search and find that which is beneficial, beautiful, and empowering about our existence. It may take a lifetime in which to do so.

I feel obliged to tell you that I consider myself a patriot. I delight in giving folks the good news about the United States. I have traveled the world, and without falling into the trap of American "exceptionalism," I sincerely believe this is the greatest country in the world.

That does not preclude telling the whole truth, as I know it, about our nation as well as my experiences therein. As a friend of mine once observed: America is great when America is good. The history of our country has been a constant struggle, sometimes in fits and starts, toward making the Constitution that underpins the foundations of the United States reflect the reality of American society. I think of the words of the Declaration of Independence: "We hold these truths to be self-evident, that all men are created equal, that they are endowed by their Creator with certain unalienable rights, that among these are Life, Liberty, and the pursuit of Happiness."

This nation was built on the labors of countless individuals of every imaginable background. My ancestors were enslaved, and the men in my family have served in the military dating back to the Civil War; they fought in nearly all of America's conflicts. The women in our clan have tilled the land, and the work of their hands has made our nation stronger.

Yet the denial of agency for those whom equality was never

"self-evident" is a discomforting paradox for those of us who love this great nation.

Harriet Tubman, Sojourner Truth, and Frederick Douglass were among the early Americans who saw the contradictions, and pointed them out. So did Abigail Adams, the wife of John Adams, one of the nation's Founding Fathers. In a famous letter to her husband, dated March 31, 1776, she implored: "I desire you would Remember the ladies, and be more generous and favourable to them than your ancestors. Do not put such unlimited power into the hands of the Husbands."

In an earlier letter, dated September 22, 1774, Adams also reaffirmed her commitment to abolition. "I wish most sincerely there was not a Slave in the province. It always appeared a most iniquitious Scheme to me—fight ourselfs for what we are daily robbing and plundering from those who have as good a right to freedom as we have."

During the 1770s, at a time when most of her contemporaries upheld racist and sexist views, Abigail Adams interceded on behalf of women and the enslaved—in ways that distinguish her even today. From a modern perspective, she was a feminist, a champion of women's rights and equality under the law, and a critical thinker. She did not shy away from pointing out her husband's hypocrisy—she noted the gap between his words and his deeds. A long line of human beings have taken up the mantle.

Much has changed. But too many things remain the same. We live in a society where, far too often, stereotypes and assumptions continue to dominate public discourse. And these false statements and more have become justification for oppression and exploitation.

I have agitated for civil rights and equality since I was a child and into my adulthood. If you think about it, all the so-called "isms"—such as racism or sexism—that would deny someone the full measure of their humanity and capacity, stem from the same source. Namely, an inability or unwillingness to see beyond the superficial, and to put someone in a box of society's making. Fortunately, change is constant. Circumstances change. Attitudes that relate to how people think about an issue can change.

I know this because people who look like me had for so long been denied even an opportunity to participate directly in the conversation about our interests. In my life, however, I have been afforded an opportunity to participate directly in that dialogue. My parents and grandparents could not even conceive of a debate about whether a woman or Black American could be the next president or vice president of the United States. We can now look back and reflect on pivotal elections that gave us women and people of color who were "firsts."

Today, we now have people of every race, color, gender, and creed in Congress. This is progress that speaks well about who we are as a society. We can evolve if we are determined to do so. This is the genius of our precious democracy. The march of history still moves forward, even though it is not linear, yet there is still much we can do to make this nation better. For starters, we must ensure that every American understands that they are entitled, as a function of their humanity, to the same rights and opportunities that their neighbor enjoys.

This is necessary as we continue to build an inclusive democracy. In the "land of opportunity," we should make every effort to extend help and support to those who have been relegated to the bottom of the socioeconomic ladder. Every American should have equal access to the resources they need to not simply survive but thrive in this great country.

Our attitudes are where it all starts and ends. If we refuse to allow narrow depictions of people to shape our judgment of them, we will unleash an opportunity for full contribution from one hundred percent of our population.

We will see movement beyond historically marginalized communities being the "first" in any field when we take off the shackles restricting opportunity and embrace the contributions and talents of every single individual.

The future is the legacy of your actions today. It is the result, not just the goal, of today's reality. And if, in this view, we keep our eyes on the lessons of the past, not out of nostalgia or as an excuse for inaction, but as a path of instruction for our decisions in present time, the actions we take will create a better future, an improved legacy, a tomorrow more in keeping with our hopes and higher values than the past we inherited.

This perspective will remind us of what we should have learned and give us tools with which to address the paradox of reconciling constant change and continuity of our values.

Shaping the answer lies in what individuals choose to do, or not do: the key is personal. It is up to each of us to engage, to do, to reach outside ourselves to shape a world we will be proud to pass on to the next generation.

My appeal to you is a simple one: choose to do something, because the most important truth lies in knowing that whether in your personal life or in the life of your community or your work, your decisions drive outcomes. You create the future with your actions in present time.

Each and every person makes a difference in shaping the direction any one person's life can take, and by extension, any one community, any one nation. As we take on each generation's issues, challenges and conflicts, we help to define the future.

We define community today. And by our actions, future generations will know us.

Your choices help to create attitudes and a climate of public opinion about the world around us. And I like to say that a climate of opinion is just like any other weather system—it depends on the hot air rising from the ground.

A climate of opinion shapes perspective as well as conduct and can change hearts as well as minds. But it starts with each one of us, sometimes in big ways, but more often in small ways.

What you say or don't say, who you say it to, whether you follow your joy or follow the crowd, all these contribute to creating an attitude and the atmosphere in which others' decisions and choices will be made.

Little steps, quiet interactions, personal connections, and contributions are sometimes all that is required to shape the opportunities and direction of another person, or community, or nation. Being a good citizen is a contribution that matters. Individual decisions are where democracy starts.

In many ways, our world is in a period of transition, moving toward a new set of societal expectations and structures. And no one can predict with certainty where this transition will go.

It is up to us to shape the landscape and expand the dialogue about civil society from "what is good for me" to "what is good for all." Every person matters and every choice you make changes the present and future for everybody else.

The reckoning that our society is right now experiencing over race, gender, wealth, sexuality, ethnicity, all call for our contributions to decide the direction the society will move, and indeed, what our country will be going forward.

Whether our society will glorify violence and greed or community and compassion, starts with you.

We can popularize the notion that real education is not a private benefit or privilege of wealth but is a public good that serves the interest of every American.

I believe it is up to each of us to create consensus that education is as much a part of our national defense as any weapons system, and that as Americans we are committed to keep our country strong by making sure our citizenry is educated.

We can live up to our responsibilities as stewards of the planet and of the next generation, and encourage people to take the blinders off and see a natural world that is far more wonderful and engaging than any make-believe. Deny it as some might, the reality of climate change is unmistakable. And, as humans lose their homes and lives from nature's inescapable fury, there can be no question that we all need to engage in a serious way around keeping our planet well and habitable.

We can begin the conversation that the Golden Rule—essentially to "do unto others" and treat people in the manner that we wish to be treated—is a universal one. And, while our differences are inherent to the human experience, we must move toward understanding, and not distinctions that serve to divide humanity or put us into conflict with one another.

We can, right here, right now, state that people have the power to recapture the values of honesty and discipline and kindness and caring, and community.

Every person matters and it only takes one person to light the spark for change. And even though we may be up against entrenched mindsets, with one and one and one, a tipping point will be reached in this world that will make our hopes a reality for someone, someday, if not for ourselves today.

The people who choose to do whatever they can to be good, and decent, and caring in their time put the "better angels of our nature" to work in our lives. Those people may or may not be known to you personally, indeed, they may not always show up in the scholarly journals and history books. But I can assure you that without the many individual and sometimes unnoticed contributions of people of goodwill to make this country what it should and could be, there would be no way that we could be here in this place in this way at this time.

The people who went before to create our present-day realities recognized that by doing for others we do for self. It is up to us to return the favor by doing as much for the next generation. When we decide to give back just a little of the good that has been given to us, we make life better for more people than we may ever know.

There can be no question that such acts of kindness are momentous and shift our society. If you participate in the conversation, you are bolstering that change.

I may not see it in my lifetime, but perhaps your generation will get to celebrate a world that will tap all the human talent available to us.

I hope you will hold up those values that honor the Divine. Truth, empathy, honesty, and love are all values and gifts we inherit from generation to generation. How those values get expressed depends on You. You decide for yourself and others, that is how the moral compass is constructed. That compass is constructed of values. It is up to you to decide how it will direct your daily life.

Finally, I recommend that you find a pursuit that inspires you, and that serves others. Focusing only on your own interests and concerns is the definition of selfishness. I hope you will choose to do for yourself and for others. By being selfless you will put more of yourself into the world, and hopefully that will preserve those values into the generations yet to be born.

You might be a savior of millions who gets in the history books, or a quiet contributor to a better life for a single person. Either way, if you choose to do, you will succeed. And, remember, that life is ever changing and what may feel like failure may not be; you have only to not give up.

Hopefully, I haven't sounded like a know-it-all, and my message to you has some value. If there is one more thing I would leave you with, it's that this life is not only fragile and complex, but a blessing. Relish the life you have. Have fun! Bring sunshine into the lives of others. Be an unabashed do-gooder and do something to uplift our collective well-being. Don't get overwhelmed by life's twists and turns, and remember that you are not alone, because every person on this planet faces challenges.

I just hope you take with you the certainty that I love you. And, God loves you even more.

EPILOGUE

January 2025

As a new year dawned, I had the honor of attending festivities that accompanied the opening of the 119th Congress. I flew in from Chicago to the nation's capital for the occasion and was excited to again be part of history.

While the House of Representatives held its own proceedings, I had been invited to attend the Senate's swearing-in ceremonies, in the place where my historic election broke barriers in the early 1990s. Although this was not my first homecoming, the day held special significance because among the veteran lawmakers and new arrivals in the chamber were dynamic women shattering glass ceilings of their own. I was delighted to join the throng of families, friends, and supporters who came from near and far to bear witness and celebrate our newest senators.

Among those taking the oath of office were Angela Alsobrooks and Lisa Blunt Rochester.

Senator Blunt Rochester had previously made history in 2016

when the longtime public servant became the first woman and person of color elected to represent Delaware in Congress. After serving in the House, she ran in the 2024 election cycle. Following a three-way race, she emerged to become the state's first woman and its first Black US senator.

Senator Alsobrooks, a former prosecutor and county executive, ran against a popular former governor in the general election. She campaigned tirelessly across the state and won decisively, becoming the first Black person to represent Maryland in the Senate.

Their respective victories meant that for the first time ever, two Black women would serve simultaneously in the Senate, a body that first convened in 1789 as part of the inaugural Congress. Talk about progress!

You see, following my single term, there was a long stretch—decades—in which not a single Black woman served among the nation's one hundred senators.

Fortunately, that lack of representation changed when Californians elected Kamala Harris to the Senate and she took office in 2017. As only the second Black woman ever duly elected to the chamber, she served successfully before being tapped by Joe Biden and elected vice president. She was our country's first woman and first Black/Southeast Asian American to hold that esteemed office in the executive branch. And, of course, we know that Harris would later be elevated to the top of a presidential ticket—a momentous achievement that continues to inspire.

Indeed, I was there in the summer of 2024 when fellow delegates nominated her at the Democratic National Convention. It was a blessing in my seventh decade to be present for another convening, and in my beloved hometown of Chicago, no less.

I've attended my fair share of these confabs in cities nationwide over the years. On more than one occasion, I have had the extraordinary privilege of being invited to take the stage and address party stalwarts and our great nation. In 2020, as the COVID pandemic raged and we mourned millions of lives lost,

I was honored to cast votes for Illinois during a virtual convention. Organizers arranged for me to tape a video segment outside the Old State Capitol in Springfield, where Barack Obama kicked off his groundbreaking presidential campaign.

Years later at the United Center arena, I joined the cheering and chanting for each VIP who took the stage: presidents and vice presidents, First Ladies and governors, as well as a newer crop of up-and-coming politicos and stars.

No matter my role at these conventions, I am always struck by the palpable sense of purpose as Americans endeavor to embrace our democracy and put one of its core principles—the right to vote—into action. It never gets old for me.

That week, I had the pleasure of meeting then-future Senators Alsobrooks and Blunt Rochester while hosting an off-site fundraising event for them. In the room as well was then-Senator Laphonza Butler of California, appointed in 2023 to replace my friend, the late Senator Dianne Feinstein. Butler came to the chamber with an impressive résumé as a labor leader and champion for women. While opting not to seek election, she ably served constituents, introduced legislation, and made the most of her tenure.

I salute the women who have succeeded me in the Senate. I am humbled by their expressions of gratitude and for graciously acknowledging me, both publicly and privately, as a trailblazer who has opened doors. We are members of an exclusive yet growing club of African Americans in the upper chamber from the Democratic and Republican parties. As of this writing, five men and women are currently serving, including Senator Cory Booker (D-New Jersey), Rev. Raphael Warnock (D-Georgia), and Tim Scott (R-South Carolina), each of them having made history in their own right. I also applaud the new generations in Congress from Illinois and beyond.

Their presence speaks to who we are as a country, and the power of possibility. And it drives home the many reasons why I value being a citizen of these United States. Topping the list

has always been the gift of democracy, and our precious freedoms as one nation under God.

Freedom of religion. Freedom of speech. Voting rights. Freedom to embrace "Life, Liberty and the pursuit of Happiness," as
the preamble to the Declaration of Independence so eloquently
states. Freedom in every conceivable form.

Reflecting upon my journey, I remember the years that followed my ambassadorship. I returned home to America feeling
reinvigorated. I could have gone back to the practice of law, or
gone the corporate route, but I sought new horizons.

I relocated and made Atlanta my base. The Southern city then
and now is a vibrant, thriving mecca. I found myself a place in
the lovely community of Buckhead and, to my delight, learned
that I was living in the same building as Mrs. Coretta Scott King.
We ran into each other periodically, and she was always warm
and gracious. Her beauty shone inside and out, as did her intellect and spirit as one of the women whose contributions were
integral to the Civil Rights Movement.

During that phase of my post-political life, my plate was full.
I was teaching civics at Morris Brown College, an HBCU in
Atlanta founded in 1881. I also did some political consulting. I
had been asked by Rev. Andrew Young—one of Dr. King's top
deputies during the Movement, and a former mayor, Georgia
congressman, and UN ambassador appointed by President Jimmy
Carter—to join his firm. Andy was one of the most committed, justice-minded individuals you will ever meet, and valuable lessons were learned in his presence.

Another good thing about living in Georgia was being within
driving distance of our family's farm in Alabama. As a proud
descendant of Southerners, I was eager to return to the homestead of my ancestors, walk the land, and develop ideas to restore the property and ensure its survival for future generations.

I was happily engaged in various pursuits when the world
changed in an instant. The 9/11 attacks shattered us, collec-

tively. Like countless others across our nation, I was in a daze, praying and mourning for all we lost on that unthinkable day.

I returned to Chicago to be near my loved ones. For a time, I practiced law and focused on being with family.

Around that time, I hit upon the idea of becoming an entrepreneur. I'd held many titles, but CEO was a novel one. My company, Good Food Organics, Inc., was launched in the early 2000s. We produced a line of coffee, tea, spices, and olive oil, which were branded as "Ambassador Organics."

The line was certified organic, certified biodynamic, and fair trade certified. Me and my tiny team worked with dedicated biodynamic farmers across the globe. The talented Whoopi Goldberg, who had a syndicated radio program at the time, was among those who interviewed me about entrepreneurship.

I invested a heap of my own money into the company. We were small and grew slowly, but the line was sold at local grocers in Chicago, select Whole Foods locations, and on Amazon. In spite of the enormous odds, I am pleased to say that my company lasted more than a decade. I spent some lean years afterward making sure that I paid off all the business debts that had accrued. Praise God, I was able to close out my books in the black.

While I was navigating in the business arena, the lure of public service still called to me like a siren song. After once touting myself as a "recovering politician" and vowing never to run for office again, I tossed my hat into the ring for Chicago's mayoral race in 2010.

My intentions were sincere. While the election did not send me to city hall, the win for me was having another opportunity to talk about the issues and connecting with voters about their concerns.

I continued my career in academia at DePaul and Northwestern Universities, gave speeches across the country, and remained committed to my perennial quest to make our communities and country the best they can be.

Along the way, I have served on numerous public boards and commissions. They range from my longtime work with Chicago's DuSable Museum of African American History, to the World War I Commission Advisory Board in honor of my maternal grandfather's military service. I am fortunate to be the recipient of several honorary degrees and multiple awards.

As of this writing, I am still engaged in civic pursuits via my appointment with the US African Development Foundation, a role which commenced under the Biden-Harris Administration.

For the past year or so, I have been traveling periodically to the African continent—from Morocco to Mauritania and beyond—endeavoring to foster community-led development that encompasses investment, capacity building assistance, and social entrepreneurism.

Whether representing America abroad or at home, my entire public life has been characterized by service and courage. I've engaged in coalition building with people of every race, color, and creed, and bringing to the public square concepts that are as practical as they are innovative. Whether pushing early in my career as a state legislator to divest pension funds from South Africa, to demanding a ban on child labor while in the Senate, I've been a consistent fighter for democracy and people just like you, throughout my public life.

I have sought with all of my heart to bring my skills and life experiences to bear on uplifting our citizenry. Fighting for folks in need. Fixing things. Righting wrongs. Endeavoring to create a renaissance in education so that our children can learn and lead. Creating jobs. Bringing forth ideas and legislation that serve every single person in our diverse society so that we all have the ability to rise higher and higher day by day, generation by generation.

Individuals who seek to hold office must reach deep into wherever it is in your personal makeup, wherever the selflessness lies. It cannot be about money. You're going to have to work long, unpredictable hours. It is doubtful that you will have much privacy.

But if you keep your eyes on the prize, and understand the greater goal, service is a glorious, enlightening endeavor. As the Good Book teaches us, loving our neighbor is required, and there is no more noble an endeavor than positive work that uplifts our communities, nation, and world. And if that's your guiding light, even in the tough times, you will be resilient because there is simply too much at stake for you to give up.

As I stated in a speech years ago, "Government is not the enemy of society; it should be a partner. An instrument of the people's will, and a facilitator of our public interest."

It may sound cliché, but I still fervently believe that each of us can make a difference in shaping the climate of opinion from which policy will change. Each of us has a role to play in directing the course our communities and country will take. Our challenge is to reach outside of our private lives to help shape the times in which we live.

Our unity is our strength. Together, we are strong. We can tell the truth and heal. As a country, we will continue to move forward as we find ways, be they minuscule or large, to come together no matter our political affiliations or differences.

Decades ago, on that fateful election night that changed my life, I quoted Illinois-born Abe Lincoln: "Let us have faith that right makes might, and that in faith, let us to the end dare to do our duty as we understand it."

I lift my heart in humble gratitude to God, the good people of Illinois, and my country, America, for the opportunity to be of service. I sincerely hope that all of my professional and personal contributions as a US senator and public servant have benefited our nation, and perhaps made the stony path a little easier to trod for those who will follow and inherit our collective legacy.

★ ★ ★ ★ ★

ACKNOWLEDGMENTS

How does one begin to express gratitude for a God-given life abounding in sweet serendipity, strong faith to bear adversity, and wondrous adventures? The task is gargantuan, but I shall endeavor to try...

To my parents, Joseph and Edna, who gave my upbringing their all. To my siblings Marsha and Joseph II, and John in heaven, whom I love without reservation. To my son, Matthew, the love of my life, precious daughter-in-law, Jennifer, and grandchildren who give me joy. To Michael Braun. To my grandparents, and all of my relatives in the Moseley and Davie families, and our courageous ancestors who paved the way.

To the many friends in my hometown, state, across the country, and around the world who have helped make my journey one to amplify.

Thank you to my mentors, most of whom have passed on, for your extraordinary encouragement and inspiration. Thank you to the good people of Chicago, Illinois, and across America who have given me their votes, shared a kind word, or sent letters, cards, and the like.

To the dedicated teachers at every stage of my public school and parochial education, my professors at the University of Illinois, and University of Chicago Law School.

Thank you to the long list of colleagues in the fields of law, politics, and diplomacy who've played a positive role in my journey. Besides the men and women of the United States Senate, they include: the legal minds who took a chance on me right out of law school; the Office of the US Attorney; the Illinois General Assembly and Cook County Recorder of Deeds Office; the US Embassy teams in New Zealand and Samoa; and the State Department. I thank everyone at the White House, House of Representatives, and colleagues in the Congressional Black Caucus.

Special thanks to the numerous advisers, staffers, volunteers, generous donors, and supporters who have been part of my campaigns.

Thank you to my team, customers, and everyone who supported my entrepreneurial vision at Good Food Organics, Inc.

I thank my Delta Sigma Theta Sorority, Inc. sisters, and the "Divine Nine" Black Greek letter organizations, as well as the many personal and professional groups to which I have belonged.

Thank you to my faith community and the unknown angels, who, along with the Holy Trinity, have truly watched over me.

This book has been years in the making. For some time, I'd given thought to penning my memoirs. I would begin in earnest, but for one reason or another, the literary muse seemed elusive.

Thank goodness for the fabulous team whose collective efforts provided me the opportunity to tell my story.

Thank you to journalist Donna M. Owens, a wonderful collaborator. I'm grateful to Silvia Mathis and Mosemarie Boyd, who joined forces to kick this project into high gear.

Thank you to Byrd Leavell and Lily Dolin, the dynamic duo at UTA. Thank you to editorial director Peter Joseph at

Hanover Square Press, Eden Railsback, and their enthusiastic team. Thanks to Christopher Bloom, Esq., and attorneys Mark O'Malley and Ted Tetzlaff; Kitty and Kevin, my publicists through the years; and Hope Daniels. Craig, Sandya, Saadia, and Adel, as well as others who've lent a helping hand. Thanks to my hardworking executive assistants and countless individuals who have helped facilitate this book and other projects.

Thank you to the US Senate Historical Office, historian Katherine Scott and team. My gratitude to senate historian emerita Betty Koed, who conducted oral history interviews with me decades ago which helped tremendously. The Congressional Record proved invaluable. Thanks to the Library of Congress, Senate Library, and the Office of the Clerk of the House of Representatives, among others for their trove of information.

For nearly five decades, my career has been chronicled by media outlets locally, nationally, and internationally. We are fortunate in America to have a free press.

I appreciate Julieanna L. Richardson, Esq., founder/executive director of The HistoryMakers who interviewed me; and WTTW PBS Chicago for interviewing me in the documentary "DuSable to Obama: Power, Politics, & Pride: Dr. King's Chicago Crusade." I thank the Chicago History Museum's Abakanowicz Research Center, where my papers are archived; Loyola University Chicago; and the Chicago Historical Society. A special thank you to my sister, Marsha Moseley-Kerman, whose research unearthed more about our family genealogy, as well as the Afro-American Genealogical & Historical Society of Chicago who shared relevant documents along the way.

Last but not least, thank you to everyone at the Carol Moseley Braun Elementary School in Calumet City, Illinois. What a magnificent honor to have a place of learning bear my name. I pray that its students will learn all that they possibly can, and use their education and talents in service to people, our great nation, and the world.

BIBLIOGRAPHY

"About." University of Illinois Urbana-Champaign. https://illinois.edu/about/index.html.

Abramowitz, Michael; Pianin, Eric; Yang, John. "Braun Reaches Agreement on Illinois Medicaid Payment." *Washington Post*, October 31, 1992.

"Ambassador to New Zealand Confirmation Hearing." C-Span, November 5, 1999. Video. https://www.c-span.org/video/?153396-1/ambassador-zealand-confirmation-hearing.

"Board Approves New Name for UIC Law." *UIC Today*, May 20, 2021. https://today.uic.edu/board-approves-new-name-for-uic-law/.

Branch, Taylor. *At Canaan's Edge: America in the King Years, 1965–68.* Simon & Schuster, 2006.

"A Brief History of Dillard University." Dillard University. https://www.dillard.edu/about/history-traditions/.

Brownstein, Ronald. "Hollywood PAC Quits to Protest Money in Politics." *Los Angeles Times*, April 13, 1997.

"Dyett, Capt. Walter Papers. Vivian G. Harsh Research Collection of Afro-American History and Literature." Chicago Public Library. https://www.chipublib.org/fa-walter-dyett-papers/.

"The Early Years | 1867 – 1904 – Mapping History." University of Illinois Urbana-Champaign Library. https://www.library.illinois.edu/mappinghistory/the-early-years-1867-1904/.

"Equality Experiment: The History of Roosevelt University." Roosevelt University. https://www.roosevelt.edu/stories/news/equality-experiment-history-roosevelt-university.

Frankie Franko & His Louisianians Discography. Discogs. https://www.discogs.com/artist/1061884-Frankie-Franko-His-Louisianians.

"The Great Migration (1910–1970)." National Archives. https://www.archives.gov/research/african-americans/migrations/great-migration.

Guinier, Lani. "Who's Afraid of Lani Guinier?" *The New York Times Magazine*, February 2, 1994.

"Hansberry v. Lee: The Supreme Court Case that Influenced the Play 'A Raisin in the Sun.'" Library of Congress, January 24, 2023. https://blogs.loc.gov/law/2023/01/hansberry-v-lee-the-supreme-court-case-that-influenced-the-play-a-raisin-in-the-sun/.

"History." University of Illinois Chicago. https://www.uic.edu/about/history/#.

"History of Wendell Phillips Academy High School." Wendell Phillips Hall of Fame. https://www.wendellphillipshalloffame.org/legacy.

"Illinois Senate Race." C-Span, November 3, 1992. Video. www.c-span.org/video/?34081-1/illinois-senate-race.

Author Interview with Mosemarie Boyd. Telephone, December 8, 2022.

Lincoln, Abraham. "Cooper Union Address." New York, New York, February 27, 1860. Speech transcript. Abraham Lincoln Online.org. https://www.abrahamlincolnonline.org/lincoln/speeches/cooper.htm.

"Madame Ambassador." *Chicago Tribune*, March 11, 2000.

Moseley Braun, Carol. "Black Excellence: Carol Moseley Braun." Interview by Aisha El-Amin. *Black Excellence. UIC Today*, September 13, 2022. https://today.uic.edu/podcast/black-excellence-carol-moseley-braun/.

Moseley Braun, Carol. "Carol Moseley Braun. She Has the Credentials. Can She Get the Votes?" Interview by Florence Hamlish Levinsohn. *Chicago Reader*, 1992.

Moseley Braun, Carol. "Explorations in Black Leadership." Interview by Julian Bond. University of Virginia, 2007. https://blackleadership.virginia.edu/transcript/moseley-braun-carol.

Moseley Braun, Carol. "Women of the Senate Oral History

Project: Carol Moseley Braun." Interview by Betty Koed. Senate Historical Office, 2017.

Moss, Marie. "Who's Got Hot Hair?" *Chicago Tribune*, January 6, 1993.

New Zealand. https://www.newzealand.com.

"Operation Breadbasket: Martin Luther King, Jr.'s Northern Legacy." Chicago Public Library, January 13, 2020. https://www.chipublib.org/blogs/post/operation-breadbasket-dr-kings-northern-legacy/.

"Our History: How It All Began—A Firm with a Powerful Story and Profound Impact." Miner, Barnhill & Galland, P.C. https://www.lawmbg.com/history-2/.

Owens, Donna M. "Ketanji Brown Jackson Celebrates Confirmation: 'I Am The Dream And The Hope Of The Slave.'" *Essence*, April 8, 2022. https://www.essence.com/news/kbj-biden-harris-white-house-celebration/.

Rybicki v. State Bd. of Elections of State of Ill., 584 F. Supp. 849 (N.D. Ill. 1984). https://law.justia.com/cases/federal/district-courts/FSupp/584/849/2270834/.

Senate Historical Office. "Hiram Revels: First African American Senator." *Senate Stories*, February 25, 2020. https://www.senate.gov/artandhistory/senate-stories/First-African-American-Senator.htm.

"The Souls of Black Folk." *Encyclopedia Britannica*. https://www.britannica.com/topic/The-Souls-of-Black-Folk.

"Union Springs." *Encyclopedia of Alabama.* https://encyclopedia-ofalabama.org/article/union-springs/.

"Women in Politics." C-Span, February 15, 2003. Video. https://www.c-span.org/video/?175136-1/women-politics.

ENDNOTES

CHAPTER 1: BARRIERS

"I do solemnly swear that I will support..." C-Span. "Sen. Carol Moseley Braun Takes Oath of Office," January 5, 1993, https://www.c-span.org/video/?c4723597/sen-carol-moseley-braun-takes-oath-office.

Gwendolyn Brooks, the U.S. Poet Laureate... Steve Daley. "Senator Braun Takes Her Place in History," *Chicago Tribune*, January 6, 1993.

After her recitation, Gwendolyn Brooks said something... Ibid.

CHAPTER 3: WE, TOO, SING AMERICA

"We, too, sing America." Langston Hughes. "I, too." The Poetry Foundation, https://www.poetryfoundation.org/poems/47558/i-too.

declared in part, "all persons held as slaves..." National Archives. "The Emancipation Proclamation," https://www.archives.gov/exhibits/featured-documents/emancipation-proclamation.

CHAPTER 4: WELCOME TO THE NEIGHBORHOOD

"To bed, to bed, you sleepy head..." All Nursery Rhymes. "To Bed, To Bed," https://allnurseryrhymes.com/to-bed-to-bed/.

CHAPTER 7: MARCHING WITH A KING

"with all deliberate speed." National Archives. "Brown v. Board of Education (1954)," https://www.archives.gov/milestone-documents/brown-v-board-of-education.

"I shall not be moved…" Hymnary. "I Shall Not Be Moved," https://hymnary.org/text/i_shall_not_i_shall_not_be_moved.

Greensboro Lunch Counter Sit-In: https://www.loc.gov/exhibits/odyssey/educate/lunch.html.

"Green for the tall straight pine trees…" Illinois High School. "Glory Days." "Chicago Parker High School 'Colonels,'" https://leopardfan.tripod.com/id706.html.

CHAPTER 8: COLLEGE AND THE COW

"Gonna ride that train to the end of the line…" Wallace Saunders. "The Ballad of Casey Jones," *Genius*, https://genius.com/Wallace-saunders-the-ballad-of-casey-jones-lyrics.

CHAPTER 9: LOVE AND LAWYERING

"So we'll live, and pray, and sing…" William Shakespeare. *King Lear*, Act V, Scene 3, https://www.opensourceshakespeare.org/views/plays/play_view.php?WorkID=kinglear&Act=5&Scene=3&Scope=scene.

CHAPTER 10: WORKING GIRL

"For unto whomsoever much is given…" King James Bible, https://www.biblegateway.com.

"Oh what a lovely precious dream…" Nina Simone. "To Be Young, Gifted and Black," *YouTube*, 2013, https://www.youtube.com/watch?v=RTGiKYqk0gY. Originally recorded in 1969.

CHAPTER 11: A BABY AND BOBOLINKS

"proud to be Hog Butcher, Tool maker…" Carl Sandburg. "Chicago," *The Complete Poems of Carl Sandburg*, January 1, 2003. For more information, please visit: https://www.nps.gov/carl/index.htm.

"Diamond in the back, sunroof top..." William DeVaughn. "Be Thankful for What You've Got," *YouTube*, June 8, 2019, https://www.youtube.com/watch?v=tSt5MaSDDj8.

CHAPTER 12: SPRINGFIELD

"I solemnly swear to support..." Illinois General Assembly. "Illinois Compiled Statutes," https://www.ilga.gov/legislation/ilcs/ilcs3.asp?ActID=431.

"O Lord, the people of Illinois with trustful confidence..." Illinois General Assembly. January 10, 1979, https://www.ilga.gov/house/transcripts/htrans81/HT011079.pdf.

CHAPTER 13: BROTHER JOHN

"There is a balm in Gilead..." Hymnary. "There Is a Balm in Gilead," https://hymnary.org/text/sometimes_i_feel_discouraged_spiritual.

CHAPTER 17: HISTORYMAKER PART TWO

"Thank you! Thank you all!..." C-Span. "User Clip: 1992 Democratic Convention—Carol Moseley Braun," July 13, 1992, https://www.c-span.org/video/?c4513851/user-clip-1992-democratic-convention-carol-moseley-braun.

CHAPTER 18: HISTORYMAKER PART THREE

I cringed hearing the term "welfare cheats..." *Chicago Tribune*. "Williamson Takes 1st Hard Swing at Braun in Attack Ad on Radio," May 12, 1992, https://www.chicagotribune.com/1992/05/12/williamson-takes-1st-hard-swing-at-braun-in-attack-ad-on-radio/.

"Hopefully tonight you'll learn why..." C-Span. "Illinois Senate Race," November 3, 1992, https://www.c-span.org/video/?34081-1/illinois-senate-race.

"Rich Williamson's been running a nasty campaign..." *Chicago Tribune*. "Braun Ad, Williamson Charges Keep Senate Campaign Heated," October 14, 1992, https://www.chicagotribune.com/1992/10/14/braun-ad-williamson-charges-keep-senate-campaign-heated/.

CHAPTER 20: CAROL VS. THE CONFEDERACY

"I wish I was in Dixie..." Daniel Decatur Emmett. "Dixie's Land," Library of Congress, 1815–1904, https://www.loc.gov/item/2023782678/.

"Mr. President," Helms said... Congressional Record—Senate, July 22, 1993, https://www.congress.gov/103/crecb/1993/07/22/GPO-CRECB-1993-pt12-1-2.pdf.

CHAPTER 21: COURTING CONTROVERSY

"Confess your faults one to another..." King James Bible, https://www.biblegateway.com.

CHAPTER 22: REELECTION

"As we pray, let us remember in silence..." Congressional Record—Senate, December 1993, https://www.congress.gov/103/crecb/1993/11/09/GPO-CRECB-1993-pt19-7-2.pdf.

"Regrettably," I said... Congressional Record—Senate, Maiden Speech, January 26, 1993.

"Dr. Elders represents the positive kind of change..." C-Span. "Surgeon General Confirmation Hearing PM," July 23, 1993, https://www.c-span.org/video/?46225-1/surgeon-general-confirmation-hearing-pm#.

"It is an unavoidable conclusion..." *Chicago Tribune.* "On Capitol Hill, a Real Rap Session," February 24, 1994, https://www.chicagotribune.com/1994/02/24/on-capitol-hill-a-real-rap-session/.

"I know I've made some mistakes..." *Chicago Tribune.* "Moseley Braun Admits 1st Term Mistakes," October 13, 1998, https://www.chicagotribune.com/1998/10/13/moseley-braun-admits-1st-term-mistakes/.

"Thanks for this opportunity. Because..." C-Span. "Illinois Senate Campaign Debate," October 4, 1998, https://www.c-span.org/video/?112743-1/illinois-senate-campaign-debate.

CHAPTER 23: AMBASSADOR TO PARADISE

"extraordinary life of breaking stereotypes..." C-Span. "House

Session, Part 2," November 4, 1999, https://www.c-span.org/video/?153356-101/house-session-part-2.

"As we're all aware..." C-Span. "Ambassador to New Zealand Confirmation Hearing," November 5, 1999, https://www.c-span.org/video/?153396-1/ambassador-zealand-confirmation-hearing.

CHAPTER 24: TAKE THE "MEN ONLY" SIGN OFF THE WHITE HOUSE

Reporter: First of all... C-Span. "Women in Politics," February 15, 2003, https://www.c-span.org/video/?175136-1/women-politics.

I have been fortunate to be the beneficiary... Ibid.

I was grateful to Americans... Archives of Women's Political Communication. "Announcement Speech for Democratic Nomination," September 22, 2003, https://awpc.cattcenter.iastate.edu/2017/03/09/announcement-speech-for-democratic-nomination-sept-22-2003/.

"Today, I am officially declaring my candidacy..." C-Span. "Presidential Campaign Announcement," September 22, 2003, https://www.c-span.org/video/?178291-1/presidential-campaign-announcement.

"the only woman and the second African American..." C-Span. "Democratic Presidential Candidates Debate," January 9, 2004, https://www.c-span.org/video/?179859-1/democratic-presidential-candidates-debate#.

"We've never had a woman..." Ibid.

I can think of no more extensive... Archives of Women's Political Communication. "A Woman President: If Not Now, When?" February 7, 2006, https://awpc.cattcenter.iastate.edu/2017/03/09/a-woman-president-if-not-now-when-feb-7-2006/.

You physically have to go to... Ibid.

At every stop, I came away positively inspired... Ibid.

...stations began to get angry... Ibid.

...the public debates, and... Ibid.

So much money is spent on... Ibid.

This is an almost-daily sampling... Ibid.

...gratifying to me that people responded... Ibid.

...experience for me. Ibid.

...laid the groundwork for me... Ibid.

CHAPTER 25: LETTER TO MY GRANDCHILDREN

"We hold these truths..." National Archives. "Declaration of Independence: A Transcription," July 4, 1776, https://www.archives.gov/founding-docs/declaration-transcript.

"I desire you would Remember the ladies..." Abigail Adams. "Letter from Abigail Adams to John Adams, 31 March–5 April 1776," *Massachusetts Historical Society*, March 31, 1776, https://www.masshist.org/digitaladams/archive/doc?id=L17760331aa&bc=%2Fdigitaladams%2Farchive%2Fbrowse%2Fletters_1774_1777.php.

"I wish most sincerely there was not..." Abigail Adams. "Letter from Abigail Adams to John Adams, 22 September 1774," *Massachusetts Historical Society*, September 22, 1774, https://www.masshist.org/digital-adams/archive/doc?id=L17740922aa.

...that a climate of opinion... Archives of Women's Political Communication. "A Woman President: If Not Now, When?" February 7, 2006, https://awpc.cattcenter.iastate.edu/2017/03/09/a-woman-president-if-not-now-when-feb-7-2006/.

...in a period of transition... The Network Journal. "Community Through Diversity," October 22, 2015, https://tnj.com/community-through-diversity/.

EPILOGUE

"Let us have faith that right..." Abraham Lincoln. "Cooper Union Address," February 27, 1860, https://www.abrahamlincolnonline.org/lincoln/speeches/cooper.htm.